JC 599 .U5 G688 2011
Gr ci c, Joseph
Free and equal

MHCC WITHDRAWN

D0558397

# FREE AND EQUAL

## RAWLS' THEORY OF JUSTICE
## AND POLITICAL REFORM

# FREE AND EQUAL

## RAWLS' THEORY OF JUSTICE AND POLITICAL REFORM

Joseph Grcic

Algora Publishing
New York

© 2011 by Algora Publishing.
All Rights Reserved
www.algora.com

No portion of this book (beyond what is permitted by
Sections 107 or 108 of the United States Copyright Act of 1976)
may be reproduced by any process, stored in a retrieval system,
or transmitted in any form, or by any means, without the
express written permission of the publisher.

Library of Congress Cataloging-in-Publication Data —

Grcic, Joseph
   Free and equal: Rawls' theory of justice and political reform / Joseph Grcic.
      p. cm.
   Includes bibliographical references and index.
      ISBN 978-0-87586-888-2 (soft cover: alk. paper) — ISBN 978-0-87586-889-9 (hard
cover: alk. paper) — ISBN 978-0-87586-890-5 (ebook) 1. Justice—United States. 2.
Democracy—United States. 3. Justice (Philosophy) 4. Rawls, John, 1921-2002—Criticism
and interpretation. I. Title.
   JC599.U5G688 2011
   320.01'1—dc23
                        2011023177

Cover photo © 2011 by Joseph Grcic

Printed in the United States

# TABLE OF CONTENTS

# CHAPTER 1. INTRODUCTION

> "If you prick us do we not bleed?
> If you tickle us do we not laugh?
> If you poison us do we not die?
> And if you wrong us, shall we not revenge?"
> —Shakespeare, *The Merchant of Venice*

For many Americans, the American Dream seems more like a vague hope than a real possibility. It is becoming increasingly clear that our society is faced with profound social and political problems. To solve these problems, we must first become aware that they exist and then look for solutions. Some of the problems are described below, and the solutions which will be defended here are based on a deeper understanding of the underlying principles of the Constitution informed by the ideas of the philosopher John Rawls.

We often hear that "America is Number One," but America is also first in some things that are not consistent with the ideals and values which define the American Dream. For example: the United States is number one in the number of people in prison (2.3 million). China, with more than five times the population, is second with 1.5 million.[1]

---

1. US Department of Justice: www.ojp.usdoj.gov; 2007; Loury, Glenn C., *Race, Incarceration and American Values*, Cambridge: MIT Press, 2008, pp. 5-6; The *New York Times*, 2/19/09, "Hispanics are Largest Ethnic Group in Federal Prisons, Study Shows," by Solomon Moore, p. A16; www.internationalheraldtribune. com 4/23/08. These numbers include those in prisons and in jails (awaiting trial or sentencing).

Although the US has only 5% of the world's population, it has 25% of the world's prisoners.[2] In recent years, 3 out of 200 young whites were in prison but 1 in 9 young African-Americans were incarcerated. Even though 137 countries have abolished the death penalty, the US has about 3,400 persons on death row. Of these, almost all are poor and 40% are African-American (African-Americans make up only 13.4% of the total population). Recent research shows beyond reasonable doubt that in the 20th century at least 39 persons (the actual numbers are certainly much higher) were executed but were innocent, and these were poor and overwhelmingly African-American.[3] More than 90% of those on death row could not afford to hire a lawyer, and inferior legal representation by overworked and underpaid public defenders has often been mentioned as a factor in miscarriages of justice.[4] Evidence shows that at least 130 people were mistakenly sentenced to death and later exonerated.[5] The lawyer and scholar Alan Dershowitz has stated, "Having no money almost ensures that you will not get justice..."[6] The overwhelming prevalence of the poor in prison and on death row helps explain the street definition of "capital punishment": "Those without the capital get the punishment." But why should the rich get better lawyers than the poor? I propose that the legal profession as we know it must be abolished and I show why this is necessary if all persons are to have

2.  Loury, op. cit. p. 5.
3.  Bedau, Adam, Michael L. Radelet, "Miscarriage of Justice in Potentially Capital Cases, *Stanford Law Review*, 1987, pp. 21-179; www.nytimes, 8/12/03; Radelet, Michael L, Adam Bedau & Constance Putnam, *In Spite of Innocence*, Boston: Northeastern Univ. Press, 1992; Adam Bedau, *The Death Penalty in America*, 4e, 1997; Adam Bedau, "The Case Against the Death Penalty" July 1992, ACLU, 5/28/08, between 1930-90, 4,016 executions of which 53% were African Americans (then 12% of the US population; between 1930-76 455 executions for rape (when it was constitutional) 90% were African American; www.innocenceproject.org reports that based on DNA evidence 232 prisoners convicted were exonerated, 70% were minorities; www.nytimes.com reports that DNA evidence freed 86 prisoners sentenced to death between 1973-89. Drug and alcohol abuse account for about 80% of the prison population and each prisoner costs about $23,876 per year while drug treatment costs range between $4.3-$7,500 per year per person. About 60% of inmates are mentally ill.
4.  Spence, Jerry, *With Justice For None*, New York: *Times* Books, 1989, pp. 112-3; Eitzen, pp. 4-5.
5.  *The Economist*, "Saving Lives and Money", 3/14/09, p. 32.
6.  Dershowirz Alan, *Fundamental Cases*, Recorded Books/Modern Scholar.com, (Course Guide) p. 20

equally good legal representation.

The US is also number one among industrialized countries in reported rapes, robbery, gun ownership, drunk driving fatalities, greenhouse gas emissions, number of cars per capita, homelessness, single-parent families and garbage produced per capita.[7] Twenty three countries have a lower per capita murder rate than the United States. The US murder rate is six times that of Germany and eight times that of Japan.[8] According to the World Health Organization, the US also leads in substance abuse (marijuana, cocaine); 15.1 million Americans are alcoholics with 22,000 alcohol related deaths yearly, and the US is fourth highest in firearm-related deaths.[9] These realities give rise to another common saying of the streets, "The rich get richer, and the poor get drunk."

The US poverty rate is also number one among developed nations. According to the most recent US government statistics, 14.3% or 39.8 million of Americans were in poverty (defined as income lower than $22,025 for a family of four) up from 13.2% in 2008. That poverty rate breaks down racially as 8.2% for whites, 10.2% for Asians, 21.5% for Hispanics, 24.5% for African-Americans and 41% for Native Americans. The latter also have an unemployment rate of 60% and life expectancy average of 45 years (78 is the expectancy for the general US population).[10] In recent years, about two million people were homeless in America at some time and homelessness is currently at a 14 year high with 49 million persons going hungry last year.[11]

America is almost number one among developed countries in the gap between the rich and the poor.[12] The US also has the highest

---

7.   Eitzen, Stanley D., *Solutions to Social Problems*: Lessons From Other Societies, 4e, Boston: Pearson Education, p. 3.

8.   www.atlanticreview.org; www.doj.gov, (Department of Justice reports 16,929 murders and 90,427 rapes in 2007)

9.   www.reuters.com, July 1, 2008; www.cdc.gov, accessed 2/8/10.

10.   www.nyt.com, Erik Eckholm, "Last Year's Poverty Rate Was Highest in 12 Years", 9/10/09; www.census.gov;

11.   www.nyt.com, Jason De Parle, "Hunger in US at 14 Year High" 11/16/09; Eitzen, D. Stanley & Janis E. Johnston, *Inequality*, Boulder, CO: Paradigm, 2007, pp. 1, 181-2.

12.   "The Rich Under Attack" *The Economist*, April 4, 2009, pp. 11-3,15;Reich, Robert, *Supercapitalism*, New York: Knopf, 2007, pp. 113-9; D. Stanley Eitzen & Janis E. Johnston, *Inequality*, Boulder, CO: Paradigm Publishers, 2007, pp. 1, 69-72; The Economist, "Ever Higher Society, Ever Harder to Ascend" 1/1/05, pp. 22-4; Newsweek Magazine, "The End of Upward Mobility?" Joel Kotkin, 1/26/09,

---

numbers of billionaires (374 out of 691) and the top .01 % of Americans are about seven times more wealthy (total assets) than the same percent in 1973.[13] The top 1% own more than 38% of the national wealth and the top 5% own or control more wealth than the bottom 95% while the bottom 40% have less than one-half of one percent of the wealth and the bottom 20% have no wealth or minus wealth due to debt.[14] A recent study by the private research group, the Organisation for Economic Cooperation and Development (OECD) reports that out of 30 developed countries studied, 26 countries have a smaller gap between the rich and poor than the US.[15]

In terms of income alone, of the most developed countries, the US is number one in unequal income distribution. Recent statistics show that 30% of the total US income goes to the top 10% of the population and 1.8% of total income goes to the bottom 10%. Another way of looking at it is that in 1978 the top 0.1% of the population took in 2.7% of total income, but in 2006 the top 0.1% took in 11.6% of total personal income.[16] The OECD reports that the average income of the richest 10% is $93,000, the highest level of all 30 OECD countries, while the bottom 10% have average income of $5,800, 20% lower than the average for OECD countries.[17] The average American annual family income is now $32,660 but it is $36,857 in Britain and $35,593 in Japan.[18] Nationally, household debt has recently grown at the fastest rate in the last twenty years and credit card debt has grown by more than 100% in the past ten years, being an average of $9,312.[19] In terms of helping the bottom 10%, Japan is number one and the US is

p. 64; James Loewen, *Lies My Teacher Told Me*, New York: The New Press, 1995, 2.24.

13. Krugman, Paul, *Conscience of a Liberal*, New York: Norton, 2009, p. 129.

14. Rothman, Robert A., *Inequality and Stratification*, 4e,Upper Saddle River, NJ: Prentice Hall, 2002, p. 101; Larry Bartels, *Unequal Democracy*, Princeton, NJ: Princeton Univ. Press, 2008, p. 1-2; Lou Dobbs, *War on the Middle Class*, New York: Penguin Books, 2006, pp. 19-20; Jeffrey D. Sachs, *The End of Poverty*, New York: Penguin Press, 2005, 305-7; www.barackobama.org, 10/9/09; www.multinationalmonitor.org, " The Wealth Divide", 10/9/09.

15. www.OECD.org

16. *Time Magazine*, "Pay Them Less? Hell, Yes" by Justin Fox, 3/2/09, p. 30.

17. *New York Times*, 11/27/08 www.oecd.org; worldwatch.org.

18. Dobbs, Lou, *Independents Day*, New York: Viking, 2007, p. 17.

19. Emmanuel, Rahm, & Bruce Reed, *The Plan: Big Ideas for America*, New York: Public Affairs, 2006, p. 37.

85th, even behind China.[20]

The numbers on upward social mobility (the likelihood of moving up to a higher socio-economic class regardless of the class of one's birth), a cornerstone of the American Dream, don't look very promising either.[21] Children from the low income social class have a 1% chance of making it to the top 5% of society but the offspring of the wealthy have a 22% chance of the same. African-American children are twice as likely to stay in the same economic class as white children from the same class. Children from the middle class have a 1.8% chance of moving to the top 5%. France, Germany, Sweden, Canada, Finland, Norway and Denmark have higher economic mobility than the US.[22]

The exponential growth of executive salaries has exacerbated the problem of class stratification. Though recent legislation in response to the subprime mortgage crisis of 2008, The Emergency Economic Stabilization Act of 2008, seeks to place some limits on some executive salaries, executive pay has grown so rapidly that the typical executive of the top 200 companies earns $11.7 million annually, which means he or she earns more in one day than the average worker earns in a year, or, in other words, 344 times the wage of the average worker. In 1980 it was only 42 times.[23] Between 2006–2008, the average total compensation for an American CEO was $18 million, an increase of 20.55% since 2006, but the average worker compensation in the same time was $36,140, an increase of 3.5%.[24] A recent survey revealed that American executives make about 22 times the salaries of comparable CEOs of Japanese firms and 17 times the CEOs

---

20. Greider, William, *Come Home, America*, New York: Rodale, 2009, p. 215; median family income was $52,000 in 2007 and $50,300 in 2008 (www.nyt.com, Eckholm, op. cit.).
21. Newsweek Magazine, "The End of Upward Mobility?" by Joel Kotkin, 1/26/09, p. 64; "Ever Higher Society, Ever Harder to Ascend" The Economist, 1/1/05, pp22-4.
22. Krugman, Paul, *Conscience of a Liberal*, p. 249; Rothkopf, David, *Superclass*, New York: Farrar, Straus and Giroux,2008, p. 71; Tom Hertz, "Understanding Mobility in America", Center for American Progress, April 26, 2006.
23. Sandel, Michael L., *Justice: What's the Right Thing To Do?* New York: Farrar, Straus and Giroux, 2009, p. 18; www.newyorktimes.com, 4/6/08; Bill Moyers, *Moyers on Democracy*, New York: Doubleday, 2008, p. 107; "Battling for Corporate America" The Economist, 3/11/06, pp. 69-71. *The Futurist*, July-August, 2009, p. 32.
24. www.publiccitizen.org, 2/18/09.

in Europe.[25] It gets worse. An executive for Merrill Lynch spent $1.22 million to redecorate his office after the company was in financial crisis and received TARP (Troubled Assets Relief Program, $700 billion) bailout money.[26] The New York State comptroller shows that it's business as usual in executive pay. It has been reported that Wall Street bankers and traders received a total of $18.4 billion in bonuses (i.e., not including salary or stock options) in 2008, the sixth largest sum in bonuses, even though it was one of the worst years on record and some of the bonuses were paid by banks which received federal bailout money.[27]

In the case of Merrill Lynch, 149 employees received $3 million or more for a total of $858 million.[28] More recently, AIG (American International Group) which received nearly $200 billion from the federal government, (making it 80% government owned) initially reported it paid $165 million in bonuses to its executives but later it was revealed that the actual bonus amount was $454 million, even though it reported a fourth quarter loss of $61.7 billion in 2008, the largest loss ever in the history of the planet.[29] Nevertheless, AIG paid 73 executives more than one million dollars (one received $6.4 million) bonuses including $33.6 million to 52 who then quickly quit.[30] This might be explained by the fact that AIG donated more than $9 million to various senators and congressmen and at least 28 members of Congress own AIG stock.[31] Goldman Sachs, a Wall Street investment firm which received TARP money in 2008 but paid it back, announced in 2009 that it would pay $11.4 billion (that's billion)

25. www.sagepub.com, "Executive Compensation: A Comparison of US and Japan" by Yuka Hayashi & Phred Dvorak, ; www.wsj.com " Japanese Wrestle with CEO Pay as they go Global" 11/28/08; "CEO Pay: Don't Look to Japan for Answers" Kenji Hall, *BusinessWeek*, 2/23/09, p. 60.
26. www.bloomberg.com, 1/23/09.
27. *New York Times*, 1/29/09 "What Red Ink? Wall St. Paid Hefty Bonuses" Ben White, pp1 & 17.
28. *New York Times*, pp B1, B8, "Nearly 700 at Merrill in Million-Dollar Club" by Michael J. De la Merced & Louise Story, 2/12/09.
29. Nagourney, Adam, *New York Times* "Bracing for a Bailout Backlash" 3/16/09, p. 1.
30. *New York Times*, 3/18/09 "418 Got AIG Bonuses: Outcry Grows in Capital" By Jackie Calmes and Louise Story, p. A1.
31. www.opensecrets.com, 3/26/09; Senator Dodd received $280,000, Obama as senator received $130,000 and Senator McCain received $59,000 in the last 20 years.

in bonuses to its employees, in addition to their average salaries of $700,000 yearly. The new bank bailout proposed by the Secretary of the Treasury, Timothy Geithner, in the amount of $2.5 trillion, reportedly includes CEO pay limits; but skeptics warn of loopholes and small print.[32]

Some of the highest paid CEOs are hedge fund managers. In 2008, one hedge fund manager was paid $3.7 *billion* and such managers have formed a club called the "Top 25" where the minimum compensation is $360 million. William Gross, a hedge fund manager, remarked concerning these high salaries, "There is nothing wrong with it—it's legal. But it's ugly."[33]

President Obama has described these bonus payments as "shameful" and an "outrage" but it is claimed that nothing can be done about it since Congress rushed to pass TARP and other bailouts but did not include provisions on executive pay limits.[34] Once again it seems our politicians lack creativity when it comes to dealing with taxpayers' money. New proposals from the White House as part of the new economic stimulus legislation (now approaching $1 trillion) call for executive pay limit of $500,000 but, of course, there will be the usual loopholes big enough to drive a truck through, a truck filled with money on the way to the executives' luxury estates.[35] The Dodd-Frank Wall Street Reform and Consumer Protection Act (2010) deals with some of these issues but, once again, critics are concerned about loopholes, enforcement and possible future repeal as has happened with other regulations in the past. One is reminded of what Barry Goldwater reportedly said about Washington's attitude to taxpayers' money, "A billion here and a billion there, pretty soon you're talking real money."

The increasing gap between the rich and poor is in part explained by recent events concerning the financial crisis. Some critics call the TARP bailout as corporate welfare, a kind of socialism for the rich or

32. *New York Times*, "Bailout Plan: $2.5 Trillion and a Strong US Hand" by Stephen Labaton & Edmund Andrews, 2/11/09, pp. A1, A21.
33. www.nytimes.com " Wall Street Winners Get Billion-Dollar Payday" 4/16/08.
34. *New York Times*, 1/30/09 p1, "Banker Bonuses Are "Shameful" Obama Declares", Sheryl Gay Stolberg & Stephen Labaton.
35. *New York Times* "Executive Pay Limits Seek to Alter Corporate Culture" by Stephen Labaton & Vikas Bajaj, 2/5/09, pp. A1, B4.

"lemon socialism."[36] When business is good, the rich keep the money; when there are problems and business turns out to be a "lemon," trillions of other people's money is lost but the corporations are deemed too big to fail; government bailouts help the rich, who get the fat bonuses, stock options, etc. But the reality is far more vast than just bonuses when one considers the report of the Congressional Oversight Panel charged with monitoring TARP money; at least $78 billion has been wasted in purchasing possibly worthless bank assets.[37]

In addition to the problems of income and social mobility, the typical working conditions of the average American worker are also troubling. The Department of Labor states that 4, 340 employees were killed on the job last year.[38] However, some estimates which include deaths from illness and injury sustained on the jobs are over 50,000.[39] Scandals include the Enron Corp., where over 20,000 employees lost their pensions and jobs in 2001 due to lies and greed of top executives; Tyco International where top managers were accused of stealing $600 million (2004) and convicted on thirty counts; and Worldcom, whose CEOs were reported to have stolen $3.8 billion (2002) after which the firm filed for bankruptcy.[40] The Wall Street financier Bernard Madoff is accused of largest securities fraud in history in the amount of $50 billion, while the SEC (Securities and Exchange Commission) was seemingly asleep at the switch. He is now in prison (his son recently committed suicide, reportedly as a result of the scandal).

The testimony of a whistleblower who tried to warn the SEC of the Madoff problem for almost ten years was not taken seriously.[41] This fact and others like it suggest to many that the Madoff scandal occurred partly because of what is called "regulatory capture", where

36. Krugman, Paul, "Bailouts for Bunglers" *New York Times*, 2/2/09 p. A19.
37. www.bloggingstocks.com 2/6/09; "The Bailout is Broken" *BusinessWeek*, 2/9/09 pp. 21-6.
38. www.sfgate.com (San Francisco Chronicle 4/27/08) Jerry Spence, op. cit., pp. 198-204.
39. Simon, David R., & D. Stanley Eitzen, *Elite Deviance*, Boston: Allyn and Bacon, 1993, p. 40; Gerry Spence p. xiii; David Newman, *Sociology*, 5e, London: Pine Forge Press, p. 265; Thom Hartmann, *Unequal Protection*, Rodale Press, 2004, pp. 184-5.
40. Hartmann, Thom, *Unequal Protection*, Rodale Press, 2004, pp. 152-3, 280.
41. *New York Times*, "At Madoff Hearing, Lawmakers Lay Into SEC" 2/5/09 p. B1

government regulators, such as the SEC, which are by law created to watch over business transactions and keep them honest, are captured or dominated by pro-industry personnel (through campaign money—Madoff and friends gave almost a million dollars, etc.) and corrupted to the point they do little or nothing (with budget cuts, insufficient personnel, etc.) to prevent large scale rip-offs.[42] In addition to the Madoff scam, the financial crisis of 2008–9 has caused losses to the pensions of ordinary workers now estimated at over two trillion dollars.[43] With the Madoff case and other revelations now unfolding of fraud and deception by billionaires, one is reminded of a saying of W.C. Fields, "You can fool some of the people some of the time, and that's enough to make a pretty good living."

Globalization has played its part as well in creating anxiety in the average worker. Corporations use outsourcing, where part of the product is made by other companies or moved to another country entirely, in search of cheaper labor and raw materials, so that manufacturing, which was about 27% of GDP in 1960s, is now about half that, and less than 10% of American labor is in manufacturing; 1.3 million manufacturing jobs have moved overseas. More and more white collar jobs are also being shipped overseas, and things don't look good since the US is 11th in spending for research and development (Germany is #1) and 23rd in quality of infrastructure. Given these dismal statistics, it should come as no surprise that the US is 84th in domestic savings (Kuwait is #1).

Now the largest mall in the world is in China and so are the largest factories and the largest public corporation and casino; the largest skyscraper is now in Dubai, in the United Arab Emirates; and the biggest movie industry is in Bollywood (Mumbai, India), not Hollywood.[44] US dependence on foreign oil has risen from 37% in 1980 to 58% in 2008.[45] This explains partly the fact that the US has had a trade deficit since 1975, and currently we import twice as much as we

---

42. "At Madoff Hearing, Lawmakers Lay Into SEC" *New York Times*, 2/5/09, p. B1 & 10; www.opensecrets.org " Madoff and Company Spent Nearly $1 Million on Washington Influence" 12/08.

43. www.moneymorning.com, 1/29/09.

44. Zakaria, Fareed, *The Post American World*, New York: Norton, 2009, pp. 2-3; Fareed Zakaria, "Are American's Best Days Behind Us?" *Time*, March 14, 2011, pp. 28-35.

45. US News & World Report, 11/3/08, p. 38.

export. Consequently, the US is now the largest debtor nation in the world, owing more than $13 trillion — much of it to the Chinese. It is not hard to understand why the insecurity of the American working class has been growing for years and is only being exacerbated by the worsening recession.[46]

Women in the US still earn on average only 77 cents for every dollar men earn; the average African-American earns 75 cents and the average Latino 71 cents. The net worth for whites is an average of $88,000, for Latinos $8,000 and for African-Americans $6,000.[47] The housing and subprime mortgage crises have increased bankruptcies and made the realization of the American dream of home ownership less likely.

Would these problems and scandals have happened or, if they did happen would they have been as severe, if workers and members of the community knew early on what was happening in these corporations? Probably not, but how could they know when executives who profited from these illegal and unethical activities did so in secret? In addition, we must take into account that there is a changing attitude to work itself. Workers have higher education want more from work than a paycheck; they are looking for interesting, rewarding work, some influence over the workplace, and an opportunity for self-development. How can the modern corporation reflect these needs and act in a more ethical manner? In other words, how can the corporation have a conscience? In chapter twelve I argue that the way to respond to changing worker demands and create a conscience for the corporation is to have workers and members of the community, in addition to stockholders, become equal voting members of the board of directors of major corporations.

Even though the US health care system is the most expensive in the world, consuming 17% of the economy, before Obama's Patient Protection and Affordable Care Act becomes law fully in 2014, an estimated 45 million Americans are without health care insurance (the number one cause of personal bankruptcies) which becomes

---

46.  Douthat, Ross & Reihan Salam, *Grand New Party*, New York: Doubleday, 2008, pp. 7, 53-5.
47.  Obama, Barack, *The Audacity of Hope*, New York: Three Rivers Press, 2006, pp. 242-3.

60 million when those with inadequate coverage are included.[48] It is estimated that this lack of coverage caused over 101,000 unnecessary and premature deaths from 2002 and 2003.[49] Medical errors alone are responsible for more than 98,000 deaths a year and medical waste, fraud and abuse were estimated at $60 billion.[50] Unfortunately, even if one has insurance and is admitted to a hospital in the US, every year about 90,000 patients die from newly evolved hard to kill bacteria and viruses contracted while in the hospital.[51] If this isn't bad enough, the survival rate for breast cancer is better in Switzerland, Norway, Britain and other countries than in the US. Seventeen people die every day in the US due to lack of organs for transplantation because an insufficient number of people donate their organs or make provision to have their organs donated at death.[52] The World Health Organization ranks the US 37th in performance of its health care system.[53] Not unrelated to this is the fact that the US is first in obesity and 34th in life expectancy of 78.6 (e.g., Japan is first with 82) and 28 countries have a lower infant mortality rate than the US.[54]

The American family has not had it easy either. The US has one of the highest divorce rates in the world. Some surveys have the US as number one in divorces; others have it second or third. Out of wedlock births have been rising, with now nearly 4 out of 10 American children being born to single mothers; 77% of women in prison are single mothers while 80% percent have been sexually and physically abused before being incarcerated. Although only about 10% of the prison population is female, it has risen 64% since 1995. The US has the lowest percentage in the West of children living with both biological parents, only 63%, and it also has the highest rate of teenage pregnancy and abortion.[55]

---

48. Emmanuel, op. cit., p. 100.
49. *Time* 12/1/08 p. 44; *Newsweek*, 3/31/08, p. 47; Emmanuel, op. cit., p. 105; *US News & World Report* "Federal Action Required" by Judy Feder, has a smaller figure of 22,000 persons per year, 2/09.
50. Emmanuel, op. cit., p. 105; www.freerepublic.com, on Aug. 12, 2009;
51. AARP Bulletin, "Killer Germs" March 2009, p. 13.
52. www.NYT.com, D. Sanghavi, "When Does Death Start?", 12/16/09.
53. www.geographic.org, "The World Health Organization's Ranking of the World Health Systems" 1/4/10.
54. *Time*, 12/1/08 p. 43; *Newsweek*, 3/31/08, p. 47.
55. *New York Times*, 3/19/09, "'07 US Births Break Baby Boom Record" By Erik Eck-

About 5.8 million children in the US were reported abused or ne-glected last year but experts estimate the real number is likely three times that.[56] Four children die every day due to abuse and neglect and more than one in six of American children live in poverty which added up to 12.3 million children recently. One in four females is sexually abused and one in six males before the age of 18.[57] Suicide is the third cause of death among teenagers (second among college students) and rising, and the suicide rate is also on the rise among baby boomers, especially middle-aged women.[58] A third of American children suffer from obesity.[59] The UN ranked the US 17th out of 20 industrialized nations in terms of the welfare of children.[60]

Although the US spends more on education on a per capita basis than any other country, the US is 18th in educational effectiveness at the secondary level and 19 countries have a higher literacy rate (Fin-land is first, South Korea, second, Netherlands, third).[61] According to a survey of employers, only 22% of employees who were recent high school graduates had adequate math skills and only 30% had suf-ficient reading skills. Motorola spends an average of $1,350 per em-ployee to teach them basic skills. Prisoners who receive literacy help have a 16% recidivism rate while those who do not get such help have a 77% chance of returning to prison.[62] In mathematical literacy, the US was 25th out of 30 developed nations (Finland is first, South Ko-rea, second, Canada, third).[63] Twenty percent of Americans think the sun moves around the earth, 6% think the moon landing was faked and only 39% believe in evolution, 66% believe the earth is about 10,000 years old (scientists hold that the earth is about 4.6 billion years old), 25% do not and 36% have no opinion.[64] In a recent survey

holm, p. A15; *USA Today*, 7/18/05, p. 12.
56. www.childhelp. org, " Child Abuse in America" (figures for 2007), 1/4/10.
57. www.teenhelp. com 1/4/10.
58. *USA News*, Oct 21 2008.
59. *Time*, 12/1/08, p. 64.
60. Johnston, David Cay, *Free Lunch*, New York: Portfolio/Penguin, 2007, p. 280.
61. UN Development Program, Human Development Education Index.
62. http://inkarceratted.intrasun.tcnj.edu, 10/11/09.
63. Isaacson, Walter, "How to Raise the Standard in America's Schools," *Time* Mag-azine, 4/27/09, pp. 32-6; Moyers, Bill, *Moyers on Democracy*, New York: Double-day, 2008, p. 238; at UC Berkeley, 47.5 % of the students are Asian-American even though they make up only about 4.9% of the US population.
64. Gallup poll, www.usnews.com 2/11/09

of teens, only 41% could name the three branches of government but 59% could name all of the Three Stooges and 59% in a recent survey could not name the Vice President.[65] This could be explained by a recent survey which shows that US college freshmen spend more time drinking than studying.[66] Americans in general watch an average of four and a half hours of television a day, which is 3/4 of their free time and 90 minutes more than the rest of the world and more than they spend in the classroom.[67]

Perhaps part of the problem with the public schools can be explained by the fact that 12% of all US students attend private schools, but 37% of US representatives and 45% of US senators send their children to private schools.[68] The cost of private schools is well beyond the reach of the middle class (yearly tuition with room and board at St. Albans, where Al Gore was a student, is now $44,457; Phillips Academy, attended by President George W. Bush, is $41,000 a year).[69] The high school graduation rate for the US is now 77% for white students and only 46% for African-Americans and 29% for Latinos.[70]

The US spends more than twice as much on prisoners ($22,000 each per year; some estimates are as high as $33,000) than on K-12 education ($11,000 average per student over 50 states). Low educational achievement and high dropout rates are associated with lower incomes, poor health and higher rates of imprisonment; two thirds of prisoners are high school dropouts. One third of Microsoft's knowledge employees in its Redmond, Washington site are from India.[71] If the US were to improve its educational performance to the top levels of nations, it would mean a rise of between $1.3–$2.3 trillion in eco-

---

65. Jacoby, Susan, *The Age of American Unreason*, New York: Pantheon Books, 2008, p. 203; Mark Bauerlein, *The Dumbest Generation*, New York: Tarcher/Penguin, 2008, pp. 17-19;Bass, Think, p. 345.
66. *USA Today*, "College Freshmen Study Booze More Than Books", Mary Beth Marklein, 3/11/09, p. 4D.
67. Gore, op. cit., p. 6.
68. Lobel, Hannah, "Putting the Public Back in Public Education," *Utne*, Jan-Feb. 09, p. 45.
69. Websites of the respective schools.
70. *Time*, 12/8/08, p. 36.
71. *The Futurist*, July-August, 2009, p. 32.

nomic production, a rise between 9–16%.[72]

Although an increasing number of countries offer free college education, in the US the average college cost (with room and board) is rising at a rate higher than inflation. Currently, a year in a private college has now risen to an average of $32,307 and $13,589 at state colleges.[73] The US has the second most expensive public universities (after Australia) and the most expensive private colleges (with yearly room and board: George Washington U. at $50,660; Notre Dame at $51,300; Stanford at $49,000; Harvard at $48,868).[74] In 1980, private college tuition was about 20% of the median family income; now it is 50%. For public colleges, it was 4%; now it is 11%—which may explain in part why the US is 12th in college graduates on a per capita basis and 6th in college enrollment (South Korea is #1).[75]

At the same time the evidence shows that a college degree is not necessarily a ticket to upward mobility unless one attends a very selective, usually private, college.[76] Middle class Americans struggle to get a degree, and then struggle to pay off their college debt for years after they graduate—if they do graduate. But wealthy Americans can get their children into an ivy league college, even if they are not exactly scholars, by donating a million dollars (or less); then they can be admitted with no questions asked about SATs or GPAs.[77] The elite know that the key to staying in the elite, next to being born into it, is to attend an elite college or university.[78] Ignoring the SATs is quite an advantage, especially since Americans' scores on the SAT Verbal have been declining since the 1960s.[79] In 2002, 29.4% of whites had a four year college degree or more while only 17.2 % of African-Americans did.[80] America was once first in college attendance, now it is

72. "The Economic Impact of the Achievement Gap in America's Schools" Report by McKinsey & Company, www.mckinsey.com, p. 5, accessed 3/20/09.
73. www.nytimes.com, Oct 23 2007
74. www.forbes.com, 3/24/09.
75. Goldin, Claudia, "Tales Out of School." *New York Times Book Review*, 2/7/2010, p. 26.
76. *Newsweek* Magazine, "The End of Upward Mobility?", by Joel Kotkin, 1/26/09, p. 64.
77. Golden, Daniel, *The Price of Admission*, New York: Crown Publishers, 2006, pp. 24-33.
78. Rothkopf, op. cit., pp. 78, 290.
79. Murray, Charles, *Real Education*, pp. 113-4
80. Hughes, *Sociology*, p. 235

ninth in the world.[81]

The political system, state and federal and all three branches have serious problems as well.[82] Primarily because of gerrymandering, where voting districts are designed to favor a certain party, only 10% of the 435 seats of the House of Representatives are truly competitive.[83] The cost of national campaign elections has skyrocketed so that the average winning House campaign costs $1.1 million and the Senate campaign estimates range between $5.6 million and $10 million. The 2008 election saw a record spending of almost $1 billion (primary and general elections) with the Obama campaign spending $712 million (raised $742) and Senator McCain $326 million (raised $357 million). President Obama's goal for the 2012 election is one billion dollars.[84] Most of these monies were collected from less than 1% of the population: private citizens who gave $200 or more; and half the donors have incomes of $250,000 or more.[85] Currently, at least 42 out of one hundred senators are millionaires and 123 out of 435 representatives.[86] Former senator Jon Corzine (D-NJ) spent more than $60 million of his own money and won. (Why would anyone spend $60 million for a job that pays $169,000 yearly?)

Although several campaign reform laws have been enacted, because of loopholes, inconsistent Supreme Court rulings, and other limitations in the law, the role of money still being contributed

81.  Emmanuel, op. cit., p. 70. What does it say about America that 45% of UC Berkeley, which some call the Harvard of the West coast, students are Asian-Americans although they are less than 5% of the population?

82.  Gore, Al, *The Assault on Reason*, New York: Penguin Press, 2007, pp. 72-82; Ernest Fritz Hollings, *Making Government Work*, Columbia, SC: Univ. Of South Carolina Press, 2008, pp. 4-5,165-7; Ronald Dworkin, *Is Democracy Possible Here?*,Princeton, NJ: Princeton Univ. Press, 2006, pp. 128-131; Mark Green, *Selling Out*, New York: Regan Books, 2002, pp. 18-9, 73; Marian Currinder, *Money in the House*, Boulder, CO: Westview Press, 2009, pp. 199-201.

83.  Kuttner, Robert, *The Squandering of America*, New York: Vintage Books, 2008, pp. 268-70; Bradley, Bill, *The New American Story*, New York: Random House, 2008, p. 203; Thomas E. Mann & Norman J. Ornstein, *The Broken Branch*, Oxford: Oxford Univ. Press, 2006, pp. 229-30.

84.  www.opensecrets.org, 2/8/09; Chuck Todd & Sheldon Gawiser, *How Barack Obama Won*, New York: Vintage Books, 2009, pp. 9-30.

85.  www.newsweek.com, Michael Isikoff, "Obama's 'Good Will Hunting'" 10/4/08; Eitzen *Solution to Social Problems*, p. 84.

86.  Green, Mark, *Losing Our Democracy*, Naperville, IL: Sourcebooks, 2006, pp. 21-28; Barack Obama Audacity, p. 109; These numbers are based on income not total assets which would make the number of millionaires much larger.

overwhelmingly by the affluent to political campaigns is a concern to many. The 2010 ruling of the Supreme Court in *Citizens United* v. *Federal Election Commission* held that limiting independent campaign spending by corporations is unconstitutional, threatens to introduce a flood of private money into campaigns. As Senator Bob Dole remarked, "Poor people don't make campaign contributions. You might get a different result if there were a 'Poor PAC' [Political Action Committee] up here."[87] Research shows that in overwhelming number of cases, the candidate who spends more in the campaign usually wins.[88] This is not a view just held by Democrats, for even Newt Gingrich, before he was Speaker of the House, said, "Congress is increasingly a system of corruption in which money politics is defeating and driving out citizen politics."[89] Republican candidate for president Senator John McCain (R., AZ) agrees, saying that American politics is "an influence peddling scheme in which both parties conspire to stay in office by selling the country to the highest bidder."[90] Even more recently Sen. Dick Durbin (D., IL.) said, "...the banks are still the most powerful lobby on Capitol Hill, and they, frankly, own the place."[91]

According to the Constitution, the purpose of the legislature is to "establish justice, insure domestic tranquility, provide for the common defense, promote the general welfare and secure the blessings of liberty." In reality, many laws are drafted, at least in part, to promote the well-being of corporations and special interests through pork-barrel provisions. Pork-barrel spending, also known as earmarking, is money set aside for special projects by senators and representatives in legislation without debate and competitive bidding. These monies, as argued by Senator McCain and others, are widely agreed to be essentially outright gifts of money to reward campaign contributors, lobbyists and special interests. Recent examples of these set asides include the "bridge to nowhere" in Alaska for $200 million, $234,000 to study wild turkeys, $500,000 for a teapot museum, $100,000 for

---

87. Kaiser, *So Damn Much Money*, p. 148.
88. Goidel, Robert K., Donald A. Gross, Todd G. Shields, Money Matters, New York: Rowman & Littlefield, 1999 Gore, op. cit.
89. Moyers, p. 184.
90. Quoted in Gar Alperovitz, *America Beyond Capitalism*, p. 11
91. www.huffingtonpost.com, accessed 4/29/09.

goat research, etc., amounting to 10,656 projects for a total of $22.9 billion in recent years and growing at an alarming rate.[92]

Leon Panetta, who served in the Clinton administration and then became President's Obama's Director of the CIA (now nominated by President Obama to become secretary of defense) has called campaign contributions "legalized bribery."[93] Panetta goes on to say that members of the House and Senate "rarely legislate; they basically follow the money... They're spending more and more time dialing for dollars... The only place they have to turn is the lobbyists... It has become an addiction they can't break."[94] The evidence confirms the old saying attributed to Mark Hanna, a wealthy businessman, who said, "There are two things that are important in politics. The first is money and I can't remember what the second one is."[95]

The reality is that the people we elect to represent our interests often vote on bills they didn't write or even read. Congressman John Conyers (D-MI) admitted it, saying about the health bill, "I love the members [of Congress]—they get up and say 'Read the bill'. What good is reading the bill if it's a thousand pages and you don't have 2 days and 2 lawyers to find out what it means...?"[96] However, most bills are carefully drafted, at least in part, by special interest lobbyists to promote their special interests.[97] Lobbyists are highly-paid agents of special interests, corporations, unions, professions, etc., hired to influence legislation and get a piece of lucrative government contracts to benefit their employers. And the number and influence of lobbyists is increasing.[98] There are now more than 35,000 lobby-

---

92. Diamond, Larry, *The Spirit of Democracy*, New York: Times Books, 2008, pp. 350-3; *New York Times*, 4\7\08; Dick Morris and Eileen McGann, *Outrage*, p. 138; Mann, op. cit., pp. 175-8; www.seattletimes.com, David Heath, 1/7/09, 12/31/08, "The Favor Factory 2008", see also www.taxpayersforcommonsense.org, www.earmarkwatch.org www.sunlightfoundation

93. Kaiser, op .cit., p. 19.

94. Ibid., p. 19

95. Moyers, p. 179.

96. www.cnsnews.com 7/27/09

97. Currindeer, Marian, *Money in the House*, Boulder Westview Press, pp. 199-202; Carville, James, & Paul Begala, *Take it Back*, New York: Simon & Schuster, 2006, pp. 142-69; "Fahrenheit 9/11" (2004) Michael Moore, Representative John Conyers (D. Michigan) made the remark about not reading bills before voting on them.

98. Johnston, op. cit.

---

ists and the spending of the lobbying establishment has grown from $1.4 billion in 1998 to $3.24 billion in 2008.[99]

One way lobbyists get influence, besides campaign contributions, (and other gifts some now illegal due to new ethics legislation) is to allow politicians to cash in their public service experience in the much more lucrative private sector. Although some legislation has been passed to limit these activities, plenty of loopholes have been left so that lobbyists can still promise politicians jobs (the "revolving door") after they leave office such as becoming lobbyists themselves, consultants to lobbyists or hiring their spouse. More than 43% of members of Congress retiring between 1998–2005 cashed in and became lobbyists (often preceded by spouses and/or children as lobbyists) making far larger salaries then they received as members of Congress.[100] Members of Congress currently make $169,300, (Speaker makes $212,000 and other leaders make $183,500) plus a generous expense account and $60,972 pension (plus Social Security), for a three day (or less) work week and over four months of vacation.[101] The politicians have also instituted an automatic pay increase system so that they do not have to go on record with their vote. If this system stays in place congressional salaries will be quietly increased this year to $174,000.

Tax laws are central to what Congress does and the tax laws generally tax ordinary workers at a higher rate than investment income and capital gains which are overwhelmingly received by the wealthy elite.[102] Warren Buffett, a billionaire and one of the richest men in the world, stated "...I'll pay a lower effective tax rate this year than my receptionist. In fact, I'm pretty sure I pay a lower rate than the average American."[103] Buffett was right; in 2003 his taxes were 15% and his receptionists' was almost twice that when FICA is included.[104] Many also don't know that the Social Security (FICA) tax, now 6.2%, is only paid on income up to $106,800, but not at all on investment income, which means the rich pay a much smaller percentage

99. www.opensecrets.org, 2/21/09.
100. www.publiccitizen.org
101. Diamond, op. cit., p. 352.
102. Johnston, pp. 288-9
103. Obama, *Audacity*, pp 189-90
104. Ibid., p. 190.

when their total income is taken into account but receive the most generous Social Security payments once they retire. (Should the very rich receive any Social Security at all?)

Recently President Obama sought legislation to curb overseas tax havens such as the Cayman Islands (where one small building is the "home" of 18, 857 firms), which corporations list as their address in order to cut their taxes. The issues are complex: although the top tax rate for corporations is currently 35%, with various loopholes and offshore registrations the resulting tax rate is only 2.3%.[105] This recalls the old saying about how law is like sausages: if you want to enjoy eating sausages, it's best not to know how they're made.

The revolving door has been spinning more rapidly recently. One third of top congressional aides became lobbyists, making much higher incomes.[106] As consultants, former members of Congress can also become directors of various corporations and make thousands of dollars for attending a couple of do-nothing meetings (in essence, vacations, golf outings, etc.).[107]

And there are, of course, the always generous speaking fees. Former presidents can make $50,000 or more per speech to various corporate bodies. These "speeches," usually a collection of old jokes, vague observations and flattery of various bigwigs present, remind many of the old Washington scam of letting someone "win" at a private poker game; both may be really bribes. Of course, with a few changes, one can give the same speech many times. And then there are the so-called "fact finding" trips for congressmen and senators which are in fact vacations paid for by special-interest lobbies, often disguised as non-profit foundations (usually funded by lobbyists and/or PACs).

The sad fact is that there is another way of paying for elections,

---

105. "Obama Asks Curb on Havens Use to Limit Taxes" by Jackie Calmes & Edmund L. Andrews, *New York Times*, 5/5/09, pp. A1 & A3.
106. *USA Today*, "Third of Top Aides Become Lobbyists" by Matt Kelley, 12/26/08, p. 1.
107. *New York Times*, "For Daschle, Lucrative Work Advising Clients Seeking Influence in Washington" 2/2/09, p. A11. Even President Obama, who campaigned against using lobbyists in his administration (e.g., nominated W. Lynn as Deputy Secretary of Defense, lobbyist for Raytheon) has made exceptions which are a concern to some, *US News & World Report*, 2/8/9 "No Lobbyists in the Obama Administration—Except When There Is One".

public financing, but many resist it thinking that it would just add more taxes. However, what opponents of public financing of elections fail to notice is that pork spending and various favors to lobbyists in legislation biased in favor of the corporate elite which the lobbyists represent have been estimated to cost each American at least $1,600 per year (real amount is likely much higher) but as little as five dollars per taxpayer would provide for public finance of all congressional elections.[108] The problem of money was well expressed by the writer Upton Sinclair, "It is difficult to get a man to understand something when his job depends on not understanding it." From a purely economic perspective, public financing makes sense and in chapter I argue that all federal and state elections should be publicly funded.

Recurring scandals dramatize the corruption and incompetence in all branches of the political realm. The 9/11/01 Al Qaeda terrorist attacks on the US, resulting in over 3,000 American deaths and massive economic losses, were clear instance of a tragic incompetence of government. Due, in part, to mismanagement by FEMA (Federal Emergency Management Administration) and other agencies, the 2005 hurricane Katrina resulted in the death of 1,836 people (705 still missing) and massive damage and property loss in the amount of $81.2 billion making it the most costly natural disaster in US history. Scandals such as that by lobbyist Jack Abramoff who pleaded guilty to felonies related to bribing public officials and cheating Native American tribes of about $80 million,[109] was overhead as saying about money and campaign contributions, "I was participating in a system of legalized bribery. All of it is bribery, every bit of it...They [representatives, senators, lobbyists] all participate, all of them."[110] (Of course, apparently, in his case, not all of it was "legal" bribery.) In a clear case, Congressman Randy "Duke" Cunningham of California pleaded guilty to taking bribes of $2.4 million. FBI agents found about $100,000 cash in the freezer of Congressman William Jefferson of Louisiana, suspected of bribery.[111] Former Governor Rod Blagojev-

---

108. Moyers, *On Democracy*, p. 73.
109. Kaiser, op. cit., p. 17.
110. Ibid., p. 18.
111. *New York Times*, 6/5/07 Diamond, Larry, op. cit., p. 348

ich of Illinois has been accused of trying to sell President Obama's Senate seat for about a million dollars. (Why do governors have the power to appoint a replacement? Why not the state assembly or a popular vote?) He was impeached and removed from office but still faces federal corruption charges. The current financial crisis and bailouts have been, according to many critics, caused in part by failure of governmental oversight, regulation and integrity which may eventually cost the American people more than two trillion dollars. A recent poll asked, "What do you think our elected representatives are: dedicated public servants or lying windbags?" and 44% responded "lying windbags."[112]

It seems that the best and brightest are not interested in seeking political office.[113] But the rich, and those who want to be rich, still are. Is politics only for the rich or friends of the rich and if so, can the rest of us expect fair representation? When, if ever, will the often quoted line by Will Rogers, "Congress is the best money can buy" be an historical relic? I argue in chapter eleven that we need a new right, what I call the right to political leave, which will give all a more equal chance to run for public office.

Democracy means rule by the people, either directly or by representatives, but do we need a bicameral legislature consisting of the House of Representatives and the Senate to represent us? During the constitutional convention of 1787, Alexander Hamilton echoed the sentiments of his fellow rich white men, who were deeply suspicious of democracy, when he argued for the establishment of the Senate as a necessary "permanent barrier" against the "turbulence of the democratic spirit"[114] Hamilton and his cronies were successful since the Senate, given the filibuster rule, is in fact an antidemocratic institution where 11% of the population can block the other 89%.[115] I argue that we do not need two houses of Congress and that we should abolish the 'Millionaires' Club,' the Senate.

This brings us to the judicial branch of the government. No justice is possible without honest, competent and independent judges,

---

112. Moyers, op. cit., p. 180.
113. Drew, Elizabeth, *The Corruption of American Politics*, pp. 22-3, 61-7; "Up the Academy" by Andrew Ferguson, The Weekly Standard, 2/9/09, pp. 10-11.
114. Quoted in David Sirota, *The Uprising*, New York: Crown Publishers, 2008, p. 125.
115. Sirota, David, op. cit., p. 135.

yet the courts, both state and federal, also face many challenges in rendering equal justice under law. Chief Justice John Roberts maintains that low pay of federal judges is reducing the quality of the federal judiciary but he does not seem to be concerned that at least six of the Supreme Court justices are millionaires with the average wealth about $10 million.[116] Despite the wealth of many judges, the practice of providing free "seminars" for judges, which are often in reality junkets or all expense paid vacations paid by those who seek favors from judges, is still a problem just as campaign contributions are for Congress and state legislatures.[117]

Lifetime appointments of federal and Supreme Court justices have been seriously questioned. Why should some keep their jobs just because they haven't died yet? Many see the appointment as undemocratic especially since their appointments are mostly based on politics not merit and because many see some Supreme Court decisions as legislation by judges, who are, in theory, chosen not to make law but apply it.[118] Why do we accept Supreme Court 5/4 rulings as authoritative when the Constitution makes no statements about what defines a definitive ruling? Should the vote of one justice define the law for millions? How trustworthy is the court which has reversed itself hundreds of times arguing, for example, for slavery and against, for segregation and against, for gay rights and against, etc. In chapter nine I argue that the justices on the Supreme Court should not serve lifetime appointments but a fixed number of years. I also defend the view that only at least 6/4 decisions of the Supreme Court would be definitive binding decisions.

Other problems concern the state courts. The US is almost unique in the world to elect almost all state judges. Their election campaigns bring the same problems as that of all elections, the influence of money by private contributors to election campaigns expecting favors in return from judges once elected.[119]

---

116. *New York Times*, Adam Liptak, "On The Subject of Judicial Salaries, A Sharp Difference of Opinion" 1/20/09, p. A14;www.jurist.law.pitt.edu, 6/11/05; Toobin, Jeffrey, *The Nine*, pp. 242-5.

117. www.nytimes.com, "Better Pay for Federal Judges" editorial, 1/31/08; Al Gore, op. cit., pp. 224-232.

118. Toobin Jeffrey, *The Nine*, New York: Doubleday, 2007, pp. 338-9; John W. Dean, *Broken Government* New York: Viking Press, 2007, pp12-21.

119. www.nytimes.com, Adam Liptak, "Looking Anew at Campaign Cash and

The constitutionally guaranteed right to a jury trial has come under attack as well.[120] The often quoted line expresses the skepticism about juries, "When you go into court you are putting your fate into the hands of twelve people who weren't smart enough to get out of jury duty."[121] As in the case of the legislature, the role of money has also contaminated the jury system as well. Wealthy defendants, in addition having the financial resources to hire the best defense attorneys, some who have been professors at ivy league law schools, also have resources to hire costly jury consultants to advise their lawyers which prospective jurors, based on scientific research, will tend to be most favorably inclined toward the accused. Is the jury system an outdated remnant of a more simple and naive bygone era? Are cases just too complicated and are people too prejudiced and ignorant to make accurate verdicts? Several countries have recently decided to abolish or limit juries.[122] Should the US abolish the jury and let judges decide cases or should we reform it? How should juries be selected, are they being compensated properly and what rights and powers should they have that they do not have now? I defend the view that the jury should not be abolished but, on the contrary, should be reformed and empowered to participate more actively in the trial.

Controversies about the jury often relate to the constitutional rule against double jeopardy. The rule against double jeopardy is the rule that no person can be tried twice for the same crime. Is the rule itself rational and consistent with the Constitution as a whole? What if new evidence is found showing the guilt of the accused that has been already found innocent? I explore this in chapter three.

The presidency is not without its difficulties either. For example, one issue that seems to emerge in every presidency is that of presidential pardons. The presidential pardon power is a constitutional power that is a unique and an unparalleled power the president has that is unlike any other power of any other federal official. The

---

Elected Judges" 1/29/08 and "Rendering Justice With One Eye on Re-election" 5/25/08, and editorials 1/19/08, 9/7/09; Linda Greenhouse, "Supreme Court Rebuffs a Challenge to New York's Way of Picking Judges," *New York Times*, p. A26, 1/17/08.

120. "The Jury is Out" *The Economist*, Feb. 14, 2009, p. 70.
121. Attributed to Norm Crosby.
122. www.nytimes.com "Jury Trials Under Attack" 12/6/08.

president can pardon absolutely anyone at any time for any reason who has or may have committed a federal crime and there is nothing, absolutely nothing, anyone, Congress, the courts or the people, can do to nullify or reverse the pardon. The checks and balances that normally apply to government actions simply do not exist in the case of the absolute power to pardon. There have been over 20,000 presidential pardons and commutations (sentences reduced to time served) in the 20th century alone.

Some of these pardons and commutations have been very controversial. The most controversial in recent years have been the pardon of Richard Nixon by President Gerald Ford in 1974 for possible criminal involvement in the Watergate scandal, the pardon of Mark Rich by President Clinton and many other pardons many of which seem in some cases to be given in return for reasons of politics, friendship or campaign contributions or contributions to presidential libraries. Other questions about pardons include the violation of the rule of law and dangerous growth of presidential power. For these and other reasons, in chapter six I explain why the presidential right to pardon should be totally abolished.

Add to these concerns the problems in the election process itself. There is substantial evidence of illegal and unethical activities such as voter suppression, bribery, ballot stuffing and other means of outright election stealing are still being practiced in the US.[123] Perhaps this helps to explain why 138 countries have a higher participation rate in elections than the US. Another factor may be that casting votes doesn't seem to mean anything as in the 2000 presidential election Al Gore who received half a million more votes than George W. Bush but, because of the electoral college, Bush became president. This is one reason why I argue for the abolition of the Electoral College. It may also be part of the reason why only 48% of US citizens on average cast a vote (non-presidential election years usually have a much smaller voter turnout.)[124]

The US is also number one in military spending, spending officially over $664 billion in 2010, but the actual defense related expendi-

123. Krugman, op. cit., pp. 24-5, 195-7; Robert Kuttner, *Obama's Challenge*, White River Junction: Chelsea Green Publishing, 2008, p. 51; Andrew Gumble, *Steal This Vote*, New York: Nation Books, 2005, pp. 326-7.
124. Bradley, op. cit., pp. 207-9.

tures are said to be over a trillion. China is a distant second in military spending with $140 billion, Russia is third with $78.8 billion, India, fourth with $72.7 billion nearly half of the total military spending of all the nations of the world.[125] The US has over 730 overseas military bases staffed with 2.5 million military and nonmilitary personnel.[126] The US also has almost as many aircraft carriers in service (11) as the rest of the world combined with Russia which has only one, China is repairing one, France has one, the UK has one and the rest of the world has a total of twelve. The national debt, now over $14 trillion, makes America the number one debtor nation, making each citizen's part of the debt more than $46,000, or about $129, 000 per taxpayer, and growing—with just the interest on the debt now is over a billion per day! (China has financed a great part of this debt and now holds trillions of US dollars, giving it what many fear is a great deal of influence in American politics.[127])

In the overall quality of life index (income, health, life expectancy, political freedoms, gender equality, job security, crime, family life, climate) the US ranks #13.[128] A recent University of Michigan study on happiness ranks the United States as 16th in happiness (Denmark ranked as #1.).[129]

But it's not all bad news. Although crime is still high by comparison to other developed countries, it has actually decreased since 1992.[130] Deaths from heart disease and cancer are also down.[131] Americans are still very generous with 70% giving to charity every year amounting to $300 billion.[132] America is also most generous (some would say too generous) in absolute dollars (but not on per capita basis) in foreign (nonmilitary) aid giving $22.7 billion recently to

125. www.washingtonpost.com, 2/6/07; US News & World Report, 11/3/08, p. 38; numbers vary depending whether special funding for wars in Iraq and Afghanistan are included or not.
126. www.alternet.org 2/19/07
127. NYT 3/14/09 p. A1, "China's Premier Seeks Guarantee From US on Debt"
128. www.TheEconomist.com/qualityoflifeindex, 2005.
129. www.michiganstudy.edu
130. Loury, op. cit., p. 4.
131. US News & World Report, "The State of America's Health" by Michelle Andrews, 2/09 p. 10.
132. Clinton, Bill, *Giving*, New York: Knopf, 2007, p. 13.

foreign countries.[133] Military aid to sixty countries amounted to $4.5 billion (and $96 billion in sales).[134] Many, but certainly not all, are pleased that America is still the dominant global military superpower.[135] And the US economy, though recently challenged by the financial crisis and other problems, is still number one in terms of total GDP ($14 trillion, total goods and services produced); China is now a distant second.[136] The African-American middle class has grown dramatically in a generation.[137]

Even though all admit that the US has serious deficiencies in K-12 education, the US still leads in the number of Nobel Prizes (but is actually tenth on a per capita basis with Sweden then #1). The US was number one in total patents for many years but now Japan is while China is predicted to become number one in 2011.[138]

America's higher education system is still world class. Most surveys still show that eight of the top ten of the world universities are still American.[139] This superiority in higher education explains American dominance in technological innovation, especially in nanotechnology and biotechnology.[140]

The election of Barack Obama, whether one is a Democrat, Republican or independent and whether one voted for him or not, shows the US still has a democratic system which is open to change and reform, which is a premise of this study. The 2008 election also saw a record voter participation of 61.6%, the highest since 1968 with 131 million voters casting a ballot.[141] The longest continuous democracy in the world and the only superpower has much to offer the world and still more to go in deciding how to use its vast power and how to fully realize a truly democratic society.

133. Wikipedia, Foreign aid article
134. www.iht.com 9/14/08. "US Pushing Through Dozens of Tough Weapons Deals" by Eric Lipton.
135. *US News & World Report Magazine*, 11/3/08, p. 38.
136. Ibid., p. 39.
137. *Newsweek Magazine*, "The End of Upward Mobility?" Joel Kotkin, 1/26/09, p. 64; Barack Obama, Audacity of Hope, New York: Vintage, 2008, p. 242.
138. Hazlett, Thoms, "We're #2?", Commentary, 12/2009; www.chinaview.com, 2/3/09.
139. Zakaria, Fareed, *The Post-American World*, New York: Norton, 2008, pp. 190-3.
140. Ibid., p. 193; see also Anthony Kronman, *Education's End*, New Haven: Yale University Press, 2007, pp. 77-85.
141. *Christian Science Monitor*, 12/16/08, p. 1.

Many Americans sensed even before these difficulties that there is a conflict between the ideology of the American Dream and the reality of America today. The American Dream was the dream of immigrants and the poor that America is a land of opportunity where one could achieve ever greater prosperity, a home and any position in society regardless of where one was from or what class one was born into if one was willing to get an education and work hard. Now only about a third of Americans believe in the American Dream and many find a disconnect between their values and the reality of what goes on in the world of politics.

The assumption of this work is in agreement with what President Bill Clinton said in his first inaugural address in 1993, "There is nothing wrong with America that can't be cured by what is right with America."[142]

Some things that I consider right with America are the fundamental ideas of the US Constitution and the ideas of the philosopher John Rawls as I understand them. Rawls has been widely considered one of the most important philosophers of the 20th century whose theory of justice develops the revolutionary ideas of human equality and liberty proposed by the founders of America. The goal of this study is to show that the full implementation of the ideals informing the US Constitution and which John Rawls (and other political theorists) have defended and expanded, would go a long way in solving most, if not all, of the problems mentioned above and preventing them from reoccurring in the future, at least to the same degree.

This does not mean that I accept all of the elements of Rawls' theory because I do not. Nor is Rawls' theory strictly needed to defend the basic ideas of this study which I believe can be defended on the grounds of the fundamental principles found in the Constitution and the Declaration of Independence alone. However, I believe the basic outlines of Rawls' theory are plausible and that his ideas shed light on the debates about the essential meaning for the Constitution.

Rawls agrees that rationality requires that to solve problems we must first become aware that they exist, define them, determine their causes and provide possible solutions for them. No society is perfect and there are many reasons why the US has the problems and chal-

---

142. Clinton, Bill, *My Life*, New York: Vintage, 2005, p. 132.

lenges it has and certainly no one has all the answers to solve all these problems but there are some ideas we need to consider.

In beginning to understand and deal with these problems, the nature of the political system will obviously play a central role. This is clear since the political system is, by definition, a system of institutions having the monopoly of power in a geographical area and the right to create, implement and enforce laws which shape all of society. The pivotal role of the political system is a given because the political system determines what is considered a 'problems' how these problems are addressed, prioritized and what resources are allocated to solve them. These questions about the proper role of government, the proper allocation of resources, the nature, and scope of rights and duties is the subject matter of political philosophy which deals with what ought the structure of government and society be, or in short, with questions of distributive justice.

We cannot escape questions of justice since we live in society with others where decisions must be made about the rights and duties of persons. Disputes concerning whether there is a right to health care, same sex marriage, abortion, privacy, euthanasia and the like, are issues of justice which continue to divide our society. To resolve these and other disputes, we need a deeper understanding of the nature of human rights and the meaning of justice and how these ideas translate into social and political structures. We also know that throughout history the questions of rights and justice have been answered in different ways, but one answer that has received much attention that may shed some needed light on these controversies is the answer given by John Rawls.

The theory of liberalism and political philosophy in general were reawakened by the publication of John Rawls' *A Theory of Justice* in 1971 and his later works continued to influence discussions of the various forms of liberal theory.[143] Liberalism is here used not in the sense of a political ideology of the Democratic Party opposed to the Republican Party and conservatism but rather as a political paradigm which incorporates much of the core ideas of both political parties and perspectives. As a political theory, it is first of all a rejection,

---

143. Rawls, John, *A Theory of Justice*, Cambridge: Harvard University Press, 1971, 1999, rev. ed.

among other things, of the traditional absolutist monarchial forms of government prevalent since the dawn of civilization and an insistence that governments must be freely chosen by the people themselves and serve their interests, needs and rights.

Some elements of liberalism can be seen in some early forms of democratic forms in ancient Athens and Rome. In England, the Magna Carta of 1215 put some limits on the king, especially in taxation matters, and gave some citizens of England some rights such as the right to trial by jury of their peers. The Renaissance of the 14th century, with its humanism, the belief in humanity's ability to reason and solve problems, also fueled the ideas associated with liberalism. Liberal thinking was strengthened by the rise of the middle class, of the Enlightenment, and the development of science, the American Revolution of 1776, the French Revolution of 1789, the development of the Industrial Revolution in the late 18th century and the rise of the nation state. Gradually the belief in the power of human reason to explain nature and free humanity from the tyranny of irrational superstition, slavery, poverty and ignorance grew.

In the Middle Ages and throughout history, religion was joined to political power and often the basis of political power. Rulers were considered either divine themselves (as in the Egyptian pharaohs) or divinely chosen, or inspired, by God. All this was to change with the development of the Protestant Reformation, instigated by Martin Luther and others, which shattered the religious unity of Europe and ushered in a religious pluralism with conflicting theological assumptions. The Protestant revolution made a union of a particular denomination with political power a source of social conflict, religious wars and political instability. It became increasingly clear that, given the widespread religious disagreements, religious beliefs could no longer be assumed as the main foundation of political power. This loss of religious agreement led eventually to the idea of the separation of church and state, that the state is not based on religion and does not promote any religious belief system but is neutral in religion. This was a revolutionary development with far-reaching implications still debated today.

Liberalism, then, is based on the central belief in human liberty, that persons (at first only men with property) are equal in having certain human rights. Human rights, as opposed to civil rights which are given by specific governments, are rights one has simply because one is human, such as the right to life and liberty and which exist independent of any government and which government must recognize and protect. Indeed, under liberalism the understanding of the state changed from an element of religious salvation to the state as simply a means for the protection of the freedom and rights of the individual.

The liberal belief in liberty and rights of individuals also claims that persons have the potential for a rational use of their liberty. The belief in human reason is also in part the basis in the belief in human equality; all persons are rational or have the potential to be rational and as such we are all equal in having some minimum of reason and can use it to increase their knowledge. The traditional beliefs in slavery, tribalism, ethnocentrism, racism and sexism, were eventually rejected as rationally unfounded. This sense of equality is not an equality of wealth or power or beauty or intelligence or charisma but a belief in the moral equality of persons. Different philosophers have interpreted this equality differently, and Rawls' understanding will be explored below.

Rawls sees himself as working in this liberal tradition of John Locke, Thomas Jefferson, Immanuel Kant, Abraham Lincoln and Franklin D. Roosevelt. He understands the liberal tradition as holding the central idea that people have certain rights and that legitimate governments can only exist if they are freely created, structured and chosen by the people for the sole purpose of protecting and helping realize the rights of the people. Although this traditional definition of liberalism is widespread, disputes arise among liberals and others about what specific rights people in fact have, what these rights mean, how they can be justified and how government and society should be designed to protect and realize these rights.

Rawls does not consider himself to be offering a completely new answer to these questions about rights or to be providing a totally new theory of justice. Rather, he resurrects the social contract model of understanding liberalism found in John Locke and others, but with several key innovations. The social contract model of justifying liberal political authority has as its core idea that the basic principles of justice are the object of an original agreement that free, equal and rational persons concerned to further their own welfare would freely accept in an initial position of equality. Rawls believes that his theory captures the essence of the social contract theories of Locke, Rousseau and Kant and deals effectively with the traditional criticisms of the contract model of political legitimacy. At the same time Rawls also wants to apply contemporary moral and epistemological insights to the discourse about ethics, rights and political authority and explore the implications of these insights.

The philosophy Rawls defends is a type of liberalism he calls "justice as fairness." As mentioned, traditional or classical liberalism such as that of Locke sought to protect individuals from a tyrannical hereditary monarchy and argued for a limited democratic government based on individual rights to life, liberty, and property. Locke argued against the then prevailing theory of political legitimacy, the theory of the "divine right of kings," that monarchs have the right to rule from God. He claimed that even if the theory of the divine right of kings was true, no one could establish that the current monarch was in fact the one the deity preferred. Locke proposed that people (for Locke this was limited to men with property) should choose their own government by free elections and the purpose of government was to protect the right to life, liberty and property.

Thomas Jefferson was deeply influenced by Locke but made some changes which in some ways foreshadow those of Rawls. In his Declaration of Independence, Jefferson stated: "We hold these truths to be self-evident, that all men are created equal, that they are endowed by their Creator with certain inalienable rights, that among these are life, liberty and the pursuit of happiness. That to secure these rights, governments are instituted among men, deriving their just powers from the consent of the governed." Although Rawls is sympathetic to the basic ideas of Jefferson's declaration, especially the idea of equality and Jefferson's changing Locke's list of basic rights from "life, liberty and property" to "life, liberty and the pursuit of happiness," Rawls does not believe that rights are "self-evident" nor does he believe in a creator, how then can democratic government be defended?

Rawls accepted the core ideas of Locke and Jefferson's liberalism that political institutions exist to protect rights, but he sought to re-examine and expand the meaning of human rights and their justification. Rawls wanted to examine what equality really means in our world today where we have a fuller and more scientific understanding of human nature, institutions and society in general. He wanted to expand the freedom of individuals by eliminating or reducing social and other conditions which he believed limit human freedom, development and opportunity. According to Rawls, conditions such as poverty, past injustices, poor health, prejudice, lack of education, even bad luck, circumstances which restrict the liberties and opportunities of many, must be addressed and rectified by political structures, to the degree this is possible. How can this form of government be justified?

For Rawls, to answer the question of justification of political authority, one must first answer the question what initial conditions are right for deciding question of justice in general. His answer is what he calls the "original position," which contract theorists called a state of nature, except that for Rawls it is a purely hypothetical or imaginary situation. It is a hypothetical state of nature or a condition without a government designed to be the conceptual context within which the competing principles of justice and forms of government will be considered and a final theory of justice agreed upon. Rawls sees the original position as a thought experiment used to clarify our intuitions about what justice is and what the basic structure of a just society should be. In other words, Rawls wants to use the original position to explore what we really mean when we say persons are free, equal and rational.

The overall design of the original position is based on ethical ideas which Rawls calls "considered judgments" and his theory of "reflective equilibrium." Rawls explains that by considered judgments he means moral judgments where our moral capacities are likely to be manifested without distortion or prejudice. Conditions conducive to making considered judgments include mental tranquility, impartiality, sufficient knowledge and similar conditions. These initial considered moral judgments, for example, would include the beliefs that slavery, religious intolerance, and racism are wrong and certain ideas about fairness and human equality.

However, considered judgments are not, according to Rawls, unchanging but rather can be modified based on his theory of justification in ethics, reflective equilibrium. Unlike the claims of some analytic philosophers, Rawls does not think there is a special method in philosophy in general or in ethics in particular; rather, moral theory must use general facts and the findings of science when relevant, and the justification of statements of ethics should pose no special difficulties for they can be established in the same manner as other statements because they are subject to the same method as other theories. This method Rawls calls reflective equilibrium.

In explaining his theory of reflective equilibrium Rawls follows the epistemology of those who view justification in scientific claims and in knowledge in general in a coherentist manner. Coherentists see knowledge as a web of belief where no belief is privileged or beyond revision or rejection but rather revision and even negation is possible in the pursuit of a consistent and more complete belief system. Rawls accepts this view of knowledge and rejects the more traditional or foundationalist ideas of justification. The foundationalist model of justification such as that held by, for example, Descartes, says that there are self-evident statements (for Descartes, "I think, therefore I am") or beliefs which are certain and from which one can build the pyramid of knowledge by the use of logic and evidence. In ethics the foundationalist approach is found in Kant's categorical imperative ("Act so that your maxim can be willed to be a universal law"), from which basic ethical principle or general moral claim Kant believed one can derive specific moral rules and principles of justice.

As a coherentist, Rawls claims that a theory of justice is justified if it is logically derived from one's considered judgments and moral principles. The equilibrium part of reflective equilibrium means that one's judgments, principles and theory are consistent and coherent. By reflective Rawls means that one not simply following social conditioning or custom but is fully aware of what one's judgments and principles are, their derivation, implications and how the principles are superior to the alternatives. Reflective equilibrium exemplifies what Rawls calls the "Socratic" nature of moral theory, i.e., "we may want to change our present considered judgments once their regulative principles are brought to light. According to Rawls, if we find that there are discrepancies between our initial convictions and principles of justice, both our considered judgments and principles can be modified to achieve a coherent belief system. The coherence aspect reinforces the idea that no belief is beyond revision but our goal must be overall consistency of all of our beliefs.

Rawls further clarifies his theory by distinguishing between "narrow" and "wide" reflective equilibrium. In narrow reflective equilibrium we seek a coherence between our considered judgments and ethical principles and the theory of justice we happen to hold. Wide reflective equilibrium exists when one has considered not only the coherence of one's judgments and theories but considers alternative conceptions of justice and all relevant facts to construct the most coherent theory of justice and belief system possible. The idea of wide reflective equilibrium is simply the idea that our beliefs, principles and theories should be ordered, consistent and based on the most available and comprehensive facts available. A coherent and rational worldview is the ultimate goal.

Rawls' idea of the "veil of ignorance" is a central feature of the original position. The veil is a metaphor for excluding information considered morally irrelevant. This information excludes specific data about one's society and individual traits including one's social class, wealth, gender, sexual orientation, race, religion, abilities, personality, intelligence, particular conception of the good, health, particular ideology, etc.

Rawls gives three reasons for the veil. First, this imaginary veil is necessary, Rawls argues, because, given our considered judgments, one must exclude information which is not morally relevant in the deliberations for determining the principles of justice. For example, to view persons as free and equal means we must exclude information about race, sex, class and other factors which differentiate persons. Second, particular information about oneself and various group interests would distort deliberations. That is, our deliberations would be distorted by ideas which go contrary to our conception of persons as free and equal. Third, Rawls wants to exclude information about ideas we need to understand better. Excluding information about a certain subject matter such as religion does not mean Rawls thinks this subject is unimportant but only that it is not relevant at this level for determining justice. Excluding information about one's religious views, if any, is Rawls' way of protecting freedom of religion by better understanding how religion fits into a just society. Excluding information about one's particular conception of the good or one's moral system is not to deny the importance of one's moral system but to realize that one's moral system is, at least in part and before critical rationality, a function of the accident of being born at a particular time and place, social class, social conditioning, experience, parental training, education and other factors which must be examined and evaluated.

Rawls sees the veil as an integral part of the original position in order to derive a theory of justice that will have sufficient universality to define the most basic structures of society. To achieve this universality one must abstract from the present social, cultural, political and natural contingencies since these circumstances may be unjust or due to unjust causes and ignorance or defined by inefficient and irrational institutions in an overarching and corrupt framework. Not to distance our deliberations from the contamination of these factors would contaminate the principles of justice deduced.

By excluding the information spelled out by the veil of ignorance, Rawls believes he has defined the person as seen in liberalism. This common core of personhood is, according to Rawls, that persons are free, equal, rational and self-interested. By free, Rawls means persons are not under the control of other persons but can make claims about their interests and rights and can change their beliefs and goals as they see fit.

By equal, Rawls does not mean that persons are equal in strength, or health or intelligence or beauty for obviously people are not equal in these senses. He means equal in the ethical sense of persons having the same basic moral rights which is based on having potentially two powers of a moral personality. For Rawls, these two central powers are a capacity for a sense of justice and a rational conception of one's good. That is, persons can understand what justice demands and can act on that basis and they are capable of forming a conception of their good, their goals and beliefs about the good life and are able to act to rationally realize those goals. Within the original position, equal also means procedurally having an equal right to suggest principles of justice and defend them and the right to critically evaluate the suggestions of others and to participate equally in the choice of the principles.

As rational Rawls means persons are capable of forming beliefs based on the best evidence and logical principles. Being rational means to act to achieve some goal and to take the most appropriate means to achieve that goal or goals.

As self-interested Rawls does not mean that people in the original position are selfish. Rather, he means they are interested in their own preservation, their welfare and can take steps to protect their own life and well-being.

The veil, by defining the core of humanity, will help yield a theory of justice which will be more stable than other theories. By stability, (discussed in more detail below) Rawls means that a structure generates support from within those who participate in it who have internalized its basic tenets without cognitive dissonance because the theory, for the most part at least, supports their wants, needs and conception of the good.

Though members of the original position are not allowed specific information about themselves, they are allowed certain very general information. General information is necessary for the deliberations to be rational and to be relevant to human nature and very general social circumstances. This general information includes, as mentioned, the conception of persons free, equal, rational and self-interested and in addition it includes what Rawls calls a conception of "primary goods."

Rawls defines primary goods as necessary means for whatever goals one may have in one's rational plan of life. These goods are certain basic rights, liberties, opportunities, income, wealth and self-respect. In other words, for Rawls, to be human is to want to be free to live ones' life, to be healthy, to have certain opportunities for education, political participation, etc., and to have the necessary property or monetary resources for a sense of security and to achieve one's goals, satisfy one's needs and maintain some degree of self-respect. Self-respect Rawls defines as the "sense of one's own worth" and "the sense that one's plan (of life) is worth carrying out." This is part of Rawls' theory of human nature, a theory every political philosophy must have, either explicitly or implicitly, since politics is about organizing persons and how one organizes persons will greatly depend on the conception one has of their nature, their potential and their limits.

As we saw, participants in the original position are not allowed specific information about themselves but they are allowed, according to Rawls, general knowledge of the circumstances of justice. Rawls explains that the circumstances of justice are the current background conditions of society and are of two kinds, objective and subjective. The objective circumstances include the fact that there are many individuals who coexist on the same geographic territory with roughly similar physical and mental powers. Consequently they are vulnerable to attack by others. Members of the original position also know general information about economics, psychology and other general and basic information. Finally, they know that there exists a moderate scarcity of natural and other resources.

The subjective circumstances are the relevant facts about the individuals who must cooperate. They know that though persons have sufficient similar needs and interests to make cooperation possible and beneficial, their life plans may and often do differ. As a result, they make claims on the limited natural and social resources which bring them occasionally into conflict. And, due to natural and moral shortcomings, their cognitive powers are incomplete and limited, their judgment often distorted by bias and selfishness. The principles of justice chosen must take into account these basic realities.

Given the design of the original position, Rawls believes that people in the original position would choose his theory of justice, justice as fairness. Justice as fairness attempts to blend the central values of liberty and equality, in what Rawls believes is a higher and a more ethical synthesis.

This Rawlsian welfare liberalism is defined by two principles in *Political Liberalism* as:

First principle: "Each person has an equal claim to a fully adequate scheme of equal basic rights and liberties, which scheme is compatible with the same scheme with the same scheme for all; and only those liberties, are to be guaranteed their fair value."

Second principle: "Social and economic inequalities are to satisfy two conditions: first, they are to be attached to positions and offices open to all under conditions of fair equality of opportunity; and second, they are to be to the greatest benefit of the least advantaged members of society." [Difference Principle] ("consistent with the just savings principle.")[144]

The first principle guarantees a democratic system where all would have the greatest liberty compatible with the similar liberty of others. These rights and liberties would include those mentioned in the US constitution's bill of rights such as the right to life, to vote, to run for public office, freedom of speech, assembly, thought, right to own personal property, freedom of religion, freedom from arbitrary arrest, and the like. (The condition that political liberties be guaranteed their "fair value" or "equal worth" was included explicitly in a later version of the two principles and will be explored below.)

The second principle deals with economic and social inequality. Why wouldn't people in the original position just agree for equal income and wealth? Rawls believes that people in the imaginary state with a veil of ignorance would not agree not absolute equality because they would understand that differences in income, wealth and social power are morally acceptable because without these inequalities all would be worse off. That is, he sees the inequalities of income and wealth as necessary incentives to motivate people to take on such burdens as education and training and the responsibilities that come with some important positions in society.

However, Rawls is clear to specify that these inequalities are just only if three conditions are met. These conditions are what Rawls calls the "difference principle," the "just savings principle" and "fair equality of opportunity." The just savings principle concerns justice between generations. It states that each generation must not only preserve the gains of culture, civilization and established just institutions, but also put aside a suitable amount of real capital accumulation for the benefit of the next generation. But justice does not demand that savings occur just so the next generation is more wealthy; the purpose of wealth and savings is to bring about "the full realization of just institutions and the fair value of liberty."

The difference principle requires that social and economic inequalities are just only if they are so arranged that they are "to the

---

144. Ibid., rev. ed., p. 266.

greatest benefit of the least advantaged." For example, we can al-low physicians to earn more than bus drivers because if physicians earned the same as bus drivers there would be fewer physicians and we would all be worse off, especially the poorest members of soci-ety. Rawls believes that people in the original position would accept the difference principle because if they found themselves in the low-est level of society, they would want any inequality to benefit them, whoever else they may also benefit. According to Rawls, the differ-ence principle demands that the amount of economic and social in-equality must be kept at the minimum while still ensuring political liberties, economic efficiency and the welfare of the lower classes, the unskilled blue collar worker.

The difference principle expresses the need to limit the gap be-tween the rich and the poor by linking the social classes. Any ad-ditional inequality, such as a contemplated tax cut, must benefit the least advantaged. Rawls believes a great gap in wealth is destructive of self-respect and diminishes the "worth of liberty" which varies greatly with wealth.

By worth of liberty Rawls means the degree to which individuals can take advantage of their rights and liberties in a social context. Wealth and education impact greatly on the worth of liberty espe-cially in participating fully in the electoral process and running for public office. The worth of liberty is diminished if one lacks educa-tion, health and if one does not have an equal chance of running for public office. This is why Rawls is concerned about election cam-paigns funding but he does not say nearly enough about this crucial problem. Furthermore, Rawls adds great inequality of wealth pro-duces greater risk of political inequality and instability because it provided an environment for justifiable envy.

The second condition on economic inequality is what Rawls calls the principle of "fair equality of opportunity." First, fair equality of opportunity does not mean equality of result; Rawls is not advocat-ing that everybody make the same income or be equally wealthy. He understands that in a free society people will make different choices, have various lifestyles and so have unequal wealth and income. Sec-ond, fair equality of opportunity includes formal equality of opportu-nity but goes well beyond. Formal equality of opportunity means the absence of legal obstacles excluding certain people from certain jobs or opportunities just because of their race, sex, sexual orientation, religion, ethnicity or other factors not relevant to job performance. For example, during legal racism and sexism, African-Americans and women, were once excluded from many jobs, colleges and other opportunities.

Fair equality of opportunity goes beyond this formal equality and would provide for equal starting social conditions for all. This means providing an equally good education, health and other conditions that influence one's chances in life. By 'equal' of course, Rawls does not necessarily mean an arithmetic equality but a set of conditions which give all an equal chance of success (within the limits of natural talents, etc, see below) which would mean giving the poor and those disadvantaged by unfavorable family circumstances, and other obstacles, extra resources for their schooling to compensate for their disadvantageous starting points. Fair equality of opportunity would also mean trying to equalize the worth of liberties such as the right to run for public office by restricting campaign funding and other measures. This is the idea conveyed by this quote from President Lyndon B. Johnson, "You do not take a person who for years has been hobbled by chains and liberate him and then say, 'You are free to compete with all the others' and still justly believe that you have been completely fair."[145]

Rawls explains fair equality of opportunity with the analogy of a race. This is not original with Rawls but can be found in the ideas of Thomas Jefferson who spoke of the need for a "natural aristocracy," a meritocracy or rule by the best in terms of knowledge and virtue as determined by equal access to education not an inherited aristocracy as was the custom throughout history.[146] President Lincoln expressed a similar view in his message to Congress in 1861, saying that the purpose of democratic government was to "elevate the condition of men-to lift artificial weights from all shoulders—to clear the paths of laudable pursuit of all—to afford all an unfettered start, and a fair chance in the race of life."[147]

---

145. Caro, Robert A., *Master of the Senate*, New York: Vintage, 2003, p. 346.
146. Jefferson, Thomas, letter to John Adams, Oct. 28, 1813.
147. Basler, Roy, ed., *The Collected Works of Abraham Lincoln*, 9 vols., New Brunswick,

For Rawls, a fair race is one where all begin at the same starting line and go as fast and as long as they can. Rawls believes that if society is to be fair, we should all have equal chance to achieve any position in society. However, the poor start far behind the starting line because they are handicapped by inferior education, poor health care, intellectually, and perhaps emotionally impoverished home environment, low self-esteem, discrimination and lack of political and social networks. The rich, on the other hand, start way ahead of the line with superior education, health care, family background, social connections and all the advantages which social class and money provide. This situation of a class stratified society without fair equality of opportunity is for Rawls, the opposite of fairness. According to Rawls, no job, profession or social position should be denied to anyone based on their parents, or what their social class, race, sex, sexual orientation, religion and ethnic background happened to be. No matter whether a person is born into a family of millionaires or to an unmarried drug addicted high school dropout with mental problems, one should have an equal shot to become whatever one desires and effort and ability allow. The two principles are intended to guarantee this kind of society as a fair race.

One additional element of Rawls' ideal of equality is his theory of natural talents. Natural talents, such as being born with the potential to sing well or being tall to play basketball well, are part of what Rawls calls the "lottery of life." The lottery of life is a way of referring to the contingencies of life and the role chance plays in people's life including one's sex, race, social class, one's parents as well as one's natural talents or handicaps.

According to Rawls, no one deserves one's talents, handicaps or one's starting place in society. He believes we should consider natural talents not as individual assets but more like social assets from which all of society should benefit, though not necessarily equally. The reasons Rawls gives for this claim about talents are twofold: a) one cannot be said to deserve them, b) they need the proper social environment to develop. One cannot deserve something one did not choose or merit in any way. Second, given any talent, which is in many ways just a potential, proper education, training and other

NJ: Rutgers University Press, 1953-5, vol. 4, p. 438.

social factors are necessary for that potential to become actual. These social factors are the contributions of society and society has some rights on the income generated by the talents. If inequality is indeed at least partly a result of causes and conditions that we do not deserve, our attitude towards our own achievement must reflect this. As Rawls sees it, one cannot take the posture of the so-called 'self-made man' who believes he has achieved everything solely through his own effort and thereby deserves all he has accumulated.

This does not mean, Rawls explains, that talented people should not profit at all from their talent and training, but only that the level of income should not violate fair equality of opportunity or the difference principle. For Rawls, justice as fairness means we share one another's fate in the lottery of natural talents and burdens and so promote social fraternity.

Now that the two principles have been defined, the relationship between the two principles must also be defined. Rawls believes that parties in the original position would agree to the priority of the first principle over the second. By the priority of liberty Rawls means that the claims of liberty are to be satisfied first and that "liberty can be restricted only for the sake of liberty." Or, in other words, the two principles do not permit exchanges between basic liberties and economic and social gains. However, there are two distinct kinds of cases where liberty is restricted; liberty may be less extensive than it could be but equal, or simply unequal. If liberty is less extensive, it must be only because it will be more extensive in the long-run. If liberty is unequal it must be so that those with the lesser liberty gain greater freedom in the future.

Rawls gives three reasons for this priority. First, each person is assured the freedom to pursue their conception of the good or way of life including religious and other personal beliefs. Second, this respect for the pluralistic conceptions of what a good life is promotes the "stability" of the society. By stability Rawls means that it likely to be affirmed and accepted by all as harmonious with and grounded in our view of persons as free and equal beings. That is, the justice as fairness is stable because, the priority of liberty protects our "self-respect" which means having a "secure sense of our own value" which freedom promotes. Third, the principles of justice promote "social union". That is, it promotes social cooperation and harmony because each person is respected and has the sense of security necessary for trust.

Rawls sums up his argument for the two principles with the following considerations. First, people in the original position would choose the two principles because they protect individual freedoms and basic equal rights. This prevents the worst case scenario of slavery, sexism, racism and other versions of denial of freedoms and equal rights. Second, Rawls believes his conception of justice is stable and would make for a society more stable than others. As mentioned above, a stable theory of justice is one compatible with human nature and thus perpetuates itself in a peaceful manner. A stable society when its laws are generally complied with and any deviation from them calls forth forces which restore stability and equilibrium. That is, the social system which is structured by the two principles tends to bring about the sense of justice it instantiates. A stable system is compatible with the citizens' conceptions of their good and hence everyone benefits in that society.

The third reason Rawls believes his theory is justified is that it protects and preserves the self-respect of individual citizens. Self-respect, as mentioned above, was the most important element of the primary goods members of the original position would seek to protect for without self-respect one lacks the confidence in oneself and one's way of life and without confidence, one would not even attempt to carry out one's life goals. By self-respect Rawls means the sense one has of one's own value and dignity, that one's life and goals are worth carrying out. Justice as fairness, Rawls believes, maximizes everyone's self-respect since everyone's good is included in the social system of equal respect and equal rights. Echoing Kant's ethics, in a Rawlsian society, each person is treated as an end in him or herself, not as a means only.

Moreover, Rawls' principle of fair equality of opportunity if implemented, would provide opportunities for full development of human potential at all strata of society. Such a society would be a true meritocracy in that all persons could contribute their maximum to the society. By contrast, a society which does not have fair equality of opportunity would not give all an equal chance to develop and so would not maximize the talent that exists potentially in society. Such as society would lose in the maximization of knowledge and technology and as such would be at a disadvantage in competition with other nations. The obvious consequence in terms of national security and ability to adapt to the environment and meet human needs is clear.

In the remaining chapters I intend to show:

The Right to a Lawyer

The trial is part of a legal system which has become so vast and complex that it requires experts to understand and use it effectively. The legal profession plays a pivotal role in the determination of justice but the quality of legal representation is not equally available across the social classes. This is due to basically two factors, individual and social: individual differences in terms of intelligence, experience or personal moral characteristics such as dedication and honesty and differences in socioeconomic background which gives individuals differential entry into colleges and law schools of varying quality and prestige. Although there are public defenders available, they are usually overworked and have a lesser quality of legal education. The wealthy have access to the highest expertise of legal representation as well as other services of investigators, researchers and the like.

I argue on the basis of Rawls' idea of procedural justice and fair equality of opportunity that the legal profession as a whole should no longer be a service sold on the free market for a fee. Rather, all attorneys should be government employees available to the public free of charge. Lawyers would be assigned cases on the basis of their expertise and availability.

Abolish the Double Jeopardy Rule

Another key element of the trial and criminal justice system is the fifth amendment of the constitution which states that no one will be tried twice or put in double jeopardy for the same crime. The purpose of the rule was to prevent the government from abusing the rights of citizens through repeated trials for the same offense. I provide several arguments against this rule based on Rawls' idea of fairness, the rule of law and other concepts.

I argue that the rule against double jeopardy violates fairness by allowing some criminals to go unpunished. Second, I claim the rule undermines rule of law and is a violation of the due process. Finally, I argue that potential abuses of allowing double jeopardy can be prevented by strengthening and reforming the use of the grand jury.

## Empower the Jury

Rawls refers to the trial as an instance of imperfect procedural justice. It is imperfect in that the procedures developed do not guarantee the correct outcome which would mean finding the innocent, innocent and the guilty, guilty. In order to make the imperfect more perfect, I argue for three reforms in the trial system. These reforms concern the structure of the jury, the nature f the right to legal representation and the rule against double jeopardy.

The trial is central to the determination of justice but its form continues to evolve. I argue that the current structure of the trial is not appropriately designed to produce the desired results, finding the guilty, guilty and the innocent, innocent, in an efficient manner and that the current jury system does not maximally reflect the values implicit in the institution nor the political paradigm of liberal democracy in which it is embedded. I argue that the jury must be given a greater and more active role in the trial. Specifically, I claim that the jury should be allowed to call its own witnesses and ask questions of all the parties involved in the trial prior to deciding the guilt or innocence of the accused. I use Rawls' ideas of fairness, persons as free and equal and fair equality of opportunity as key components of this argument.

## Abolish the Electoral College

The US Constitution specifies that the President of the US is not to be chosen directly by the people but by what has come to be called the Electoral College. The Electoral College is constituted by electors chosen by the legislatures of each state and the District of

Columbia. I claim that the Electoral College is an undemocratic institution which should be abolished because it is inconsistent with the underlying principles of the constitution and the basic ideas of John Rawls' theory of justice. The Electoral College introduces an undefined variable into the basic structure and violates the Rawlsian idea of a stable society and public reason. A stable society, in brief, is a society which is structured in a manner consistent with human nature and generates the virtues needed for its perpetuation and social justice. Rawls' idea of public reason specifies that public discourse must be structured so that it only involves constitutional essentials of the basic structure. Since the Electoral College need not respect the majority vote of the citizenry nor publicly justify its vote, it violates the idea of public reason of citizens as free and equal and political discourse must be public and consistent with the principles implicit in the basic structure. It also undermines stability since it is not sufficiently structured to necessitate procedures consistent with the principles of the basic structure.

Abolish Presidential Pardon

The constitution provides that: "The President...shall have power to grant reprieves and pardons for offences against the United States, except in cases of impeachment." A pardon removes any possibility of punishment for crimes committed against the United States for the person receiving the pardon and cannot be reversed. The pardon can be given before indictment, during prosecution or after conviction and extends to every type of offence against the United States including civil and criminal felonies, misdemeanors, imprisonment, fines, penalties, forfeitures and even treason. The president also has the power to commute sentences or substitute a lesser punishment.

I argue that the presidential pardon is a remnant of a theocratic political paradigm such as the divine right of kings that must be abolished. More specifically, I argue that it is inconsistent with the underlying principles of the constitution, namely, that it is a violation of the rule of law, equal protection of the laws, due process and the separation of powers.

Abolish the Senate

The US Senate consists of two senators for every state, regardless of population. As currently defined this is inconsistent with the basic principles of equality as understood in one person one vote implied in the US Constitution, many Supreme Court rulings and as defended by Rawls. This and other reasons point to the abolition or fundamental restructuring of the Senate.

Limit the Power of the Supreme Court

The US Supreme Court is the most powerful court in the world not only because it is the highest court of the most powerful state in the world but primarily because of the power of "judicial review." The power of judicial review, generally considered to have been established by Marbury V. Madison (1803), is the sweeping power to declare unconstitutional acts of state legislatures, Congress, state and federal courts and acts of the President.

The argument defended in this chapter is that judicial review and other factors give the Supreme Court excessive power not explicitly justified in the Constitution. This power needs to be curbed by requiring that court decision, assuming the current number of nine justices, consist of a super majority of a minimum of six votes, not the current five, to decide cases in a constitutionally normative manner.

Abolish Lifetime Appointment of Supreme Court Justices

Currently justices to the Supreme Court are given lifetime appointments to serve on the court. I argue that the independence of the judiciary is important but that the practice of lifetime tenure of judges is irrational and violates the rule of law, the ideal of meritocracy, and the Rawlsian ideas of procedural justice. I contend that lifetime appointment of Supreme Court judges should be eliminated and replaced by appointments limited to a set number of years.

Electing or Selecting State Judges

Many states elect state judges but this is only one of five different ways of selecting state judges. I argue that electing judges is open to many abuses and should be abolished. I claim that the best system for selecting judges is through an expansion of the civil service merit based system. Only this method is most consistent with the ideals of the rule of law, stability, legitimacy and meritocracy.

## Reduce Private Money in Election Campaigns

The current campaign finance reforms do not go far enough in providing what Rawls calls the equal worth of liberty required by his theory. I claim that current laws would need to change to virtually prohibit the role of private money in election campaigns. But this is enough to provide for the equal worth of liberty, what is needed is what I call "political leave."

## Expand the Right to Run for Political Office

For Rawls, democracy is defined as a political structure where, among other elements, free and equal persons freely decide who has political power and how they are to exercise that power. Rawls also believes that political equality of rights is compatible with economic inequality of income and wealth. I believe that Rawls' proposals for reconciling economic inequality and political equality are inadequate and incomplete.

I argue that reconciliation of equal political rights and economic inequality would require far more radical structural changes in the political and economic system. Among other reforms, I believe what is needed is the implementation of the right to what I call "political leave." This is the right of any adult to be a candidate for public office, the right to have the campaign publicly funded and the right to return to one's place of employment (or equivalent employment) at the end of the campaign or term in office. I believe this reform, if realized, would end the domination of political elections by the social and economic elite who unfairly and overwhelmingly constitute the political class. This reform would amount to an extension to Rawls' idea of fair equality of opportunity which is needed for the safeguarding of equal worth of rights.

Expand Employee Rights

For persons to be moral they must have a conscience. A conscience exists when individuals internalize the values of their society and control their behavior to conform to those values. In a corporation, the corresponding entity for a conscience is a democratized governing structure where workers, together with stockholders and the community, run corporations. This institutional structure would actualize Rawls' theory of justice more fully than the current corporate management structure.

The Contradictions of Libertarianism

Many objections to the reforms defended in the book are based on the ideology of libertarianism.

Libertarianism is a theory of minimal government such as held by the Tea Party and similar groups. I argue that this ideology misconstrues the meaning of freedom and would, if fully implemented, lead to a serious reduction of freedom for most people and undermine society's ability to adapt and survive as a stable society.

Conclusion

These implications of the deep values of the constitution and the ideas of Rawls call for major restructuring of the American political system. These ideas are not totally new for they represent the implications of what Jefferson called a natural aristocracy based on meritocracy, the ideas of Lincoln as he fought against slavery and racism and FDR's call for what he called "the second bill of rights" which included a guarantee for a home, medical care, education, job with a living wage, and what he called the "economic bill of rights." The realization of these rights and the reforms defended here would go a long way to counteracting what Rawls calls "the lottery of life" and help actualize more fully the democratic values of liberty and equality which are the foundation of our Constitution.

## Chapter 2. The Right to a Lawyer

> "A jury is a group of individuals chosen to decide who has the
> better lawyer."
> —Anonymous

Calvin Burdine, a 31-year-old white male, was on trial in Texas in 1984 for the murder of his gay lover. He faced the possibility of the death penalty but unfortunately his court appointed lawyer did not inspire confidence. In fact, as everyone in court could see, his lawyer was asleep many times during the trial. In addition, Mr. Burdine, an openly gay man, was referred to by his lawyer in court as a "fairy" and "faggot" several times. In his closing argument the prosecutor stated that prison would not be too unpleasant for a gay man. After Mr. Burdine was found guilty, he appealed to the state court of appeals for a retrial due to the fact that his lawyer was asleep during the trial, the Texas court ruled that the constitution did not require that one's lawyer stay awake during trial and denied a new trial. Burdine appealed to the US Court of Appeals which did demand a new trial.[148]

Recently it was found in North Carolina that 16 death row inmates had lawyers who were later disbarred. These findings prompted a lawyer to comment that a major problem with the death penalty was "poor people getting lousy lawyers."[149]

---

148. Bragg, Rick, "New Trial is Sought for Inmate Whose Lawyer Slept in Court", www.NewYorkTimes.com, 1/23/01.
149. Dewan, Shaila, "Releases From Death Row Raise Doubts Over Quality of De-

On the other side of the social spectrum is O. J. Simpson's 1995 trial for the murder of his ex-wife Nicole Simpson and Ronald Goldman. O. J. Simpson's legal fees for his murder trial are estimated to have been between $5–6 million, which included paying for a Harvard law professor's advice and at least one other lawyer's fee of $100,000 a month.[150] Simpson was acquitted of the murders.[151] And these are certainly not all of the cases of this type.[152]

A study by the ABA concluded "There are two criminal justice systems in this country. There is a whole different system for poor people. It's in the same courthouse-it's not separate-but it's not equal."[153] It is fact like these which lead Rawls to discuss different types of injustice. The most radical injustice would exist if what Rawls calls the basic structure of the society, the fundamental distribution of rights and duties, were itself unjust, as a slave or sexist society, for example, would be. Even if the basic structure were just, the specific laws and acts of the legislative body could be inconsistent with the basic structure. This could be due to the ignorance, incompetence or bias of the legislators. Though laws may be fairly drafted, the lack of proper enforcement or implementation can also result in injustice. For example, the police, judges and courts may themselves be incompetent or prejudiced or structured so as to unfairly discriminate against a certain individual or group. Because of the type of society we live in, our legal system has become so vast and complex that it requires experts to understand and use it effectively. Hence, even if the laws are formulated fairly and even if the judges and jury are impartial and competent, the lack of legal counsel of sufficient competence and integrity can result in an unjust decision by the court. If a defendant lacks legal representation or has representa-

---

fense" The *New York Times*, May 7, 2008, pp. 1, A17.

150. www.time.com, Elizabeth Gleick, et. al., "Rich Justice, Poor Justice" 6/19/95.

151. O.J. Simpson was found guilty of the murders in a civil trial in 1997; the court awarded the Goldman family $33.5 million but they received almost none of the money since almost no Simpson money could be found. In 2006 O.J. Simpson came out with a book about the murders, *If I Did It*, in which he explains how he might have done the murders. Due to various challenges it was published by the Goldman family. Simpson is currently in prison on unrelated charges.

152. www.newyorktimes.com, "Durst Cuts Ties to Family for 65 Million" Charles Bagli, 2/7/06.

153. Ibid., p. 2.

tion of a significantly inferior caliber vis a vis the opposing attorney, then the guilt or innocence may not be correctly determined or the prescribed penalty may be unfair. It is at this point that the chain of justice may have its weakest link.

The legal profession clearly plays a pivotal role in the determination of justice. As understood here, lawyers constitute a profession in that they are a group of persons whose function in society presupposes a substantial period of formal education consisting of significant theoretical content. In addition they largely regulate themselves and enjoy material affluence and social prestige usually accompanying individuals who meet the essential needs of persons, e.g., health, knowledge and justice.[154] In their professional capacity, lawyers perform several roles in society.[155] They may counsel others in drafting various documents such as leases, wills, contracts, etc. Attorneys may also serve as intermediaries in negotiations between various parties in disputes as in labor/management discussions. However, next only to the actual formulation of laws, the role that is most crucial in matters of justice is that of trial advocacy in an adversarial judicial proceeding. In this context, lawyers represent their client in a court of law when their client is involved in some dispute with one or more persons. It is obvious that the nature of this legal representation can have significant impact on whether the rights of individuals are protected.

In the US today, attorneys sell their services in the marketplace to those who can afford to pay. Furthermore, the profession, as all professions, consists of members who are not equally well trained or experienced or competent in their knowledge and application of the law. This is due to basically two factors, individual and social: individual differences in terms of intelligence, experience or personal moral characteristics such as dedication and honesty and differences in socioeconomic background that gives individuals differential en-

---

154. Wasserstrom, Richard, "Lawyers as Professionals: Some Moral Issues" in *Ethics and the Legal Profession*, Davis, Michael; Elliston, Frederick eds., Buffalo: Prometheus Books, p. 131.

155. Bayles, Michael, "Principles for Legal Procedure," *Law and Philosophy*, 5, 1986, pp. 33-57; Golding, Martin, *Philosophy of Law*, Englewood Cliffs: Prentice Hall, 1975, pp. 108-122. Abel, Richard, "Socializing the Legal Profession," *Law and Policy Quarterly*, Vol. 1, No. 1, January, 1979, pp. 13-17.

try into colleges and law schools of varying quality and prestige.[156] Putting it bluntly, affluent and well connected individuals have access to the best lawyers with an extensive staff of specialists to defend their clients in court, whereas the poor have no similar access or no access at all.[157]

In addition to these socioeconomic factors, there are certain institutional realities of the courts that give the affluent special advantages.[158] Attorneys representing wealthy individuals have occasion to use the court system more frequently than others and as such develop informal relations with court personnel which often facilitates their transactions. In addition, the advantaged often have long term lawyer-client relationships that solidifies the lawyer's loyalty to the client as opposed to individuals who use lawyers on an episodic and isolated manner. Furthermore, the present court system is overloaded with cases that cause delays which, in turn, raise costs which the poor are less able to bear. Finally, given the present political realities, the financial resources of lawyers of the well-to-do provides the opportunity by way of lobbying and campaign contributions to influence the making of substantive rules that decide outcomes. This kind of long term strategy is useful to the social elite but usually unavailable to the disadvantaged and infrequent user of the courts.

Procedural justice consists in the implementation of certain principles of justice (as specified by the basic moral framework) to the exercise of political authority. Procedural justice in the form of due process is a set of rights whereby one's other rights and duties are determined by the court according to a specified mechanism, the trial in this case. The mechanism is established to ensure that the state acts justly, i.e., consistently with the basic structure, in abridging the rights of the accused. As such, due process is grounded in those moral principles that give legitimacy to the exercise of political power.

Due process is not a right like the right to life, liberty or property.

156. Rawls, John. A *Theory of Justice*, Cambridge: Harvard UP, 1971, pp. 83-7. Auerbach, Jerold S. *Unequal Justice*, New York: Oxford UP, 1976, pp. 4-12, 40-60; Larson, Magali S. *The Rise of Professionalism*, Berkeley U. of California Press: 1977, pp. 166-177; Jencks, Christopher and Riesman, David, *The Academic Revolution*, New York: Doubleday, 1968, pp. 150-3.

157. Bayles, op. cit. pp. 41-50; Baker, C. Edwin, "The Ideology of the Economic Analysis of Law," *Philosophy and Public Affairs*, Fall 1975, pp. 6-48.

158. Bayles, op. cit., pp. 50-53.

The right to liberty, for example, does not imply that every reduction of individual liberty is unjust; the incarceration of criminals is not obviously unjust. The right to due process is unique in that there seems no just way by which the state can deny a person due process.[159]

We thus come to the following question: What are the necessary conditions and structures to correctly and fairly determining the guilt, innocence or liability of individuals in a class stratified society and profession? ('Class stratified' here means that certain individuals have certain advantages and disadvantages simply because they are born into a certain family in a certain social and economic situation, not that there is no mobility between classes.) These structures will, in part, consist of what is termed 'procedural justice'.[160] These procedures consist of several rules. First, there must be a particular dispute where specific individuals are involved. Secondly, a third party, such as a judge or dispute settler, is present; no one is to be judge in his or her own case. In addition, the dispute settler must not have a private interest in the outcome, only to objectively determine the guilt or innocence of the parties involved. The settlement of the dispute takes place in a forum where information about the dispute is heard, the courtroom. The dispute is settled according to substantive legal principles and rules based on all the relevant information presented. Procedural justice is constructed so that only the guilt or innocence of the parties involved is used as a basis for determining justice.

The nature of procedural justice in the context of a trial can best be clarified by comparison with other types of procedures. Rawls'

---

159. Galanter, Marc, "Why the 'Haves' Come out Ahead: Speculations on the Limits of Legal Change," *Law and Society Review*, 9, Fall 1974, pp. 98-104. Bedau, Hugo Adam, Radelet, Michael L. "Miscarriages of Justice in Potentially Capital Cases," 197; Harold Laski, *A Grammar of Politics*, New Haven: Yale Univ. Press, 1931, pp. 565-7.
160. Hare, R.M., *Moral Thinking*, Oxford: Clarendon Press, 1981, pp. 1 56-7; Westen, Peter, "The Concept of Equal Opportunity," *Ethics*, 95, July 1985, pp. 838-841; Barry, *Political Argument*, New York: Humanities Press, 1965, chap. 6; Nelson, William, "Equal Opportunity," *Social Theory and Practice, Vol.* 10, No. 2, Summer 1984, pp. 168-70; Plamenatz, John, "Diversity of Rights and Kinds Of Equality," in *Equality*, Pennock, J. Roland, Chapman, John W. eds., New York: Atherton Press, pp. 87-93.

discussion is helpful here.[161] He contrasts pure, perfect and imperfect procedural justice. Pure procedural justice occurs when there is no criterion for the correct outcome independently of applying the procedure correctly. Examples of this are found in certain games of chance as in tossing dice. In this game there is no way to determine who wins or loses except by throwing the dice and seeing the result (assuming the dice are fair, of course). Perfect procedural justice is characterized by as a situation where there is an independent criterion for the correct outcome prior to the procedure being carried out. An illustration of this would be the equal division of a cake among two or more persons. Here the person who cuts the cake takes the last piece, thus ensuring a fair division. By contrast, imperfect procedural justice is exemplified by a trial. Here, the outcome desired is that the accused be found guilty if and only if he or she has committed the crime. The trial is the mechanism to determine this but no trial procedure is infallible so as to guarantee the correct outcome each time. Hence, a trial is an example of imperfect procedural justice for there is an independent criterion for the correct outcome, i.e. the guilty should be found so and the innocent, found innocent; but no procedure can ensure this absolutely. This may be due to the unavailability of sufficient and impartial information concerning the alleged action or the veracity, impartiality or competence of the individuals involved. The goal of justice, then, is to design procedures that are more likely to give us the correct outcome; the more reliable the procedures the more one is warranted in believing the punishment decided upon by the court is justified and deserved.

The adversary trial system is an instantiation of procedural justice. The structural features of this model are based on the assumption that truth concerning guilt will emerge from the struggle between two contesting parties who present their side in an impartial tribunal. One maximizes the probability of arriving at the correct outcome to the extent one can insulate this tribunal from irrelevant conditions and factors. That is, one should not be found guilty or in-

---

161. Resnick, David, "Due Process and Procedural Justice" in Pennock, J. R., & Chapman, J.W., eds. *Due Process,* Nomos 18, New York: NYU Press, 1977, p. 208; Ibid., Scanlon, T.M., "Due Process," pp. 94-97. Luban, David, "Political Legitimacy and the Right to Legal Services," *Business and Professional Ethics Journal,* Vol. 4, Nos. 3-4, pp. 43-68.

nocent simply because one is of a certain race or sex or of a certain economic status. Furthermore, if one's economic status prevents one from having a lawyer or from having a lawyer of sufficient and comparable competence to that of the opposing attorney, then too the trial process is adulterated by an external and irrelevant factor.

These procedures must be carried out within certain economic and moral constraints.[162] One should, for example, strive to minimize the cost of the legal procedure in terms of reducing cost of personnel and materials. However, this minimum must not be so low as to unreasonably increase the probability of error, i.e., convicting the innocent or acquittal of the guilty. These moral costs must be minimized to the degree possible within certain economic parameters.

In addition to the instrumental value of procedural justice described above, these procedures also have an intrinsic value.[163] The instrumental value rests on the procedures as means to determining guilt or innocence; the intrinsic values are values the procedures have independently of the correctness of the outcome. These "process benefits" involve values such as dignity, fairness, participation and social harmony. Procedural justice is founded on the peaceful resolution of conflict as opposed to dueling or some violent conflict resolution based on brute strength and as such it promotes communal harmony. The dignity of the participants is promoted if they are given some sense that they have some control over their lives and destiny. This cannot take place if individuals are not able to participate meaningfully in the trial. This means the presence of competent legal counsel is crucial. If the parties involved cannot understand the process they are less likely to accept the settlement as correct and fair.

The argument presented here thus far is as follows: if there exists a society where there are widespread inherited privileges of status and wealth that are passed down from one generation to the next and if these privileges often allow one to attain a quality of education superior to that of others in lower socioeconomic levels and if these differential levels of professional training give the privileged advantages in the courts through better legal representation, then

---

162. Rosenfeld, Steven B., "Mandatory Pro Bono" in Davis, op., cit., pp., 391-427.

163. Bayles, Michael, *Professional Ethics*, Belmont: Wadsworth Publishing Co., 1981, pp. 43-50.

that society, to that extent, is unjust. It is unjust because the only relevant factors in determining a correct decision in a court of law are the facts of the case and the law, not whether one is able to afford a Harvard law professor as an attorney.

These theoretical considerations are supported by substantial empirical data. As Bedau and others have argued with respect to capital punishment, racial and economic factors play a significant role in who is found guilty and how severely he or she is punished. It seems clear from the evidence that poor black male rapists were more likely to get the death penalty (when it was constitutional to do so) than white male rapists, thus reaffirming the street definition of 'capital punishment' as "Those without the capital get the punishment."[164]

In addition to the above argument based on procedural fairness there is also the argument based on equal opportunity. The general conception of equal opportunity holds that individuals must not be prevented from being considered for positions or denied certain rights on the basis of traits that have no relevance to the ability to perform adequately in those positions. In other words, equal opportunity means the absence of certain obstacles in pursuit of some goal.[165] These obstacles could be natural (lack of innate ability), socioeconomic (lack of education or wealth) or legal (the law prevents one from attaining it, e.g., women prohibited from voting). The full meaning of equal opportunity varies with respect to the overall political theory one accepts, yet most political theorists would accept that, minimally, equal opportunity means the absence of legal impediments to attaining one's goal. For example, if there is no law that specifies that women cannot vote, then men and women have equal opportunity to influence the election by voting. Of course, this formal equality can be undermined by certain background social and economic conditions such that, say, women do not have an equally good education or the leisure time to pursue political affairs. These background injustices of the past (racism, sexism) live on in the present perhaps not in the formal legal sense but socially and economically so that certain individuals cannot take full advantage of their rights and

---

164. Abel, op. cit., pp. 12-23.
165. Galanter, op. cit., pp. 135-45; Harold Laski, *A Grammar of Politics*, New Haven: Yale UP, 1931, 565-7.

opportunities. It is clear from the preceding argument that even this formal understanding of equal opportunity is vitiated in the manner it is implemented in a judicial system that does not provide equal chance to equally competent legal counsel to protect one's rights as specified by the law.

The formal sense of equal opportunity is related to the 'rule of law'. The rule of law means individuals are judged impartially as dictated by the written law, not according to the whims and caprice of those in power. The rule of law means the consistent administration of laws. However, consistent administration of laws cannot occur when administration involves legal advice of radically different value and competence arising from the background social circumstances of economic and educational inequality.

If the argument given above is correct, then one must consider possible reforms to address the problem. One possible answer would involve the government regulation of fees that trial lawyers can charge making sure that everyone can afford legal counsel. This would include free legal services for the most indigent. In fact, this last proposal has been implemented by Congress in 1974 when it founded the Legal Services Corporation to provide free legal services for the poor.[166] This proposal would enable everyone to have legal representation but it would not provide equal legal representation since the best lawyers would still be inaccessible to the disadvantaged.

Another approach would allow full laissez-faire market mechanism to apply to the legal profession with advertising and competition. This would probably significantly lower the cost of legal advice compared to the present system of minimal advertising and minimal competition. Again, this would not provide equally good legal counsel for all, since there would still be price differences that would put the affluent on the advantage. Nor would increasing "pro bono" services adequately address the problem since it would not eliminate the advantages of those who have access to superior legal advice on a consistent basis.[167]

Other proposals have included various insurance schemes or the

---

166. Abel, op. cit., p. 15.
167. Wasserstrom, op. cit., p. 132.

requirement of mandatory service to the disadvantaged for a few years after graduation for all lawyers.[168] These suggestions are helpful but, again, they do not provide for equal legal services across social strata.

The only solution to this problem is the abolition of the legal profession as it currently exists.[169] Legal representation must become a free social service provided by the government just as police and fire protection, health and education are provided by the state and paid for through general tax revenues. Lawyers would be assigned cases on the basis of expertise and availability not on the ability of the customer to pay. If more than one lawyer is qualified to defend or prosecute a client, then a lottery would be used to decide.

Finally, the issue of equal access to legal aid has a political dimension. The courts are institutional facilities for the implementation of authoritative legal norms promulgated by Congress. Given the present system of campaign contributions, lobbying and prevailing class origins of the legislators (many of whom are lawyers themselves) requires that we consider the possibility of whether the formulation of these norms may themselves be slanted to favor the affluent. The partial solution here would involve the public financing of campaigns and increased lobbying by the organized poor to promote and express their needs and perspectives.

A just society is one where the justice of the basic structure is fully implemented into every level of society in a consistent and thorough manner. If the basic structure does not permeate the structure of law from legislation, enforcement, adjudication and legal representation, then, to that degree, the society is unjust. A just society must be one where, as Rawls puts it, the "lottery of birth" should not reduce one's chances in a court of law.

---

168. Abel, op. cit., p. 21.
169. Ibid., p. 25.

# Chapter 3. Abolish the Double Jeopardy Rule

"The common law says wrong guilty verdicts can be wrong,
but wrong not guilty verdicts cannot be wrong."
—Evan Whitten

Brenda Schaefer was an ordinary, likeable and attractive young lady who lived with her blue collar parents outside Louisville, Kentucky. She married the first young man she ever dated, right after graduating high school in 1971; she worked part time as a cashier. The first tragedy she and her parents had to endure was the murder of her brother Jack, to whom she was very close. Brenda divorced her first husband, dated a couple of men, and years later her parents had to endure another tragedy, the brutal murder of Brenda herself at 36. Brenda was tortured and killed by her boyfriend in 1988 in his new girlfriend's house, which they tested beforehand to make sure Brenda's screams could not be heard by the neighbors. Shortly thereafter, the boyfriend was arrested and tried for murder on strong circumstantial evidence but was found innocent.

After the trial was over conclusive evidence was found showing that Brenda's former boyfriend was indeed the murderer. Pictures taken by his new girlfriend clearly showed the boyfriend tying, gagging, raping, sodomizing and finally ending Brenda's short life by forcing her to inhale chloroform. However, the rule against double jeopardy prevented putting the boyfriend on trial again for the same crime.[170] Is this justice?

The fifth amendment of the US Constitution states, ". . . nor shall any person be subject for the same offense to be twice put in jeopardy of life and limb." Known as the double jeopardy rule, it means that no one shall be tried twice for the same offense after an acquittal. Nor can the state try the same person for the same crime after a conviction with the intent of seeking a more severe punishment.[171]

Justice Hugo Black in *Green* v. *United States* (1957) gave the classic justification for the rule against double jeopardy. The rationale is based on the understanding that the state, unlike individuals, has vast resources at its command to use against the accused if it wishes. To prevent this ordeal of embarrassment, expense, anxiety, insecurity and the possibility of the innocent found guilty, the rule against double jeopardy was adopted by the federal constitution and, later, by most state constitutions as well.[172]

The argument presented here against the rule of double jeopardy consists of several elements: 1.) The rule is arbitrary and irrational; 2.) It undermines the rule of law ideal; 3.) It violates equal treatment under law; 4.) The rule violates Rawls' idea of fairness and the ideal of a well-ordered society; 5.) Instead of the rule against double jeopardy, potential abuses of governmental power can be made less likely by restructuring the grand jury.

The argument has two basic parts. One part will examine the validity of the rule against double jeopardy from the point of view of the ideas of the rule of law, due process and equal protection of the laws. The second part will apply Rawls' ideas of fairness and the "original position" to the problem of double jeopardy.[173] I consider the two approaches mutually reinforcing by bringing to light different dimensions of the controversy.

The rule against double jeopardy is arbitrary and irrational. No human endeavor in an important domain is allowed only one attempt

---

170. Hill, Bob, *Double Jeopardy*, New York: Avon Books, 1995. (Mel Ignatow, the boyfriend, did testify in court during the first murder trial. He was later tried for perjury based on this testimony and did go to jail.)
171. Constitution of the United States, fifth amendment.
172. *Green v United States* (1957) 355 US 184.
173. Rawls, John, *A Theory of Justice*, Cambridge: Harvard University Press, 1971, pp. 17-22; *Political Liberalism*, New York: Columbia UP, 1993, pp. 5-6, 356-63; *Justice as Fairness*, Harvard UP, 2001, pp. 14-28.

to achieve a desired goal, to require it in such a crucial matter as justice seems arbitrary. A possibility the framers of the constitution apparently did not consider is that in serious criminal cases two trials might be allowed in some cases while less serious cases and civil cases, only one trial could be permitted.

Rationality means, among other elements, that beliefs should be supported by sufficient evidence and that relevant evidence cannot be intentionally ignored. Therefore, it is irrational to ignore relevant evidence in all criminal cases, especially as it applies to situations that affect the basic structure of society.[174] The rule against double jeopardy sometimes forces the state to act irrationally by ignoring evidence that is relevant to the guilt of a person once the person has been mistakenly found not guilty by the first trial.

The ideal of the rule of law expresses the value that law is supreme and that all members of a society are subject to the law and to various consequences for violating the law. On this view, law is a system of universal normative rules governing social relations and enforceable by the political system.

The meaning of the rule of law can be clarified by distinguishing it from the 'rule of men' and the 'rule by decree.' A rule by men or persons would mean rule by whim and prejudice and as such lacks, among other factors, the consistency and predictability a modern complex society needs. A complex and diverse society implies the need for a rational legal system consisting of general rules to structure society and guide human behavior. A rational society needs consistent rules consistently applied to be stable and enable individuals to make plans and carry out endeavors with some degree of security which rule by decree cannot provide.

To be sure, the rule of law has been subject to valid criticisms from various schools of thought.[175] We cannot discuss the entire debate here but many have been skeptical about the notion of the rule of law as too abstract arguing that one cannot extricate law from the social, cultural, linguistic, psychological and political contexts within which it is created, formulated, interpreted and applied. Though the law is a social practice and as such malleable to some degree by

---

174. Rawls, *Theory*, pp. 90-5.
175. See for example *Jurisprudence* by S. Sinha, St. Paul: West, 1993.

these forces, with some exceptions, it is assumed here that the law generally is not necessarily totally obscured by these forces. These external forces are more a factor at the more abstract and constitutional level of legal dispute, not the more specific level of law which is the majority of legal situations. To abandon the very idea of the rule of law ideal would be tantamount to abandoning the idea of a written law and would lead to rule by decree and certainly to social chaos in a modern complex society.

The rule of law suggests the need for due process or a set of necessary and sufficient conditions for correctly and fairly determining the guilt and innocence of individuals. Rawls calls the trial an instance of "imperfect procedural justice" since the goal of the process is to find the guilty guilty and the innocent innocent, but there is no perfect procedure which guarantees such an outcome; but clearly there are better and worse procedures.[176]

The rule against double jeopardy undermines the rule of law and procedural justice in at least three ways. The double jeopardy condition places an undue burden on the state to show the guilt or innocence of an individual in a single attempt. Given the social, institutional and personal limitations of prosecutors, juries and judges, the system fails at times and allows guilty individuals to go unpunished.[177] For the guilty to suffer no undesired consequences reduces the power, legitimacy and effectiveness of law.[178]

The second way in which the rule against double jeopardy conflicts with the rule of law is that sometimes prosecutors are reluctant to indict at all because of the rule. They are loath to bring charges because they are not sure if more evidence may come forth later which would make a stronger case but, if they proceed with an indictment sooner, they may not get a conviction but would be prevented from attempting the case again with the new evidence.

The double jeopardy exclusion undermines due process since the rule does not allow the process to come to a rational completion in some cases. The process that is due must reflect the socio-economic realities of the judicial system as it relates to the desired goal just as,

---

176. Rawls, *Theory*, pp. 85-8.
177. Examples would include the case of Robert Durst, accused of murder in 2001.
178. Rawls, *Theory*, pp. 453-62.

say, scientific method reflects the fallibility of humans in suggesting hypotheses, testing them and, if unsuccessful, formulating new hypotheses, retesting and so forth.

The equal protection of the laws concept, in essence, is a requirement that the law be applied consistently without respect to characteristics that are irrelevant to the purpose of the law, the determination of basic rights and duties, penalties and opportunities. What is relevant is determined by the underlying principles that inform the system of laws and the ideal of equal protection is the requirement that the law should be implemented in a manner consistent with these underlying principles.

The rule against double jeopardy violates the equal protection clause in its implementation in a social context in two ways. First, it violates equal protection because those who have the financial resources are able to enlist the services of superior legal representation (and other personnel such as investigators, jury consultants, etc.) which enhances the chance for the guilty to be found innocent. Given a free market system of allocation of professionals such as attorneys, the private sector has in general been able to attract highly qualified attorneys and pay them more generously than the government can. As a result, the state may be at a disadvantage in criminal trials where wealthy individuals are indicted. Second, state prosecutors are often overworked and lack the experience and training the top trial lawyers from the private sector have. It seems clear that the reality of class society permeates even the court system and undermines the equal protection clause.[179]

Fairness, for Rawls, is central to justice and implies a correct structuring of distribution of goods and burdens that would be agreed upon and accepted by free and equal persons under the right circumstances.[180] Rawls explains his conception of justice as fairness with his thought experiment version of the state of nature, called the "original position." This hypothetical choice situation is defined by three basic elements, namely, a definition of the 'people' in the original position, the "veil of ignorance" and the general knowledge

179. Grcic, Joseph, *Ethics and Political Theory*, Lanham: U. Press of America, pp. 207-9, 2000.
180. Ibid., p. 208.

he allows the people in the original position to have. The veil of ignorance expresses some of Rawls' ideas of the necessary structures of the decision-making framework for defining the nature of justice. This fictional veil is Rawls' way of specifying the relevant knowledge conditions of the original position.

The central concept in justice as fairness is the mutual acceptance and agreement of basic rules of social organization which Rawls believes is a necessary condition for any just community.[181] Given these conditions, Rawls believes the principles of justice chosen would be: "Each person is to have an equal right to the most extensive total system of equal basic liberties compatible with a similar system of liberty for all; and social and economic inequalities are to be arranged so that they are both: "to the greatest benefit of the least advantaged consistent with the just savings principle" and "attached to offices and positions open to all under conditions of fair equality of opportunity."[182]

The reason people in the original position would choose these principles is that they provide for what Rawls calls "primary goods." Primary goods are "what a rational man wants whatever else he wants"[183] That is, they are necessary means to fulfilling one's plan or goal of life, whatever these happen to be. These goods include rights and liberties, opportunities and powers, income and wealth and self-respect. The two principles would be chosen by rational self-interested persons as the best way for each to secure their ends. Though persons in the original position don't know their particular conception of the good they do know they have a rational life-plan and to achieve this end they prefer more primary social goods.

The members of the original position would not accept the rule against double jeopardy for the following reasons. First, since they are allowed general knowledge, they would know that they are far more likely to be a victim of crime than a perpetrator of it. As potential victims, they would realize that their primary goods are in jeopardy and as such would want crime deterred and criminals punished, as the rule of law demands. They would also be concerned about ex-

---

181. Ibid., p. 256.
182. Ibid., p. 302
183. Ibid., pp. 90-5.

cessive prosecution and so would agree to some restrictions on governmental indictments (as explained below.)

Second, members of the original position would also know that they are not likely to be affluent but more likely in the middle class. This means they would not want the wealthy to have an unfair advantage in evading the consequences of their criminal acts. Nor would they want a tyrannical government since they would lack the resources to adequately defend themselves against false charges, hence the restrictions discussed below.

Third, the current practice violates Rawls' ideas of a stable and well-ordered democratic society because of three facts.[184] A well-ordered democratic society is one where citizens are treated as free and equal and special priority is given to basic rights as specified by the two principles of justice and the basic institutions encourage the virtues of fairness and mutual trust. First, people in the original position would know that there exists a class divided society and would see that the rule against double jeopardy places an undue burden on the state especially in cases where the accused are affluent and have resources to get their desired result. Second, the people in the original position would also know the general limitations of the basic institution of criminal justice. They would know how the trial system in reality works given the human weaknesses in general and of the jury and judge in particular. The moral and intellectual limitations exacerbate the social class problem to undermine the reliability of the judiciary.

The third fact that would lead members of the original position to see the irrationality of the rule against double jeopardy is based on the fact that one is more likely to be a victim of a criminal act then a criminal. Given this, they would be concerned that those found guilty can appeal but society is not given the same right since it, under the current system, cannot re-try those found innocent but later evidence shows could be guilty. The hypothetical persons of the original position would further reason that if the state can err in finding the innocent guilty and thus gives the right to appeal to those found guilty, it seems rational to conclude that the state can also err in finding the guilty innocent in which case it would seem fair that

---

184. Ibid., pp. 453-62, *Justice as Fairness*, pp. 8-10.

the community must have the right for another trial.

These three conditions weaken what Rawls calls the ideal of a stable and well-ordered society and as such do not strengthen mutual trust or encourage the public virtues of fairness. However, people in the original position would not abandon the rule against double jeopardy without requiring that there be conditions put in place to prevent possible abuses of power by the state. The restructured grand jury is the solution to this problem.

The grand jury must be distinguished from the trial jury.[185] The grand jury, as is it currently practiced, is a group of individuals called by the government to hear evidence in a criminal matter and to decide whether there is sufficient evidence for the government to issue an indictment. A judge instructs the jurors concerning their rights and responsibilities and jurors hear witnesses under oath and, unlike a regular trial, can ask questions of the witnesses. If the grand jury decides there is enough evidence to bring an indictment, then if the person does not plead guilty, a trial is called for with a different set of persons who will constitute the trial jury and will decide the guilt or innocence of the defendant.

Analogously to the rule against double jeopardy, the grand jury's purpose is to protect the people from abuse of power by the government by restricting indictments the state can issue. Currently the grand jury is called by the office of the prosecutor but it can become an instrument of the community.

The rule against double jeopardy can be abolished if the grand jury is restructured so that the power of calling the second trial is placed in the hands of the community. After an initial trial resulted in an acquittal, laws relating to the grand jury must allow the grand jury be reconstituted by a decision of the citizens if new evidence comes to light which casts serious doubt on the accuracy of the original acquittal. This reform of the grand jury and elimination of the rule against double jeopardy would go some distance in preventing gross injustice.

The rule preventing double jeopardy is based on a desire to avoid violating the rights of citizens. The goal of the founders was valid

---

185. See, e.g., Brenner, Susan W. "The Voice of the Community", in *Virginia Journal of Social Policy and the Law*, 67, Fall 1995, pp. 11-61.

but the means they chose was too blunt an instrument to meet the needs of justice. The problem overlooked by the framers of the constitution is that they seem to have been oblivious to the violation of equal rights that arise from a society radically divided by economic resources and income.[186] The grand jury properly used can act as a buffer between the tyranny of the government and the consequences of losing what Rawls calls the "lottery of life" by being born on the wrong side of the tracks that lead some innocent to prison and some guilty, to freedom simply because they happen to be the lucky winners of the lottery of life.[187]

---

186. See "Meritocracy in America," *The Economist*, pp. 22-4, 1/1/05.
187. Rawls, *Theory*, p. 93.

# Chapter 4. Empower the Jury

"A jury is a group of people who will judge you but were not smart enough to avoid jury duty."
—Anonymous

Skepticism about the jury system is as old as the jury itself but do we want to get rid of it, keep it as is or reform it? A look at the history of this controversial institution may shed some light.

The origins of trial by jury are go as far back as ancient Greece and Rome, the Norman conquest of England in 1066 and the Magna Carta of 1215 which further institutionalized the idea of a trial by one's peers. The right to a jury trial gradually replaced the medieval system of trial by ordeal where the accused faced some physical challenge such as attempted drowning, burning at the stake or an actual battle with an opponent. The will of God was said to be revealed in these trials where the deity would protect the innocent from death or serious harm. The replacement of the trial by ordeal by trial by jury represented the growth of the ideal of equality, the greater empowerment of the people, a limit on autocratic political power and a more rational judicial system but, it will be argued, this development has not gone far enough in the direction of democratic participation.

In the early stages of the development of the trial, the jury was not to serve silently. In its nascent stage, the jury was selected from the local community where the alleged crime occurred and was to consist of persons who were familiar with the accused in order to provide any relevant information about the dispute, in addition to weighing the evidence for and against the defendant. In this sense the original concept of the jury, now sometimes referred to as a petit jury, was more of the nature of the grand jury rather than the current nature of the trial jury.[188]

In the US, trial by jury is guaranteed by the Constitution in federal and state criminal cases and some civil cases; however, originally, only white men with property could serve on a jury. The size of the jury has varied and the requirement for unanimity has also fluctuated generally being required for serious federal criminal cases but less so for civil cases.[189]

The thesis argued for here is that the current structure of the trial is not appropriately designed to produce the desired results in an efficient manner. Further, the current jury system does not maximally reflect the values implicit in the institution nor the political paradigm in which it is embedded. I argue that the trial jury must be given a greater and more active role in the trial. Specifically, I claim that the jury should be allowed to call its own witnesses and ask questions of all the parties involved in the trial prior to deciding the guilt or innocence of the accused.

Prior to defending the thesis of a participatory jury, a brief sketch of the current judicial procedures will be helpful.[190] Although most criminal cases in the US are settled by plea bargaining, the trial system has been instituted to provide a framework for determining the guilt and innocence of persons charged with crimes. If there is to be a trial, prospective jurors are called and the voir dire process takes place where jurors are questioned by the prosecution and defense to determine their suitability for the trial. Currently, the function of

---

188. Devlin, Patrick Sir, *Trial by Jury*, London: University Paperback, 1966, pp. 8-17. The grand jury, unlike the trial jury, is a group of citizens called by the government to hear evidence in a criminal matter and to decide whether there is enough evidence for the government to issue an indictment. If the grand jury decides there is enough evidence to bring an indictment, then if the person does not plead guilty a trial is called for with a different set of persons which will constitute the trial jury will decide the guilt or innocence of the defendant.

189. Hall, Kermit L., ed., *The Supreme Court of the United States*, New York: Oxford University Press, 1992, pp. 632-4.

190. Williams, Jerrie, *Constitutional Analysis*, St. Paul: West, 1979, pp. 75-80.

the jury, which in theory represents the community, is to establish whether the facts presented in court are credible and sufficient to determine that the accused committed the alleged crime. After voir dire the jury is impaneled, or defined and sworn in after which the trial can begin.

The actual trial typically begins with the prosecutor stating the case against the accused who must prove the guilt of the accused. The defendant and his or her lawyer then respond to the prosecutor and seek to establish that the prosecutor has not proved guilt beyond a reasonable doubt, in a criminal trial, or by preponderance of the evidence, in a civil trial. Witnesses are called and cross examined. Rationality requires that all relevant evidence for and against the claim of guilt or innocence must be presented and evaluated.

When both sides have completed their presentation, the summation begins. The summation is the summary of the case against the accused and the summary of the evidence by the defendant against the prosecutor's claims. After this, the jury is charged and instructed by the judge as to the law and the rules they must follow in their deliberations. Finally, a decision must be made whether the individual is guilty or innocent of the charges and, if guilty, certain consequences or some form of punishment must be determined and implemented as specified by the legal system operative at the time the trial is taking place.

It is argued here that the mentioned structure of the jury trial should be reformed so that the jury can call witnesses and ask questions during the trial proceedings. Once the jury has finished questioning, then both sides may offer their summations after which the jury deliberates in private.

A rationale for the jury trial in general, as opposed to trial by judge(s), is needed. This rationale, it will be argued, will also justify a more active jury. The general rationale for the jury system is based on instrumental and intrinsic considerations. The instrumental values rest on the procedures as a reliable means to determining guilt or innocence of the accused, the values of legitimacy of the judicial system and social stability. The intrinsic values or process benefits are values the procedures have independently of the correctness of the outcome. The intrinsic or "process benefits," the jury embodies values of dignity and fairness which the trial can enhance and instantiate if properly structured and implemented.[191]

The concept of dignity involves the ideas of treating people with respect as bearers of certain rights such as the right to autonomy, free speech, or the right, as Kant would articulate, to be treated as an end in him or herself, not as a means only.[192] The jury in theory represents the community which is, in an important sense, also an injured party in any crime since the crime challenges the established laws of the community. As an injured party dignity suggests it has the right to present its side and defend itself. Given this understanding, dignity is not present if all affected parties are not able to participate equally in the trial where their interests and rights are in question.

Under the present system, the jury, representing the community and the sovereignty of the people, is in an essentially passive role through the trial proceedings (prior to the jury being charged) and has only the right to react to the evidence it has heard and seen. The value of dignity would be enhanced if the jury could participate in a more active manner if properly structured and implemented. To keep those mostly directly tied to the community in a passive role in the presentation and questioning of evidence demeans the community to what one may call the tyranny of the professionals, the lawyers and judges. Though the prosecutor, and the judge, are said to represent (in some sense) the community, there is no valid reason consistent with dignity why the community's speech must be mediated by the prosecutor exclusively (especially given the reality of the political and bureaucratic system, see below).

The process benefit of dignity is closely related to that of fairness but fairness emphasizes the idea of rational agreement. As Rawls explains it, fairness implies equality, free agreement and mutual benefit.[193] A fair procedure would mean one where the rules, of an institution or society in general, would be freely and publicly accepted by all rational persons and impose on themselves equally. That the

191. Bayles, Michael, "Principles for Legal Procedure," *Law and Philosophy*, Vol. 5, 1986, 33-43.
192. Kant, Immanuel, *Foundations of the Metaphysics of Morals*, L. W. Beck, trans. New York: prentice Hall, 1989, pp. 23-6.
193. Rawls, John, *A Theory of Justice*, Cambridge: Harvard University Press, 1973, pp. 3-8.

jury, which in theory represents the community and which the entire judicial process serves, would freely agree to an exclusively passive role seems implausible, especially given the non-ideal realities of the socio-political system. It seems unlikely that any group of persons engaged in such a central social function would limit themselves to such a limited role knowing how imperfect the judicial process is in general.

The instrumental values of the jury rest on it as a means to the goals of a democratic society. First, as mentioned above, the current trial system is founded on the peaceful resolution of conflict as such it promotes communal harmony.

Second, a jury trial can protect what Rawls calls "primary social goods," goods every rational person wants since they are necessary means to any rational goal.[194] Rawls specifies these goods as: rights, liberties, opportunities, income, wealth and self-respect. In Rawls' idea of the original position and the veil of ignorance, specific information about individuals is excluded for reasons of fairness, the members of the original position would not decide to limit themselves in the judicial process where their rights are in question. This is especially true since the hypothetical members of the original position are allowed to have general knowledge about their society which would inform them of the distorted nature of the democratic system (see below). The greater empowerment of the jury as a representative of the community will enhance the fairness of the proceedings and safeguard primary social goods.

Thirdly, a jury trial makes bribery less likely. Depending how judges are selected, they may be more or less subject to bribery or corruption. If the judges are elected, then the need for campaign moneys may influence the judge. The outright bribery of the judge will be less likely with a jury system since it is easier to bribe one person than twelve; something the ancient Athenians knew well when they decided on a jury of 501.[195] Moreover, a judge may be biased and rule in an unfair manner but it is less likely for a group to share the same bias (especially if properly selected through voir dire) and as

---

194. Ibid., p. 22.
195. Devlin, op. cit., p. 159.

such can be a counterbalancing force to bias.[196]

The value of intelligibility means the trial should be understandable to the community and the average person involved in the trial. Currently the mere presence of the jury motivates the parties involved to present their side clearly but this right to enlightened understanding is seriously compromised by the current trial system. Rationality requires that all relevant evidence be examined concerning the truth or falsity of a statement or the guilt or innocence of a person. The inability to ask questions (except of the judge after being charged) of the relevant parties and call witnesses limits the jury to a passive role and as such does not have the opportunity to enlighten itself during the presentation of the evidence by asking pertinent questions thus increasing the chance for a faulty verdict.

Moreover, the lack of opportunity to ask questions can also conceal the jury's ignorance and prejudice. Denying the jury the right to ask questions is to deny them the opportunity to rectify their ignorance and reduce or eliminate prejudice before the deliberations begin.

Furthermore, the argument for the jury in general and the more empowered jury, cannot be oblivious to the social context in which the judicial processes occur. Given the current realities of a class stratified society, cultural differences, circumstances and conditions of the various classes may not be generally understood. If the jury had the right to ask questions it would increase the intelligibility of the trial to the jury and others involved in the trial such as the accused and the public.

The jury system with a more active jury can improve the ethical character of the jurors and society in general. The trial is an opportunity for jurors and the general community to learn about the law and participate in the affairs of the community. The jury is based on the autonomy of citizens and thereby encourages the citizenry to be more knowledgeable and active in civic affairs.[197]

A key argument for the active jury and its role in a democratic society is based on the understanding of how formally democratic societies actually function. Various political theorists argue plausi-

---

196. See also *Duncan v. Louisiana*, 391 US. 145 (1968).
197. De Tocqueville, Alexis, in Hall, op. cit., p. 633.

bly that contemporary 'democracies' are only democratic in a limited and weak sense.[198] The ideal definition of democracy has an informed electorate determine their common good and have elected representatives who come from widely diverse parts of society, help bring this good into reality in a selfless and efficient manner. There are several reasons why this is an idealized and misleading model of democracy.

Evidence and common experience show that complex societies are not fully democratic. The democratic ideal of universal active and informed participation of the electorate choosing the most qualified representatives from candidates of the highest intelligence, virtue and impartiality is far from the reality. Criticisms of contemporary democracies point out that contemporary advanced societies require a vast hierarchical bureaucracy to administer and rule. Bureaucracy requires an educated elite with specialization and division of labor. The general ignorance, irrationality and apathy of the masses strengthen the entrenched rule of the societal and bureaucratic elite even in a society that is in theory democratic. At best, what passes for democracy is a competition for power by members of the elite influenced by lobbyists and private campaign contributions who manipulate the populace through corporate (elite owned) mass media, sound bites and vague and misleading promises.

In addition to the problem of the ruling bureaucratic elite, there is the general reality of a class stratified society whose members have radically unequal opportunity to become members of the ruling elite. A class divided society with unequal opportunity further exacerbates the limitations of the democratic model and puts in jeopardy the judicial system. What all societies thus far lack is what Rawls calls "fair equality of opportunity" the real opportunity to equal education and other social values to develop one's potential to enter the ruling class.[199] This is another reason why in the original position where hypothetical individuals do not know their class membership would not agree to enhance the power of the elite.

Given the current political and social system as seen by these theorists, judges, prosecutors and attorneys are members of an elite

---

198. Social theorists such as Joseph Schumpeter (*Capitalism, Socialism, Democracy*), William Domhoff (*Who Rules America?*), among others.

199. Rawls, op. cit., pp. 35-9.

alienated from the ordinary community. There is a form of professional inbreeding where many prosecutors and defense attorneys become judges hence strengthening their characteristic as an isolated
and elite professional and socioeconomic class far removed from ordinary citizens. Empowering the jury would lessen the power of the
elite from exercising undue influence on the welfare of the accused
who are usually from a class very distinct from that of the elite.

By participating in the process, the jury helps to counterbalance
this reality of diminished democracy. The jury that is representative
of the community introduces a direct democratic dimension missing
in the political process. In a quasi-democratic system distorted by
the bureaucratic elite and class society, the jury system is a safeguard
against unjust and nondemocratic state power. In this sense the jury
serves as an expanded application of the checks and balances idea
and the separation of powers established in the Constitution. The
purpose of checks and balances is to limit government and protect
the sovereignty of the people. A more active jury would be a more
direct way for the citizenry to express their sovereignty and check
a government that tends to be dominated by an elite. The abolition
of the jury or the maintenance of a passive jury would enhance state
power and make more possible the abuse of that power and diminish
the legitimacy of political power. The jury, analogous to the division
of power and federalism, provides an additional set of checks and
balances where the community directly assesses the validity of laws
as it sees it.

Regardless whether one accepts the bureaucratic elite theory
of modern democracies, the legal system in any society is imperfect
and is, in varying degrees, unjust, incomplete, underdetermined and
vague. The law promotes social order through peaceful dispute settlement and the facilitating of necessary social change, however, all
legal systems have limitations, some which are based on the nature of
language itself, the law, human nature and some based on the intrinsic nature of institutions.

Language is a necessary tool of social order and communication
but one that is also limited. It is generally agreed that language, no
matter how sophisticated and complex, cannot fully avoid the problems of vagueness and ambiguity. The legal system as a set of state-

ments of various levels of generality cannot but be contaminated by these intrinsic limitations of language.[200]

Research shows that errors in the trial process as it currently exists are due to certain human problems. One major cause of trial errors (about 25%), i.e., finding the innocent guilty, is overzealousness of the prosecutor plus police incompetence and corruption.[201]

Additional institutional limitations include the conservative nature of bureaucracies and institutional inertia. Bureaucracies are by nature slow to make necessary changes and tend to favor the status quo since any change is construed as possible loss of power or position by its members. Secondly, laws are by nature a reaction to a problem and as such a time gap exists between the law and the problems it seeks to address. Thirdly, law, also by necessity, is a system of general rules which cannot anticipate all situations in their unique particularities. In an increasingly pluralistic society, this consideration should carry substantial weight.

The active jury can help minimize some of these deficiencies of law. As members of the community, the jury can 'complete' the law as it sees necessary, disambiguate vague laws and ignore unjust laws. Although the actions of the jury are, to be sure, not immune from error or bias, as representatives of the community which the law is, in theory, designed to serve, they have a right to address the limitations of the legal system.

Jury nullification can be an instance of this power. In jury nullification the jury de facto ignores the instructions of the judge by refusing to apply the relevant laws and decides on acquittal. Though rare, jury nullification can be an example of a jury reacting to a legal system it sees as unfair, antiquated or improperly implemented.[202]

In participating in the justice system and enhancing the democratic dimension of the process, the jury enhances the legitimacy of the process and, by implication, the legitimacy and stability of the political system as a whole. By participating in the system in an ac-

---

200. See Dworkin, Ronald, A *Matter of Principle*, Cambridge: Harvard Univ. Press, 1985, pp. 49, 230-1, & *Law's Empire*, Cambridge: Harvard Univ. Press, 1986, pp. 8-9, 87-9.
201. Huff, C. Ronald, Arye Rattner, Edward Sagarin, *Convicted But Innocent*, 1996, London: Sage, p. 64.
202. See the John Peter Zenger case, in Hall, op. cit., pp. 633, 765.

tive and central manner, the jury implicitly accepts the judicial system and by implication, the political structure within which it is embedded. Furthermore, if juries make unpopular decisions, the animosity the public would have directed toward the government is directed toward the jury which melts back into the general population thus dissipating the negative feeling which otherwise might persist.

Any rationale for the jury system cannot be complete without an analysis of the criticisms of the jury in general.[203] It has been argued that jury duty is an unfair burden placed on the citizenry. The pay is low and the trial may be long separating the jurors from their family and normal routine.

Part of the response to this claim is to raise the pay of the jurors. Another is that the added power of the jury would enhance the prestige of the jury and make it more attractive to many but not all potential jurors. The manner of selection must also be evaluated; individuals should be sought who are representative of the community and more likely to be willing and able to do well on the jury.

Another criticism is that the jury lacks the needed knowledge to perform well in the trial. Critics contend the jury is selected from a pool of average citizens most of whom lack higher education or legal education which will lead to inaccurate verdicts. A trial by judges, by contrast, would be a trial by individuals knowledgeable and educated in the necessary areas needed to perform their function.

There are several responses to this claim. First, although in the current practice jurors tend to be selected who have little or no prior knowledge of the case, originally, the knowledge of the jury was valued as essential to the just resolution of the case. Jurors today are more educated and they receive instruction from the judge as necessary. Moreover, defenders claim, the jury needs no special knowledge to perform its function. Rationality, common sense and lived experience are enough to apply the law and make judgments of justice. The fact that the jury is more likely to be from the social class of the accused then the judge or the prosecutor given the jury special insights other may not have and since the purpose of the trial is to find all the relevant evidence, it seems irrational that one element of the trial not

---

203. Litan, Robert E., ed., *Verdict*, Washington, DC: Brookings Institution, 1993, pp. 103-133; Adler, Stephen J., *The Jury*, New York: Random House, 1994, pp. 41-5.

be allowed to ask pertinent questions.

Another concern is the possibility that a more active jury will take more time and so add cost to the proceedings. It is possible that a more active jury will take some additional time during the trial but it may save time during the deliberations since it will presumably have a better understanding of the issues. Although time and cost are relevant, if a more active jury does enhance process values and improve instrumental values, the some added time seems a reasonable risk to take.

As for the accuracy of the jury, the evidence by its very nature cannot be conclusive but there are some relevant findings.[204] As mentioned above, an overzealous prosecutor and police corruption and incompetence are the major causes of judicial error. Evidence shows about 81% of verdicts agree with the judge's opinion. The 19% includes 15% where the judge felt the accused was guilty but the jury found him or her innocent and in only 4% of the cases did judges believe innocent people were found guilty.[205]

Moreover, these statistics of course do not prove the jury is only 81% accurate, for one cannot assume the judges are 100% accurate. One could also argue that the accuracy of the jury could be greater since it is more difficult to bribe a jury of twelve than one judge. In addition, the guilty can appeal the decision to a higher court often decided by judges alone. Finally, a judge can set aside a jury verdict (except an acquittal in a criminal case) if the judge believes the verdict is manifestly in error and request a new trial.

Questioning by the jury would expose the possible ignorance of the jury which can then be rectified by the judge and the attorneys. In addition, historically, the jury does not and need not give reasons for its verdict.[206] The questioning period would indicate indirectly the likely rationale forthcoming from the jury and suggest possible appeals to the defendant if found guilty.

Another criticism is the potential bias and prejudice of the jury.

---

204. Kalven, Harry, Hans Zeisel, *The American Jury*, Boston: Little, Brown, 1966, pp. 5, 417-25. Eyewitness misidentification was the major reason for error in about 50% of the cases, see Huff, op. cit., p. 64.

205. Kalven, op. cit., p. 45.

206. This should be changed since in the case of guilty verdicts especially, the rationale of the jury can be helpful in appeals.

First, the process of selecting jurors, known as "voir dire," is designed to identify prejudiced jurors through questioning by the attorney and/or judge and eliminate jurors believed to be biased or otherwise inappropriate. Again, if the jury were allowed to ask questions, biased would be revealed and corrected.[207]

Studies reveal that current juries suffer from confusion, boredom and frustration.[208]

The right to ask questions would alleviate to some degree most of these concerns. It would reduce confusion by asking and receiving answers to questions, it would reduce boredom which leads to poor concentration since having a dialogue between the prosecutor, defense attorney and judge will add intellectual stimulation. Frustration is the result of confusion, impotence and boredom and will also be mitigated by the changes proposed here. Empirical evidence shows that active involvement with any material enhances memory and understanding.[209]

Another issue is that the jury can violate the rule of law by misunderstanding the law or simply ignoring the law as in jury nullification. First, though not explicitly mentioned in the Constitution, the jury in the US originally had the right to make judgments of law not just judgments of fact.[210] Second, the rule of law, though important, is by no means an absolute; justice is a higher standard than the rule of law. Finally, jury nullification is extremely rare and can be reversed in some cases by the judge.

A related criticism of the more empowered jury contends that the jury may ask inappropriate questions or act inappropriately and so jeopardize the fairness of the proceedings. It is possible that the jury may ask questions or call for witnesses who violate the rules of procedures and evidence in such a manner that a mistrial might be declared. One answer is to argue that this is simply a necessary risk and that the benefits outweigh the costs.[211] Another response is to

---

207. In response to these issues many judges have suggested that juries be eliminated in complex cases. (See Litan, op. cit., p 379.)

208. Adler, op. cit. p. 46.

209. Myers, David G., *Exploring Psychology*, New York: Worth Publishers, 1990, pp. 206-7.

210. See *Sparf & Hansen v. United States*, (1896).

211. Japan is reintroducing the jury trial with a lawyer on the jury; see Robert E. Precht, "Japan, The Jury," *The New York Times*, Dec. 1, 2006, p. A29.

have the jury submit questions and list of its own possible witnesses to the judge prior to taking any action court. (Currently the jury can ask questions of the judge only after the jury has been charged.) The judge would then evaluate the questions or action as to their appropriateness and if the judge decided the question or action is inappropriate or illegal he or she must explain the reasons to the jury. The judge should explain that to ask a clearly illegal question (or ask for inadmissible witnesses) would mean a mistrial and a new trial. If the defense attorney agrees with the judge, then the jury should refrain from asking such questions or calling for legally unacceptable witnesses.

Conclusion

Participating in a jury trial is one of the most direct political powers citizens have in a democratic system. The democratic ideal is founded on the idea of moral equality which holds in essence that rational adult persons can make and have the right to make judgments about central political matters. An empowered jury can perform this function more fully and instantiate the values of a democratic society in greater degree. No justice system is perfect but we must choose the best among the alternatives after considering the advantages and disadvantages of all possible systems.

# Chapter 5. Abolish the Electoral College

"The people are uninformed, and would be misled by a few designing men."
—E. Gerry

In the 2000 presidential election Vice President Al Gore received 543, 895 more votes (50,999,897) than George W. Bush (50,456,002) but George Bush became President of the United States. This was not the first time this happened and may not be the last. Is this democracy?

The US Constitution specifies that the President of the US is not to be chosen directly by the people but by what has come to be called the Electoral College. The Electoral College is constituted by electors chosen by the legislatures of each state and the District of Columbia. The number of electors is equal to the number of senators and representatives the state has in Congress. There is only one constitutional restriction as to the identity of the electors, "No Senator or Representative or person holding an office of trust or profit under the United States shall be appointed an elector."[212] Further qualification, if any, for being an elector are determined by state legislatures.

The constitution does not require that electors vote as the majority or plurality in their state has voted. Currently, only 16 states require that the electors vote for the winner of majority or plural-

212. US Constitution, Article II, Section 1, 2.

ity vote. The US Supreme Court has determined these 16 states are within the constitution but there is no clarity what would happen if some elector chose to ignore this state law. In fact, there is evidence that the framers of the constitution expected the electors to vote according to their own judgment and conscience. When the Electoral College meets, about six weeks after the election, a majority of 270 electoral votes out of 538 is needed to win the presidency. Failing this, the election is thrown into the House.

The rationale of the founders for creating the Electoral College was practical and theoretical. On the practical side, the Electoral College seems to have been decided upon as a compromise to appease the small and slave holding states who felt a direct election of the president would place them in a weakened position.[213]

Some defended the Electoral College because it promotes the value of geographic distribution since predominantly rural states have more power than urban and more populous states with the Electoral College than without. The underlying idea seems to have been that the winner of the presidential race should have wide appeal geographically including rural as well as urban states. This geographic appeal was seen as promoting the stability and unity of the nation.

A pivotal rationale for the college was to be found in the thinking of individuals such as Alexander Hamilton who were suspicions of mass democracy and saw it as potentially mob rule by an uneducated, widely dispersed, and selfish populace. They feared that private property would be placed in jeopardy by direct popular vote for president.[214] They saw the Electoral College as consisting of mature, affluent wise men that had the best interests of the country when they deliberated.

The argument against the Electoral College presented here has two parts, one based on the political ideas of John Rawls and one based on more general considerations.

Let us consider the specific rationale for the Electoral College. First, contrary to Hamilton's assumption, the population is far more educated and sophisticated than at the time the Constitution was

---

213. Slaves were to be counted as 2/3 persons as part of the compromise as well.
214. Hamilton, Alexander, in Lodge, H.C., ed., *Federalist Papers*, New York: Putnam & Sons, 1888, p. 425.

written. Democratic theory, as will be explored more fully below, is not based on whether the populace is educated or wise but on the right of each adult person to certain basic equal moral rights and respect. Communication has improved and other institutions such as mass education and mass media have developed to strengthen social cohesion.

Second, the other main justification for the College, that it would be a deliberative body of wise or at least better informed individuals who would select the president and vice president in a rational manner, has not been implemented. The electors are not chosen because of their wisdom, even if that were possible, since there is no generally accepted legal definition of "wisdom." In fact, the electors are chosen for their loyalty to their political party.

Third, the Electoral College is inconsistent with the idea of democratic rule. The undemocratic aspects of the institution are obvious in that the votes of the Electoral College as a whole have not always corresponded to the winner of the national popular vote.[215]

A further problem exacerbates the Electoral College as an institution is that of unfaithful electors. Unfaithful electors, at least seventeen so far, are those who did not cast their vote as they promised or as the majority of popular vote dictated. At times these electors acted as they did in exchange for personal favors from those elected.[216]

The problematic and anomalous aspects of the Electoral College are made more perspicuous by comparison with what John Rawls calls a democratic "well-ordered" and "stable" society.[217] A democratic society according to Rawls is one where a society is a "well-or-

---

215. Six times the winner of the popular vote did not win the majority of electoral votes. Twice the decision for president was thrown into the House of Representative as provided by the 12 amendment. (In 1824, Andrew Jackson won plurality but lost to John Quincy Adams in the House election; in 1876, Samuel J. Tilden won the popular vote but not the presidency; Benjamin Harrison won by electoral votes in 1888 even though Grover Cleveland won the popular vote. Given the current legal situation, there is a probability of one in three that there will be a lack of consistency in the popular and electoral vote if the margin of popular votes is less than 300,000. If the margin is less than 1.5 million, the probability of an inconsistency is one in four.

216. Dahl, Robert, *How Democratic is the American Constitution?*, New Haven: Yale Univ. Press, 2003, pp. 79-82.

217. Rawls, John, *A Theory of Justice*, Cambridge: Harvard Univ. Press, 1971, pp. 453-62.

dered," and a "fair system of cooperation," where citizens are defined as "free and equal." By "equal" Rawls means equal as "moral persons" which means they have equal rights as specified by the first principle and "a conception of their good and capable of a sense of justice."[218]

According to Rawls, a democratic society would be based on Rawls' two basic principles of justice. The first principle states "each person is to have an equal right to the most extensive basic liberty compatible with a similar liberty for others." And the second principle holds: "social and economic inequalities are to be arranged so that they are both a) reasonable expected to be to everyone's advantage, and b) attach to positions and offices open to all."[219]

The Electoral College is a violation of the first principle in two senses. First, the college denies the general population the right to select the president and vice president directly and as such jeopardizes the basic structure as defined by the two principles. Second, the Electoral College gives smaller states a disproportionate and unequal influence in the college. States with small populations are constitutionally guaranteed a minimum of three electoral votes (two senators and at least one representative). Thus, for example, in the 1988 election, one electoral vote in Alaska for every 66,705 voters while in New York, there was one elector for every 178,604 votes. Individuals in smaller states have greater power to determine the presidency than members of larger states, a violation of equal basic rights as specified by the first principle.[220]

The two principles would form the foundation of a well-ordered society. This is a society where there is a conception of justice which the citizens know and accept and the basic structure of society satisfies these principles in general. In addition, citizens have a sense of justice so that they apply these principles and act accordingly for the most part.[221]

Clearly the Electoral College contradicts Rawls' idea of a democratic society. It is simple not a "fair" system where individuals participate in good faith in a process of electing the president but their

218. Ibid. p. 19.
219. Ibid. p. 60.
220. Polsby, Nelson, Aaron Wildavsky, *Presidential Elections*, New York: Free Press, 1991, p. 43.
221. Rawls, John, *Justice as Fairness*, Cambridge: Harvard Univ. Press, 2001, pp. 8-9.

votes may be completely ignored by the electors.

Secondly, the Electoral College does not treat citizens as free and equal since only some individuals, the electors, are allowed to legally vote for the president and vice president.

The idea of a well-ordered society implies a basic structure defined by the two principles exists. The Electoral College contradicts the idea of a basic structure since it is under-determined and functions at the discretion or whimsy of many individuals at many levels. At the level of selecting electors, there are inconsistencies and once electors are chosen their decisions are essentially open-ended and undefined. In practice, the Electoral College is an undefined variable that can function outside the parameters defined by the basic structure. If the vote is thrown into the House, there are no restrictions to how the representatives may vote and thus great uncertainty and under determination by law. Secondly, the House vote is subject to bartering, and possible bribery, further removing it from the basic principles which inform the constitution.

The Electoral College also conflicts with the third requirement that the basic institutions encourage the virtues implicit in the basic structure, namely fairness and trust. Since the Electoral College can, except in the cases where limited by state law (though constitutionality of this is uncertain as mentioned), act in virtually any way it chooses, it conflicts with the principles constitutive of the basic structure and especially fairness.

The Electoral College belies the electoral process as it currently exists. The campaign process takes place as if the citizens choose the president and vice president which is not necessarily the case. Hence, the presidential campaign is a misrepresentation and as such do not encourage the values of fairness. Fairness of social cooperation exists when individuals freely accept the terms of their collaboration and the " idea of reciprocity or mutuality: all who do their part as the recognized rules require are to benefit as specified by a public and agreed-upon standard."[222] Rawls adds that "The idea of cooperation also includes the idea of each participant's rational advantage or good."[223] Certainly the idea of rational advantage is not observed

---

222. Ibid., p. 6.
223. Ibid., p. 6.

by the Electoral College since it allows the process and the result of selecting the chief executive officer who may not accept or act in accordance with the basic structure of constitutional well-ordered society.

A stable society according to Rawls is a society which meets three conditions. First, a stable constitutional society is one which must "...fix, once and for all, the basic rights and liberties, and to assign them a special priority."[224] Second, the basic structure of the society is the basis of "public reason" and the basic institutions encourage the virtues of "public life" and "fairness." By "fairness" Rawls means that institutions satisfy the two principles of justice and that one has "voluntarily accepted the benefits of the arrangement or taken advantage of the opportunities it offers to further one's interests."[225] And third, a stable society is one where "its basic institutions should encourage the cooperative virtues of political life." These virtues are those of "reasonableness and a sense of fairness, and of a spirit of compromise and a readiness to meet others halfway."[226]

The Electoral College is clearly incompatible with Rawls idea of stable society. Specifically, it conflicts with the first requirement that the basic rights be "fixed." The Electoral College is fundamentally under-defined that the rights specified in the basic structure of the constitution are open to violation. The Electoral College may vote (depending on state law) for any person, not necessarily the winner of the popular vote or even the loser of the popular vote, they may choose someone else entirely.

The Electoral College also conflicts with the second requirement of a stable society in two ways. First, it conflict with the idea of what Rawls terms "public reason."[227] Public reason is an ideal of democratic citizenship and fairness where citizens agree that political discourse in a just society will be open and public and in terms of the basic rights and duties embodied in the mutually acknowledge principles defining the basic structure. Public reason is public in three ways: 1.) Pertain to the reasoning of citizens as free and equal; 2.) It is

---

224. *A Theory of Justice*, p. 454; Rawls, *Political Liberalism*, New York: Columbia Univ. Press, 1993, pp. 38-40.
225. *A Theory of Justice*, pp. 110-12.
226. *Justice as Fairness*, p. 116
227. *Political Liberalism*, p. 213

open and public discourse about the general good and social justice 3.) The content of the discourse is given by a public conception of justice and the basic structure.[228]

The content of public reason involves constitutional essentials and basic justice to be settled by political values alone. The legitimacy of public reason is based on whether or not it uses concepts and principles constitutive of the overlapping consensus. Public reason does not apply to private deliberations about comprehensive doctrines but only to political and constitutional essentials of the basic structure.

The Electoral College is fundamentally a violation of public reason. The college does not respect citizens as free and equal since the average citizen does not elect the president. The college may function independently of the values implicit in public reason and not engage in public debate at all. Public justification of electoral votes cast, whether in conformity to the majority or not, is not required by law. The Electoral College functions in a manner not engaging with public reason or based on the content of the basic structure but in private deliberations. Certainly a free and equal people would not agree to the idea of a system of election which operates in an anomalous manner out of no necessary relation to the basic structure.

The Rawlsian ideal of fairness and a well-ordered and stable society all assume the ideal of the rule of law. The rule of law ideal sees laws as necessary normative general statements that apply over a given domain the rule of law implies the need for a rational legal system consisting of general rules to structure society and guide human behavior. A legal system as seen by the rule of law ideal is a complete and consistent interrelated network of norms specifying how members of the community should behave and how the legal system and governmental institutions themselves should function.

To be sure, the rule of law as opposed to the rule of men is an ideal abstraction. It is an abstraction since laws, of course, are written in language vague to various degrees which must be interpreted and implemented by imperfect and variously biased persons. Nev-

---

228. Ibid., *Political Liberalism*, pp. 223-225; Samuel Freeman, ed., *Collected Papers: John Rawls*, Cambridge: Harvard Univ. Press, 1999, pp. "The Idea of Public Reason Revisited," pp. 573-590.

ertheless, the rule of law sets limits to these variables and provides somewhat stable parameters which make possible law as a guide to human action and as the basis of social order.

The Electoral College clearly violates the ideal of the rule of law. As already indicated, the college is not well defined in structure or function in several respects. The college is inconsistent with the democratic ideals of the constitution in that the winner of popular vote not necessarily winner of the electoral contest.

The anomalous nature of the Electoral College brings forth a dilemma. If the electors vote for the candidate who has received the most votes, they are redundant. If they do not, and, as already indicated, there is no legal guarantee the electors will vote as those who voted for them expected them to, then the college is undemocratic and inconsistent with the basic structure. Hence, there is no justification for the Electoral College as it is inconsistent with democratic principles and the rule of law.

If the above arguments are sound, then the Electoral College should be abolished through a constitutional amendment. The president and vice president should be elected directly by the free vote of the citizenry. The college violates the rule of law, the democratic principles implied and expressed in the constitution and is contrary to Rawls ideas of a well-ordered society, a stable society and the idea of legitimacy implied by these Rawlsian ideas. The Electoral College makes a mockery of every basic value the constitution stands for. It is an anomaly and lacunae within the basic structure one of the last remaining vestiges of the undemocratic and inegalitarian elements in the constitution.

# Chapter 6. Abolish Presidential Pardon

> "Of all presidential perks, the pardon power has a special signifi-
> cance. It is just the kind of authority that would attract the special
> attention of someone obsessed with himself and his own ability to
> influence events."
> — Barbara Olson

Gerald Ford was chosen by President Nixon to be his vice president after Vice President Spiro Agnew resigned in the wake of bribery allegations and tax evasion in 1973 (to which Agnew pleaded
no contest). Ford became president when President Richard Nixon
resigned the presidency on August 9, 1974, due to the Watergate
scandal. President Ford soon thereafter pardoned Nixon in Septem-
ber 1974, even before Nixon was charged with any illegality. Many
speculated that there was an agreement between Ford and Nixon for
the pardon in exchange for the resignation of Nixon, but both denied
these claims.

One thing is clear: by pardoning Nixon, President Ford unilaterally decided to deny the American people the right to put Nixon
on trial and discover all the information this would have revealed.
Nixon's campaign for president was based on law and order, but was
his pardon an instance of the rule of law and justice? Double jeopardy
is not allowed as the Constitution is now, but single jeopardy is.

There have been other questionable presidential pardons. President George H.W. Bush pardoned many involved in the Iran Contra

scandal (illegally trading arms for release of American hostages held by Iran and providing weapons to the Nicaraguan Contras) during Reagan's administration. Other pardons in the thousands by other presidents have been debated, questioned and denounced but none have ever been overturned. Should any man or woman have such a power?

Checks and balances, limited power, rule of law and government by the people are all part of the American political tradition but these ideals overlook an important power off the president. Few people know that the US President has a kingly power, a power that monarchs have had since the dawn of history, the power of pardon. It is an absolute power, a power which cannot be nullified or overturned, ever or by anyone.

The Constitution of the United States provides that: "The President ...shall have power to grant reprieves and pardons for offences against the United States, except in cases of impeachment." [229] A pardon removes any possibility of punishment for crimes committed against the United States for the person receiving the pardon. The pardon can be given before indictment, during prosecution or after conviction. It extends to every type of federal offence against the United States including civil and criminal felonies, misdemeanors, imprisonment, fines, penalties, forfeitures and even treason. The president also has the power to commute sentences or substitute a lesser punishment. [230]

There are just two limitations or conditions on the president's power to pardon. The main limitation is that the president cannot pardon someone who is being impeached including if the president is being impeached. [231] A further condition was added in *Burdick* v. *U.S.,*

229. Constitution of the United States, Article II, Section 2.
230. Presidents Lincoln and Jackson gave over 200,000 pardons, F.D. Roosevelt gave thousands and President Truman gave over 10,000 for various offenses including draft evasion and desertion. In more recent cases, President Ford pardoned President Nixon, President Carter pardoned over 10,000 Vietnam war draft evaders, President Bush, among other pardons, pardoned former Secretary of Defense Caspar Weinberger of charges about his role in the Iran–Contra affair, and more recently President Clinton provoked controversy in several of his pardons—many of which he issued just before leaving office. In cases not involving the federal government, state governors generally have equivalent power to pardon.
231. An impeachment is a trial of a government official by the Senate for various

where the Supreme Court ruled that a pardon is not valid until it is accepted by the person being pardoned.[232] Pardons can also be conditional in that they can be given only if the person being offered the pardon agrees to some terms.[233]

It is also clear from the Constitution and historical practice that Congress cannot limit the president's power to pardon. "This power of the President is not subject to legislative control. Congress can neither limit the effect of his pardon, nor exclude from its exercise any class of offenders. The benign prerogative of mercy reposed in him cannot be fettered by any legislative restrictions."[234] In *Schick v. Reed*, the Supreme Court ruled that the pardoning power flows from the Constitution and can only be limited by a constitutional amendment.[235] As mentioned, only the political tool of impeachment can limit the power to pardon. The impeachment limit can itself be overridden since it is only effective if the president is still in office.[236]

The judiciary also has a minimal role in the pardon process. The administration of pardons is housed in Department of Justice where cases for the president to consider are prepared. This role however is only advisory and does not bind the president in any way. The judiciary has never reversed a presidential pardon.

The framers of the constitution had a rationale of sorts for giving the president the power to pardon. Its original purpose was to correct miscarriages of justice, offer mercy and restore social order. In the early years of the republic, communication was slow and neither Congress nor the federal courts were in session most of the year. The reasoning at that time was that only the executive could deal with matters of urgency. For example, in cases such as the Whiskey Rebellion in 1794 where farmers in Pennsylvania rose up in protest of new liquor taxes, President Washington pardoned the perpetrators to restore social peace and forestall further rebellions. The actual

---

crimes committed while in office.
232. *Burdick v. U.S.* 236 U.S. 79, 80 (1915).
233. For example, when President Nixon pardoned Jimmy Hoffa, it was made with the condition that Hoffa not associate further with the Teamsters Union.
234. Ex parte Garland, 71 US 333,380, 18 L. Ed. 366 (1866).
235. (419 US 256 (1974))
236. In the recent cases involving former President Clinton, his last-minute pardons would make impeachment impossible.

practice of giving pardons has been used often and has involved hundreds of thousands of persons through the years.

The thesis of this chapter is that the presidential pardon is a remnant of a theocratic political paradigm of the divine right of kings that must be abolished. More specifically, I argue that it is inconsistent with the underlying principles of the Constitution; specifically it is a violation of the rule of law, equal protection of the laws, due process and the separation of powers.

The rule of law as a standard for a just and rational society has a long history. The rationale for the rule of law draws on many considerations. It is a principle which rejects of the practice of rule by decree or rule by issuing specific commands. Rule by decree as a form of maintaining social order may have some use in a small tribal group but it is generally considered impracticable in a large, complex and modern society. The rule of law stabilizes social interaction and provides norms for social order. The idea of an institution itself would be impossible without the rule of law for institutions are defined by rules. The rule of law sets a limit on governmental power and promotes a stable social structure within which persons can pursue their goals with some security and predictability. Plato defended the rule of law against the rule of men arguing that public servants, as public servants, must serve the law which serves the common good.[237]

Aristotle claimed that men are subject to emotion and bias while the law, if properly formulated, was a product of reason. For Aristotle, the rule of law means the sovereignty of law over the arbitrary and biased rule of persons. Without just laws, Aristotle went on to explain, community is not possible and without the social order of community, the proper raising and moral education of the young is impossible.[238]

A legal system as seen by the rule of law ideal is a complete and consistent interrelated network of norms specifying how members of the community should behave and how the legal system and governmental institutions themselves should function. The rule of law ideal sees laws as normative general statements that apply over a given domain. Laws specify how individuals within that domain and

---

237. Plato, *Laws*, 715d.
238. Aristotle, *Nicomachean Ethics*, 5.6.5; 10.9.8-9; *Politics*, 3.6.13, 3.10.5, 3.9.3-5, 3.10.10.

under a certain description should behave. The ideal of the rule of law expresses the idea that all members of a society must obey the law and that no one is above or below the law but all are subject to various forms of punishment for violating the law. The rule of law implies the need for a rational legal system consisting of general rules to structure society and guide human behavior. These basic norms which define the fundamental rights and duties of persons John Rawls calls the "basic structure."[239]

To be sure, the rule of law as opposed to the rule of men is an ideal abstraction. It is an abstraction since laws, of course, are written in language vague to various degrees which must be interpreted and implemented by imperfect and variously biased persons. Nevertheless, the rule of law sets limits to these variables and provides somewhat stable parameters which make possible law as a guide to human action and as the basis of social order.

Legal systems exist to achieve some purposes or values and to varying degrees embody those values and purposes. Ideally, a rational legal system would be one which has a certain content and structure that are well ordered, complete, consistent, factually supported and which maximally embodies those values and help actualize the values and achieve the chosen purposes of that community.

The rule of law requirement deals with the formal aspects of the legal system not the substantive content of law. The idea of the rule of law is compatible with any number of specific legal systems with varying ideas of justice. For the purposes of this argument, we will assume the U.S. constitution and its underlying principles as generally interpreted as the relevant substantive legal system.

The implementation of the rule of law implies the existence of due process. The concept of due process requires that certain rules and procedures exist in implementing the law. Due process places a limitation on government requiring that a formal process must be completed before government can act adversely against any person.

---

239. Rawls, John, *A Theory of Justice*, Cambridge: The Belknap Press, 1971, p. 7; Rawls' definition of a legal system adds some other relevant elements, namely, "a coercive order of public rules addressed to rational persons for the purpose of regulating their conduct and providing a framework for social cooperation," p. 235; *John Rawls: Collected Papers*, Cambridge: Harvard University Press, 1999, pp. 118, 495.

The constitutional basis of due process is found in the Fifth and Fourteenth Amendments. The Fifth Amendment protects individuals from the federal government by prohibiting the denial of "life, liberty and property without due process of law." The Fourteenth Amendment is addressed to the states holding that governmental actions must conform to orderly and regular processes. It is a process as John Rawls states "reasonably designed to ascertain the truth" about the guilt or innocence of the person in question.[240]

The rule of law and due process exist as the necessary conditions for correctly and fairly determining the guilt and innocence of individuals. Rawls calls the trial an instance of imperfect procedural justice since the goal of the process is to find the guilty guilty and the innocent innocent, but there is no perfect procedure which guarantees such an outcome. Nevertheless, the ideal of procedural justice consists in the implementation of certain principles of justice (as specified by the basic moral framework of the society) to the exercise of political authority. Procedural justice in the form of due process is a set of rights whereby one's other rights and duties are determined by the court according to a specified mechanism, usually a trial. The mechanism is established to ensure that the state acts consistently with the basic structure or constitution, in abridging the rights of the accused. As such, due process is grounded in those moral principles that give legitimacy to the exercise of political power in that community.

Procedural justice has an instrumental as well as an intrinsic value. The instrumental value rests on the procedures as means to determining guilt or innocence. These procedures understood instrumentally consist of several rules. First, there must be a particular dispute where specific individuals are involved. Secondly, a third party, such as a judge or dispute settler, is present; no one is to be judge in his or her own case. In addition, the dispute settler must not have a private interest in the outcome, only to objectively determine the guilt or innocence of the parties involved. The settlement of the dispute takes place in a forum where information about the dispute is heard, the courtroom. The dispute is settled according to substantive legal principles and rules based on all the relevant information presented.

240. Rawls, op. cit., p. 85.

Procedural justice is constructed so that only the guilt or innocence of the parties involved is used as a basis for determining rewards and punishment.

Prima facie, the pardon does not seem to violate due process. The pardon does not seem to take away anything but gives or returns what was lost or threatened. In the instrumental sense, due process relates to those who are accused and need protection usually provided by a fair trial. In the intrinsic sense, due process embodies the basic process values of the legal system which prevent the arbitrary power of government and ensure social order. Due process, then, includes not only the rights of the accused but the rights of the community and (alleged) victim's to be heard and participate in the process.

The intrinsic or "process benefits" of procedural justice are implicit values relevant to the pardon issue. These are the values instantiated by the process and assumed by the process. These process benefits involve values such as respect for the autonomy of and dignity of persons, fairness, the right to participation, and social harmony among others. The autonomy and dignity of the participants are promoted if they are given some sense that they have some control over their lives and destiny. This cannot take place if individuals are not able to participate meaningfully in the trial. Moreover, if the parties involved cannot participate in it, they are less likely to accept the settlement as correct and fair. The pardon as it currently exists does not require the participation of the community in the process, indeed, as we saw, there is no legally necessary process at all.

The inability of the community to participate directly in the process is the denial of the process value of fairness. Fairness is closely related to rationality in this context for fairness means, at the minimum, that both sides of any dispute must be heard. Rationality, among other conditions, requires that the evidence for and against a claim or person must be known and evaluated before a decision about the credibility of some claim or person can be decided. But it is clear that the community is not allowed to state its case directly in the pardon process. To this degree the pardon process is also irrational.

Another central benefit of the process is that it makes the procedures more intelligible to both parties. The more rational a process is the more intelligible it is. Rationality, in turn, is a rule-governed mental process. This clearly leads to the conclusion that for a process to be rational it must be rule based and rule governed. As already argued, the presidential pardon is not rule governed.

Ideally, all disputes should be resolved once and for all. This is the process benefit of finality. The purpose of legal procedures is to resolve disputes at a minimum economic cost compatible with the goals of the process. Since the pardon procedure is not transparent to the general public, it does not promote the ideal of finality as questions may always linger about the propriety of the pardon.

It is clear that the presidential pardon as currently constituted is a violation of the rule of law and the intrinsic or process values implicit in due process. As we have seen, with the exception of impeachment, there are no limits to whom and what crimes the president may pardon. The pardon is not limited by the recommendations of the department of justice, by Congress nor by the courts. Indeed, the pardon has no legally necessary procedures attached to it and as such is potentially an anomalous function of the presidency. Possible victims are not given a hearing and the community is not consulted as it normally is through a jury. It is reminiscent of the divine right of kings and rule by decree more appropriate for a tribal theocratic chief than a leader of a modern democratic society.[241]

The concept of the rule of law has been generally held to require the separation of powers and the independence of the judiciary. The concept of the separation of governmental powers into the legislative, judicial and executive branches is based on the idea that government consists of functions which should be exercised by different groups of persons within government. The reasons for the separation defended by Aristotle, Locke and others are threefold: to promote government efficiency; to limit government; and to ensure that the rule of law is supreme. The rationale for division of powers is based

241. Summers, Robert S. "Evaluating and Improving Legal Processes—A Plea for 'Process Values'," *Cornell Law Review*, v. 60 n.1, Nov. 1974, pp. 1-52; Bayles, Michael, "Principles for Legal Procedure", *Law and Philosophy*, 5, 1986, pp. 33-57; Resnick, David, "Due Process and Procedural Justice", in *Due Process*, Nomos 18, J. Roland Pennock & John Chapman, eds. NY: New York University Press, 1977, pp. 206-228. The speculations about former president Clinton's pardoning Mark Rich as related to contributions to the Democratic Party and other contributions speak for themselves.

on the assumption that different governmental functions require different skills which can be performed more efficiently by different groups of persons. Secondly, to concentrate all governmental functions in one group increases the likelihood of abuse of power. Each branch of government is intended to keep the other in check and within the law. Third, the above two conditions make more likely the ideal of the rule of law will be operative.

Each branch of the government has a specific function. The role of the judiciary is to determine whether laws have been violated and to assign the proper punishment. As already mentioned, the ideal of the rule of law when applied to the judiciary requires a certain institutional structure and that certain procedures obtain in the judicial process.

These institutional structures must incorporate some degree of independence of the judiciary from the other branches of government. Judges must not be intimidated or fear undesirable consequences for acting in a manner displeasing to the other branches of government. The only relevant factors would include factors relating to the guilt and innocence of the person under indictment and the content of the law. This independence preserves the functional integrity of the institution, i.e., it enables it to perform its function with minimal interference. To be sure, the independence cannot be absolute for all branches of government must operate within the parameters of the legal system and act consistently with the basic structure.

The idea of separation of powers includes in its American implementation the idea of "checks and balances." Checks and balances are practices and powers designed to preserve the separation of powers as well as promote the ordered governmental action consistent with the basic structure and the rule of law. The use of checks and balances is a way in which each branch of government exercises some power and influence over the others so preventing any one branch from becoming dominant. The current use of checks and balances includes the veto power of the president over legislation (and the possible override of the veto by the legislature), judicial review of legislation by the courts to establish consistency with the basic structure or constitution and the impeachment power of the Senate over federal judges, congressman and the president. In addition, both the executive and the legislature have a role in the selection of the judiciary, the first in nominating judges and the senate in confirming them.

The division of powers and checks and balances are ideas which have historically come to include the idea of judicial review. Judicial review is the right of the Supreme Court to examine the legislative actions of the state and federal legislatures and executive branches to determine whether they are constitutional. Though not expressly mentioned in the Constitution, ever since *Marbury v. Madison* (1803), the right of the Supreme Court to so act has not been questioned.

If the above considerations are valid, then the presidential pardon as it currently exists is a violation of the separation of powers, checks and balances and judicial review. With the exception of impeachment, as has been mentioned, the pardon power of the president is not subject to judicial review. The court has no rights to deny a pardon even though it may violate many explicit laws and implicit values of the constitution. It seems clear that the current form of the presidential power is a usurpation of the role of the judiciary making the president judge and jury combining as it does the legislative and judicial function in the presidency. This unilateral and essentially unchecked power of the presidency threatens the consistency and unity of the government for it is independent and beyond the scope of legal restraint of the other branches of government.

Closely associated with the idea of the rule of law and due process is the equal protection of the laws. The unifying idea underlying these notions is the assumption that consistency is a necessary condition of rationality and a rational legal system. It draws on Aristotle's idea that equals should be treated equally and unequals, unequally.[242] Though this general idea is widely accepted, the controversy emerges over what are relevant characteristics by which equality and inequality should be determined.

Originally, the equal protection clause of the Fourteenth amendment was instituted to deal with the aftermath of the abolition of slavery and intended to exclude racial classification of persons. The basic idea of the equal protection of the laws has evolved reflecting changing conceptions of human nature and equality. In essence, it is

---

242. Nicomachean Ethics, 1131a,b.

a requirement that the law be applied consistently without respect to characteristics that are irrelevant to the purpose of the law, the determination of rights and duties, penalties and opportunities. Increasingly the courts have excluded property, race and sex, and more recently sexual orientation, as irrelevant in assigning rights and duties based on the equal protection clause.

The implicit logic of the equal protection clause points to factors beyond that of race and sex as irrelevant in the application of the law. The inherent values of the concept of the equal protection of the laws extend to exclude matters of social class and political influence. One's wealth, campaign contributions or social position should have no role in determining whether one gets a pardon or not. The reality is, given the current electoral and political systems, not all persons have equal access to the ear of the president and consequently are not in an equal position to become eligible for a pardon. In any case, the idea of the equal protection of the laws should not be based on the judgment of one person beyond the reach of the rule of law and procedural guidelines. Hence, it is clear that the power of presidential pardon as currently implemented is open to the possible violation of the equal protection of the laws.

The incoherence of the current presidential pardon power can be shown by a kind of reductio ad absurdum. The reductio argument shows the invalidity of some argument or concept by deriving a contradiction from it. As currently implemented, the presidential power of the pardon in principle gives the president the legal power to pardon all federal prisoners. The president can empty all federal prisons and there is nothing that any governmental institution can do to reverse this action. Though the president could of course be impeached and if convicted the pardon could not be reversed.

I consider this possible consequence to be a reductio ad absurdum of the pardon power. The present power implies a consequence which contradicts the basic principles of the legal system of which it is an integral part. The pardon power could undermine the entire federal legal system. This reveals the conclusive flaw implicit in this arbitrary, capricious and anomalous power.

We shall assume that the need for some kind of pardoning process is necessary to correct miscarriages of justice. Four possible solutions to the problems associated with the current presidential pardon have been proposed.[243] One solution is the total abolition of the presidential pardon, another is review of the pardon by congress and the third is review of the pardon by the judiciary and the fourth is the review by both congress and the Supreme Court.

The last three options assume that there is a need of some power of the president to pardon. But what is this need? In cases of the miscarriage of justice federal courts have the power to stay execution and release or retry the convicted. Unlike the early days of the republic, communication is swift and reliable and the courts and congress are in session for longer periods. In cases of an emergency, a federal court can act and if not, the president has special powers independent of the pardon power in times of national emergencies.

If the above arguments are persuasive, there does not seem to be a good reason to maintain the presidential pardon as a power of the presidency. The pardon is a lacuna in the normative web of the legal system and the rule of law. Its continued existence shows the legal system to be underdetermined and incomplete. It makes the legal system irrational for it allows the undermining of the system with impunity by an agent virtually beyond any checks and balances. The pardon power is irrational for it is a poorly defined variable subject to minimal norms which exist to prevent arbitrary power. A constitutional amendment should eliminate this last remnant of the divine right of kings.

---

243. See Mondale, Walter, "Harnessing the President's Pardon Power" *American Bar Association Journal*, January 1975, V. 61, pp. 107-8.

# CHAPTER 7. ABOLISH THE SENATE

"What do you call a lawyer who has gone bad?"
"Senator."
—Anonymous

About two thirds of the current senators are millionaires, which may explain why the US Senate is also called the "Millionaires' Club." On average, a run for the Senate costs about $10 million but former Senator Corzine (D-NJ) spent more than $62 million in his Senate campaign and won, spending $48 million more than his competitor — which confirms the general rule that the candidate who spends more usually wins. The current structure of the Senate allows that the largest state in the US, California, with about 37 million population and Wyoming, the smallest population with about half a million, to have equal votes in the Senate. This means that the voter in Wyoming is about 74 times as powerful as the voter in California when they vote for senator; is this equality? Because of these facts, it is possible given the current constitution and rules that the 21 least populous states, representing only 11.2% of the national population, can block all legislation in the Senate; is this democracy?[244] Let us look at this matter more closely.

According to the US Constitution the legislative power of the federal government is constituted by the bicameral Congress made

---

244. Sabato, Larry, A More Perfect Constitution, New York: Walker & Co., 2007, p. 25.

up of the House of Representatives and the Senate.[245] The constitutional convention of 1787 agreed on the two chamber system as a compromise, usually known as the Great Compromise, between the demands of the large populous states which wanted representation based on population only and the small states which wanted equal representation regardless of population. At one point the small state of Delaware threatened to secede and join another country if the compromise was not agreed to by the large states.[246] The compromise consisted in representation in the House to be based on population and elected directly by the people of each state and to serve for two years and the Senate was to have two senators per state (originally to be chosen by state legislatures until the Seventeenth Amendment of 1913 when citizens were empowered to vote directly for their senators) who would serve six years. It was further agreed that the entire House would stand for election every two years and only one third of the Senate would stand for election every two years.

The differences between the House and Senate are greater than just those based on how members are selected and the length of their tenure. The House and the Senate have many of the same legislative powers but the Senate has special powers denied to the House. For example, the House has the power of impeachment in that the House can charge the president, vice president and other federal officers with treason, bribery and "high crimes and misdemeanors" but the Senate has the right to try impeachments with two-thirds of the Senate needed for conviction. The Constitution also gives the Senate the exclusive right to approve or reject presidential appointments for federal judgeships including the Supreme Court, ambassadorships, cabinet posts and treaties with foreign nations.

Although not explicitly mentioned in the constitution, Senate rules also allow the filibuster which gives the Senate power to block proposed legislation. The filibuster is a Senate rule which allows a

---

245. US Constitution, Article 1, Section 1.
246. Farrand, Max, *The Framing of the Constitution of the United States*, New Haven: Yale Univ. Press, 1913, p. 91, see also Max Farrand, *The Records of the Federal Convention of 1787*, New Haven: Yale University Press, 1966, 4 Vols., vl, 397-404, et al.; Forrest McDonald, *Novus Ordo Seclorum* Lawrence, KS: University Press of Kansas; Akhil Reed Amar, *America's Constitution*, New York: Random House, 2005, pp. 36-7.

senator or group of senators to speak in the Senate chamber as long as they wish unless the supermajority of 60 senators agrees to bring the debate to a close.

Many reasons for the current structure of Congress and the existence of the Senate were given during the constitutional convention and subsequently. One of the main justifications offered for the Senate is the idea of federalism.[247] There are many forms of federalism but in general it is defined as a division of power between the central and regional governments for the purpose of protecting individual freedom and state or regional autonomy and a limited central government. Other characteristics of federalism include a written constitution, bicameralism or two legislative bodies, rights of smaller or regional units to participate in the amending of the federal constitution and to unilaterally participate in amending their own constitution, and a decentralized government.[248] The written constitution is needed to specify the nature of the power sharing between the central government and the lower state or regional units.

In this context of federalism, the defenders of the Senate saw it as representing the sovereignty of the states which was central in the Articles of Confederation. After the declaration of independence in 1776, the Articles of Confederation were drafted in the summer of 1777 and were de facto adopted in November, 1777 (and adopted de jure in 1781), became the basic laws of the colonies until the Constitution was adopted in 1788 and formally went into effect in 1789. The Articles gave the states much more autonomy and the Treaty of Paris (1783) which formally ended the Revolutionary War (1775–1781) had referred to the thirteen colonies as individual states and to be sure the founders were suspicious of anything they perceived as a powerful central government.[249] However, it is generally agreed that the Articles failed for several reasons: they denied the federal government the right to tax, there was no independent central leadership, there was no right to regulate interstate and international commerce and any change in the Articles required unanimous agreement of every

---

247. Amar, op. cit., p. 37.
248. McDonald, op. cit., p. p.45.
249. Madison, James, *Notes of the Debates in the Federal Convention of 1787*, New York: Norton, 1987, pp. 147-9.

state. Shays' Rebellion of 1786 in Massachusetts, consisting of hundreds of angry farmers and Revolutionary war veterans protesting high taxes and other matters, was a vivid reminder of some of the problems with the Articles.

Another argument for the Senate used during the constitutional convention was the widespread distrust of democracy which was closely related to the concern of the affluent members for the security of private property.[250] The relatively wealthy members of the convention, who were in the majority, were concerned about the masses who had little or no property. Representatives to the convention such as Luther Martin and Gouverneur Morris claimed that the new legislature should represent property and wealth as well as people.[251]

Many of the affluent felt they needed to be protected from the majority who were not wealthy but often envious of those who were. Senators, who were as noted above initially elected by state legislators who were themselves constituted overwhelmingly by the affluent, would, it was believed, protect the interests of the wealthy.[252]

Related to distrust of mass democracy is the belief on the part of some of the founders in what they saw as the need to have more deliberation on pending legislation to slow down the legislative process. The senators' longer term of office of six years was intended to allows a more rational leisurely reflection on legislation and produce what they believed would be better laws. Slowing legislation was seen as necessary to reduce the impact of the masses that were judged to be more emotional and less rational.

James Madison argued in a similar vein that the purpose of the Senate was to protect the people against the rulers and to protect the people against themselves. People needed to be protected against themselves due to their "want of information as to their true interests" and their shortsighted passions.[253] Madison also claimed that

---

250. Ibid., p. 189; Jackson Turner Main, *The Upper House in Revolutionary America 1763-1788*, Madison: Univ. of Wisconsin Press, 1967, pp. 202-7; Robert Middlekauff, *The Glorious Cause*, New York: Oxford University Press, 1982, pp. 618-21.
251. Farrand, Max, *The Framing*, op. cit., pp. 108-111; Howard Zinn, A *People's History of the United States*, New York: Harper Perennial, 1995, pp. 95-101.
252. Farrand, op. cit., Vol. 1, p. 422.
253. Carey, op. cit., pp. 319-321; John Adams, "Thoughts on Government," in Paine, Thomas, *Common Sense*, E. Larkin, ed., Broadview Press, Ontario: Canada, 2004, p. 210.

the Senate was necessary to prevent tyranny of the majority.[254] He argued that without the Senate the populous states could dominate the less populous states. The final rationale for the Senate was the practical one that, apparently, without it there would have been no agreement between the states and no constitution at all. There is substantial evidence that the smaller states were reluctant to join a union where they felt weaker than and threatened by the larger states.[255]

The argument for the Senate on the basis of federalism is unconvincing for several reasons. First, it must be noted that there are different means of implementing the idea of federalism. As mentioned, federalism means a sharing of power between the central and local governments, but it does not necessarily imply the implementation agreed to by the convention in designing the Senate. Federalism can also be promoted by the checks and balances of the three branches of the federal government, the independence of the judiciary, frequent regular elections at state and federal levels, freedom of the press and the Bill of Rights which became amendments of to the Constitution in 1791. To be sure, the arguments for the Senate during the constitutional convention were made prior to the agreement to include the Bill of Rights to protect individual freedoms and state rights but it can be argued that the Bill of Rights promotes the values of federalism and answers many of the fears founders had about a central government that may become a threat to liberty without the Senate. Moreover, the President had the veto power which could be used to protect the smaller states if needed.

The founders were concerned to avoid the abuses of the British monarchy and saw federalism as part of the protection of the sovereignty of the states but, again, the Senate is not necessary for that purpose. First, federalism does not by definition require that subdivisions are to be treated as equal or sovereign and the mere fact of agreement to a central government the states agreed to limit their sovereignty. Article VI of the Constitution has the "supremacy clause" which holds that federal law is supreme over state laws. The

254. Lee, Frances E., & Bruce Oppnheimer, *Sizing Up The Senate*, Chicago: University of Chicago Press, 1999, p. 16.
255. Farrand, *The Framing*, op. cit., pp. 95-7.

same article requires that all national and state officials swear to support the federal Constitution. Further, the preamble to the Constitution declares "We the people," not "We the States," and even granting some validity to the claim of state sovereignty, still only the original thirteen states could claim some degree of sovereignty, not the majority of the states, which were added to the union after the constitutional convention. Since these later added states did not enjoy any semblance of sovereignty as the original colonies may have under the Articles of Confederation, they cannot claim it as part of the defense of the Senate. Rulings by the Supreme Court such as US v. *Curtiss-Wright* in dealing with foreign nations and other rulings strengthen the federal government at the expense of the states. The Seventeenth Amendment (ratified 1913) mentioned above, required direct election of senators by the citizens of the each state and as such represent the people of the state not the states as sovereign entities. This amendment implicitly affirmed the core idea of democracy, the sovereignty of the people, not the states.[256]

As for bicameralism in general, there is no proof that it is essential for the protection of liberty or democracy. Indeed its history suggests a fear of mass democracy as was the case in ancient Rome from which the English term is derived (meaning 'old men'). The ancient Roman Senate was a group of wealthy landowners and aristocrats and the senate continues to generally reflect a class divided society. Further, there is substantial evidence that the Senate in practice generally protects the interests of the wealthy to a disproportionate degree. The Senate is often referred to as the "millionaires club" since it has a large percentage of millionaires, far larger than the general population.[257] Due to this wealth, many senators spend their own money to finance their campaigns and overwhelmingly, the candidate who spends the most in the campaign wins.[258] Campaign election costs for senators is far greater than representatives where House members election campaigns costs less than million whereas senate campaigns in recent years is between $3–10 million.[259] Even with the cur-

256. Lee, op. cit., pp. 116-8.
257. Amar, op. cit., p. 413.
258. Goidel, Robert, Donald A. Gross, Todd G. Shields, *Money Matters*, Lanham, MD.: Rowman & Littlefield, 1999, pp. 38-9.
259. Green, Mark, *Losing Our Democracy*, Naperville, IL: Sourcebooks, 2006, pp. 21-2.

rent laws regulating campaign funding, the need for greater funds opens the possibility of bias to favor campaign contributors.

One reason for bicameralism has been to represent minorities, but that was not the rationale given by the founding fathers unless one considers the wealthy a minority that needs protection. Small states did not then and do not now represent any definable minorities, rather it is the more populous states which have large groups of minority members.[260] Indeed, in the case of minorities, the Senate has come to have the opposite result. The Senate gives rural states disproportionate power and since rural states tend to be more conservative and thus more Republican, the Republican Party is over represented in the Senate and has thereby disadvantaged the Democratic Party.[261]

The Senate as a guard against the tyranny of the majority is unconvincing for it could in reality result in a far worse tyranny, the tyranny of the minority. In addition to the factors already mentioned such as the judiciary, the Bill of Rights, the press and the presidential veto, the Senate as currently constituted could block the will of the majority. This is possible with the use of the filibuster so that the 21 least populous states, though representing only 11.2% of the national population, can block all legislation in the Senate.[262]

The distrust of democracy argument including the idea that legislation needed to be slowed and distanced from the irrational masses, has no validity especially under current social conditions. This argument undermines the idea of the sovereignty of the people, the very basis of democracy. (This argument will be further developed below in the discussion of Rawls.) Secondly, the claim has far less relevance currently given the far greater level of education of the citizenry. Further, the increased role and power of the press makes this assumption unwarranted especially since senators are in reality certainly not chosen on the basis of wisdom and virtue but on power, wealth, charisma and connections. The growing power of the internet to make governmental processes open to the public also reduces the need for structural slowing of the process. Current social, economic and technological conditions are more dynamic and fast paced requiring more

---

260. Lee, op. cit., p. 21.
261. Ibid., pp. 23-6.
262. Sabato, Larry, *A More Perfect Constitution*, New York: Walker & Co., 2007, p. 25.

accelerated responses than during the agrarian period of history. If there were still concerns with stability, the term of office of House members could be extended to four years with only half the House coming up for election every two years.

The pragmatic argument that the Senate was necessary to achieve agreement on a constitution by the part of small states is fundamentally flawed for several reasons. First, one could argue that agreement was reached at too high a price since it violated the equality of persons (developed below). Another response already alluded to is that the founders were not considering the power of the Bill of Rights to protect their autonomy and interests. The founders could not anticipate the development of the country and its population growth which would potentially lead to consequences that would exacerbate the tensions between the states.

Finally, there is nothing unchangeable about a bicameral system as evidenced by the fact that many nation states have moved from bicameralism to a unicameral system. Unicameral systems have been defended as more responsive to social problems and less costly since they require fewer personnel and reduce redundancy. There does not seem to be anything essential in democracy which requires a bicameral legislature as evidenced by Great Britain which is effectively a unicameral since the House of Lords, which consists of mostly inherited seats of wealthy aristocrats, is generally ceremonial.

Given that the rationale provided by the founders is not sufficient let us consider Rawls theory of justice in relation to the Senate as currently structured. The Senate as currently defined violates Rawls' first and second principles. Recall the first principle reads in its final version, "Each person has an equal claim to a fully adequate scheme of equal basic rights and liberties, which scheme is compatible with the same scheme for all; and in this scheme the equal political liberties, and only those liberties, are to be guaranteed their fair value."[263] Political liberties are a subset of what Rawls calls "basic liberties" (which include freedom of thought, speech, religion, of association, fair trial, right to vote and run for public office, personal property, etc.) "to hold public office and influence political decisions."[264]

---

263. Rawls, *Liberalism*, op. cit., p. 5.
264. Ibid., p. 327.

The Senate as currently structured is a violation of Rawls' ideal of persons as free and equal and the equal and fair value of political liberties. Rawls' idea of persons as equal means that each person is to count as one and no more than one and has the right to vote where each vote is to have equal value regardless of race, sex, religion, class or state of residence.[265] But this is clearly not the case since, as mentioned above, the largest state in the US is California, with about 37 million population, and Wyoming is the smallest with a population of about half a million. This means that the voter in Wyoming is about 74 times as powerful as the voter in California when they vote for senator. The Senate violates equality for it allows that votes for Senator to be of grossly different value between the vote cast in a low population state and that cast in a large population state. In effect, then, the Senate grants greater political power to individuals in low population states.

Furthermore, as mentioned, the Senate as currently defined with the use of the filibuster, is open to the possibility of violating majority rule in favor of minority rule. This minority would be predominantly rural, white and conservative.

Moreover, this inequality of the worth of political liberties results in the violations of Rawls' second principle. Recall the principle states "Social and economic inequalities are to satisfy two conditions: first, they are to be attached to positions and offices open to all under conditions of fair equality of opportunity; and second, they are to be to the greatest benefit of the least advantaged members of society."[266] The inequality in political representation leads to unfairness in the distribution of federal funds to states which impacts negatively on Rawls' fair equality of opportunity and difference principles. Given the imbalance of power, the more populous states receive a disproportionately lower per capita tax money than smaller more rural states which have a lower percentage of poverty.[267]

The Senate also adds substantial costs to the running of the gov-

---

265. See also US Supreme Court decisions *Reynolds v. Sims* (1964) and *Wesberry v. Sanders* (1964) arguing for "one man, one vote."
266. Rawls, op. cit., p. 6.
267. Given the continuing tendency of immigration to concentrate in some states more than others, the lack of representation of these groups has a great potential for destabilization of society. (See Lee, op. cit., pp. 20-1.)

ernment in term of the personnel and bureaucracy it involves.[268] These funds could be used to help what Rawls calls the least advantaged.

Finally, the Senate unnecessarily slows the democratic process. Some historians claim that an egregious example of this delay was the abolition of slavery itself and the Civil War. Prior to the Civil War erupting, the House repeatedly tried to outlaw slavery but was blocked by the Senate, (most senators were slave owners and so were many House members also) which contributed to the conditions which lead to the horrors of the Civil War.[269]

If the above argument is sound, then the Senate as currently defined is inconsistent with the basic principles of equality implied and expressed in the Constitution and as defended by Rawls. And, given the continuation of current demographic and population trends this inequality will be exacerbated, and given that it conflicts with the principles of Rawls' theory of justice which articulate and develop the values of the Constitution, then the Senate must be abolished or fundamentally reformed.

Several reform proposals are possible to lessen the power of the Senate and enhance the power of the House which embodies the democratic values more fully or make the Senate more democratic. As mentioned, the Senate has more powers than the House, such as voting on appointments to the Supreme Court, which powers could be taken from the Senate and given to the House.

Another proposal could keep the Senate and the minimum two senators but add a senator for each million population.[270] However, this could make Congress too large to be effective. Still another proposal would limit term of office of senators to four years thus making it more responsive to the population but this would leave untouched the basic electoral inequality. Another suggestion would make House supreme by giving it the power to initiate legislation. The Senate could be limited to vote on constitutional amendments only and to act in an advisory capacity at other times as the House of

---

268. Hill, Steven, *10 Steps to Repair American Democracy*, Sausalito, CA: Polipoint Press, 2006, p. 107.
269. Ibid., p. 107.
270. Ibid., p. 108.

Lords does in Britain. Another possibility is to require a 2/3 majority in the Senate to override a House vote, but this does not fully eliminate the inequality of the Senate.

However, the probability of the abolition of the Senate or basic reform seems low for one main reason. The Constitution states that "No state, without its consent, shall be deprived of its equal suffrage in the Senate."[271] Though this may make the abolition of the Senate almost impossible, but not absolutely impossible, for, let's not forget, white men gave women and African-Americans the vote when white men had all the votes. Second, although its outright abolition may be unlikely, altering and reducing the power of the Senate is not.

The Senate is a remnant of a world and an ideology that have been transcended and transformed by greater access to education, advanced technology and a more pluralistic and dynamic society. The idea of the Senate has also been nullified by an evolving moral consciousness informed by an enhanced view of human equality and a greater trust in a democracy. The contemporary conception of democracy is not based on the assumption that the wealthy are more wise nor is it founded on Plato's analogy of the ship of state in a vast and dangerous ocean where the philosopher/kings are the ones in charge because they have the knowledge and virtue necessary to pilot the ship to a predetermined port. Rather, in the Rawlsian paradigm, society is not a ship but an ocean filled with many ships all going to the port of their choice.

---

271. US Constitution, Article 1, Section 3.

# CHAPTER 8. LIMIT THE POWER OF THE SUPREME COURT

"The most important rule in constitutional law is that with five
votes you can do anything."
— Associate Justice William Brennan

The disturbing part of the above quote is that Brennan was not far off when he said the court could do "anything." This is why the US Supreme Court has been said to be the most powerful court in the world. Only the president has more power but the president is elected for four years at a time but the justices of the Supreme Court are not elected and enjoy lifetime appointments with the average length of tenure now over 25 years. Too many justices have served while in poor health and with reduced mental capacity while most have been white, male and very wealthy and even the current court has at least 6 multi-millionaires.[272]

The problematic nature of the power of the Supreme Court was succinctly put by Justice Charles Evans Hughes: "We are under a Constitution but the Constitution is what the judges say it is..." The argument defended here is that judicial review and other factors give the Supreme Court excessive power not explicitly justified in the Constitution. The power of judicial review is the sweeping power the court has to declare unconstitutional acts of Congress and state

---

272. Toobin, Jeffrey, *The Nine*, New York: Anchor Books, 2008; Bob Woodward, Scott Armstrong, *The Brethren*, New York: Simon and Schuster, 1979.

legislatures, state and federal courts and acts of the President. This power needs to be curbed by requiring that court decision, assuming the current number of nine justices, consist of a supermajority of a minimum of six votes, not the current five, to decide cases in a constitutionally normative manner.[273] The first argument for the rule of 6/3 is based on the fact that the Constitution does not specify the number of justices the Supreme Court must have nor does it specify the kind of majority required to definitively decide cases. Moreover, the history of decision making in the Supreme Court shows it to be an evolving practice. During its early years the justices of the Supreme Court, following the English courts, delivered their opinion seriatim[274] that is, each justice stated his opinion with no majority opinion per se being defined. During Justice Marshall's tenure as Chief Justice (1801-1835) the court began offering a single "opinion of the court" to make the decision more authoritative and compelling. This practice did make clearer what the opinion of the court was and hence increased the power and influence of the court.

The second argument for the 6/3 rule is that judicial review is a major power enhancing function of the Supreme Court which is not explicitly granted by the Constitution but was claimed for the court by Justice Marshall in his opinion in *Marbury* v. *Madison* (1803).[275]

The historic origins of the notion of judicial review can be found

---

273. Though not argued for here, the "rule of four" which requires that four justices agree on which petitions would receive a hearing in the court, the justices developed themselves and is not specified in the Constitution or any act of Congress should be changed to the "rule of five." Justice Hughes quote from speech to the Chamber of Commerce, Elmira, N.Y., May 3, 1907.

274. White, G. Edward, *The Marshall Court and Cultural Change*, Vol. 3-4, New York: Macmillan, 1988, pp. 182-191. To be sure, judicial review also has established limits though generally these "limits" are not well defined. The court can hear only actual disputes not consider purely intellectual queries. Secondly, only those with "standing," i.e., a stake in the outcome can be heard in the court. Thirdly, the court does not hear "political questions" which are of three main categories. First, the court does not hear cases about proper procedures for amending the constitution. Secondly, the court does not hear cases concerning guarantees to each state a republican form of government (Article IV, Section 4). Thirdly, cases concerning foreign affairs such as the recognition of foreign countries, are not within the scope of the Supreme court. And finally, the rule of "ripeness" holds that a case must be ready to be heard by the Supreme Court if other avenues of appeal have been exhausted. (O'Brien, David M., *Constitutional Law* and Politics, 4e, New York: Norton, 2000, p. 115.)

275. Marbury v. Madison, (1803) (5 US 137).

in English common law.[276] Judicial review has been defended by asserting the existence of a divine law or natural law higher than positive law to which positive law must conform to be valid. Secondly, the notion of due process found in the Magna Carta of 1215 holding that the king was not above the law has also been viewed as implying judicial review. Thirdly, the idea of the social contract as found in John Locke and in the Declaration of Independence held that there are certain natural rights which define and limit government and that it is the job of the courts to define these rights. These historical justifications are the background of Marshall's defense.

In the historic case of *Marbury* v. *Madison* (1803), Justice Marshall gave the classic defense of judicial review.[277] Marshall argued that the purpose of the Constitution was to create a form of limited government and that judicial review performs that function. However, critics have pointed out that judicial review is just one instrument for limiting government, there are others, such as regular elections, checks and balances and the Bill of Rights. Secondly, Marshall noted that justices take an oath to support the Constitution. This is true but all judges, members of Congress and presidents take the oath to defend the Constitution. And thirdly, Marshall argued that the supremacy clause of the Constitution, Article 6 states that the Constitution "shall be the supreme law of the land." However, the supremacy clause does not necessarily imply the existing practice of judicial review since most constitutional historians believe that clause was addressed to the state legislatures and state courts. Marshall's case for judicial review, then, is not compelling.

Another defense of judicial review is related to the idea of federalism. Federalism is not clearly defined but is understood as a sharing of governing power between the states and the federal government. Justice Oliver Wendell Holmes argued that the court must have the power to declare a state law unconstitutional if the union is to be preserved.[278] This may well be so and the Judiciary Act of 1789 explicitly gives the court this power, but it does not mean that federalism

---

276. Williams, Jerre, *Constitutional Analysis*, St. Paul: West, 1979, pp. 2-11.
277. Ibid., pp. 16-23.
278. Hall, Kermit L. *The Supreme Court of the United States*, New York: Oxford University Press, 1992, pp. 405-9.

implies that the Supreme Court must have the power to declare an act of Congress unconstitutional.[279]

Judicial review is also problematic for reasons dealing with the political nature of the appointment and confirmation process and the very nature of the Constitution itself.[280] The Supreme Court is political in the broad sense that its decisions influence the distribution of rights, duties and interests of millions of citizens. The court is also political in the narrow sense by being influenced by partisan ideologies. Justices are appointed by the president for at least partly political reasons in that presidents seek justices whose ideology and understanding of the Constitution is consistent with their own. Presidential election campaigns use the idea of likely Supreme Court appointments as reasons to vote for or against a candidate. The nominees are voted on by the Senate often along party lines. During the Senate review process appointees are questioned and examined to determine their judicial philosophy and overall ideology to determine their political leaning and likely future rulings once on the court. Moreover, without an appointment with a mandatory specific end point, justices often postpone their retirement until a president with similar political ideology is elected and nominates a replacement with like ideology. Empirical studies support the reality of the role of political ideology in court decisions.[281]

There are other concerns with the court as well. The court as a formal institution has rules which structure and define its role within the federal structure and society as a whole. However, within every institution there are customs, personalities, friendships and ideological differences which also play a role in the functioning of the court. The role of the "swing" vote on the court is a concern. The swing voter is usually considered a "moderate" or "independent" voter who sometimes votes with one ideological group and at tomes with another. For example, the now retired Justice Sandra Day O'Connor, is

279. Haskins, George Lee, *Foundations of Power: John Marshall, 1801-15*, Vol. 2: *History of the Supreme Court of the United States*, New York: Macmillan, 1981, pp. 182-5.
280. Davis, Richard, *Electing Justice*, New York: Oxford University Press, 2005, pp. 7-9.
281. Sunstein, Cass, et al., *Are Judges Political?*, Washington DC: Brookings Institution Press, 2006; Richard Posner, *How Judges Think*, Cambridge: Harvard University Press, 2008, pp. 269-323.

a justice who was not an obvious member of any camp or ideological group of the court. The power of the swing justice is great in a 5/4 rule system. No justice, with his or her ideological preferences and personality should influence the court's decision to such a degree. A rule of 6/3 would reduce the power of any one justice and thus make the decision less a reflection of the ideology or idiosyncrasies of one judge and make the decision have a broader rationale as well as shift power to the states in the event a majority of six is not attained.

The personalities, ideologies and limitations of the justices raises related problem, the possibility of error. In a 5/4 controversial ruling on gay rights in *Bowers* v. *Hardwick* (1986) Justice Lewis Powell voted with the majority. Later after he retired he admitted he "probably made a mistake."[282] The Bowers decision was overturned later in *Lawrence* v. *Texas* (2003). Of course the rule of 6/3 would not have given a decision in favor of gay rights at the time of Bowers, but it would have left it up to the states and since most states had at that time already legalized adult consensual sodomy, the negative ruling may have stopped other states in attempting to legalize the same.

The nature of legal reasoning raises an additional concern about the decision making of the Supreme Court. Legal reasoning is by no means a deductive science but rather inductive and analogical.[283] Legal decisions must take into account the Constitution, the various statutes, the facts, and precedent. Analogical arguments are based on treating like cases alike; but no two cases are exactly alike. Which cases are deemed "alike" depends on the "facts" and the "relevant" legal principles; both aspects are at least in part a function of the justices' ideology or interpretive theory. Precedent or the rule of stare decisis is not a foolproof guide, either, since justices may ignore and overturn precedent, which they have done often. It seems fairly clear that all interpretations and reasoning involve presuppositions and to attempt to prove every presupposition involves an infinite regress. This inexactness of legal reasoning adds another level of indeterminacy to the court.

Another feature of the court relevant to the nature of its decisions

---

282. Hall, op. cit., p. 80; see also Bob Woodward and Scott Armstrong, *The Brethren*, New York: Simon & Schuster, 1979.
283. Tribe, op. cit., pp. 87-96

is that the court does not function in a mechanistic or scientific manner when it interprets and applies the Constitution. First, no objective standards alone, such as the results of a civil service exam, are used, required or possible in appointments to the Supreme Court. An objective exam would not be possible, first, because constitutional principles and statements, especially those concerning the Bill of Rights, are often abstract, vague and incomplete and hence difficult to interpret accurately, and the idea of "accurate" is itself problematic. Indeed, many have argued that a constitution must be vague and indeterminate in part to be relevant and useful in future unforeseen and, to the framers, unforeseeable circumstances.[284] Even Justice William Rehnquist stated, "The framers of the Constitution wisely spoke in general language and left to succeeding generations the task of applying that language to the unceasingly unchanging environment in which they would live... Where the framers...used general language. They [gave] latitude to those who would later interpret the instrument to make that language applicable to cases that the framers might not have foreseen."[285]

Historians agree that the actual drafting of the Constitution was a compromise between differing ideologies and conflicting interests which necessitated vagueness as a precondition for consensus.[286] The ambiguity, vagueness and flux of language and social, cultural, moral and scientific change, further exacerbate the problem of meaning and interpretation.

The historical origins and brevity of the Constitution have produced various conflicting theories as to its proper interpretation. Theories of the interpretation of the Constitution are complex but for the purposes of this essay a brief characterization is necessary.[287] Those who favor what is sometimes called "strict constructionism" seek a more constrained court and believe that the power of the court can be curbed by adopting "textualism" as a method of interpreting the Constitution. Textualism holds that the literal text, not intent or some assumed underlying unstated principle of the Constitution

---

284. Amar, Akhil, *America's Constitution*, New York: Random House, 2005, pp.7-28.
285. Tribe, Laurence, & Michael Dorf, *On Reading the Constitution*, Cambridge: Harvard University Press, 1991, p. 13.
286. Amar, op. cit., p. 34.
287. Hall, op. cit, pp. 183-7.

must be the standard for interpreting the Constitution if the rule of law and unwarranted judicial activism is to be controlled. Textualism denies that the actual words are vague and indeterminate to such a degree as to be useless. Rather it holds that the semantic meaning of the words of the Constitution is sufficiently clear to allow definitive judgments in most cases. Without textualism, there would be no reason to have a constitution at all, defenders of this view hold.[288]

There are problems with textualism as a means of interpreting the Constitution and limiting the court. Though some terms of the Constitution are clear, such as limiting a president's term to "four years," there are also pivotal terms in the Constitution such as "equality" and "rights" which have an open texture and are fundamentally indeterminate. Another difficulty is that even when the terms are fairly clear, it is not always sufficient to determine meaning. An example often given is the First Amendment which clearly states "Congress shall make no law...abridging the freedom of speech, or of the press..." To take this amendment at its literal meaning would imply that there would be no laws on perjury, libel or falsely yelling 'fire' in a crowded theater. The response defenders of textualism usually make is that is not what the framers "intended." Thus textualism must go beyond the lexical semantic meaning and appeal to the intentions of the writers to clarify meanings. This introduces the theory of interpretation known as "originalism."

Originalism is the view that interpretation of the Constitution must be based on the original intent of the framers.[289] This view of the Constitution, like that of textualism, is defended by those who seek to limit the courts power. For example, in passing the Eighth Amendment prohibiting "cruel and unusual punishment" the framers did not intent to outlaw the death penalty since we know they practiced it extensively in their time. The intent clarifies meaning which can then be used to judge cases.

Originalism has its critics as well.[290] It is not clear whose inten-

---

288. Scalia, Antonin, *A Matter of Interpretation*, Princeton: Princeton University Press, 1997, pp. 126-7.
289. Bork, Robert H., *The Tempting of America*, New York: The Free Press, 1990, pp. 143-50; Whittington, Keith, *Constitutional Interpretation*, Lawrence: University Press of Kansas, 1999, pp. 3-4.
290. Hall, op. cit., pp. 187-9.

tions we must uncover, the framers or those who voted for it. Often the intentions are not clear or are conflicting. Moreover, the intentions may be considered immoral by contemporary moral standards such as the apparent intent of the framers to limit voting rights to white men with property.

There is also the theory of the "living constitution."[291] Those who support the living constitution theory do so because they refuse to impose what they see as the dead hand of the past on contemporary society. They claim the Constitution must be interpreted according to the evolving moral understanding and social realities of the times. For example, the debate on the Eight Amendment and the death penalty must be interpreted in the light of the current scientific understanding of the causes of crime, the nature of human psychology and the emerging moral consensus. To reject this understanding of the Constitution would lock the court into being ruled by the dead with their acceptance of slavery, denying women the vote, and other immoral practices according to the expanding contemporary moral consensus.

Though the theory of the living constitution has many supporters, there are also difficulties with this view.[292] First, it tends to weaken the meaning of the Constitution as a clear limit on government and as constituent of the rule of law. It also seems to negate the amending function built into the Constitution and replace it by the ideological perspectives of the justices. This view of the Constitution would make the judiciary another legislature. As Scalia quotes approvingly, "Judge-made law is ex post facto law, and therefore unjust."[293] The Constitution as a meta-rule or a framework for governmental functioning seems to be weakened by this theoretical approach.

There are other theories of constitutional interpretation but none are generally accepted. As Justice Scalia has stated, "We American judges have no intelligible theory of what we do most."[294] The lack of consensus and indeterminacy not only at the level of constitutional meaning but also at the meta level of the appropriate method of in-

---

291. Ibid., pp. 190-2.
292. Ibid., p. 191.
293. Scalia, op. cit., p. 10.
294. Ibid., p. 14.

terpretation make the court's functioning itself more indeterminate. Moreover, even if there were an agreed upon theory of interpretation, there seems to be no legal way to compel justices to apply this theory in their actual deliberations. Hence, the court is again without sufficient structure and the rule of law is in jeopardy but there is a way out of this apparent impasse.

The living constitution theory is right in that it is often impossible to know exactly what the framers intended. And even if one could know the intent with some reliability, it may be immoral, irrelevant or unwarranted by contemporary consensus. The textualists and originalists are also right in that to depart from the text of the constitution is, to varying degree, legislate but this is inevitable. It is inevitable for three reasons. First, it is impossible to know with certainty what the framers intended for to establish the intent implies other conditions and complications. It requires that the context in which the document was created be understood and clarified. The context includes the cultural, philosophical and political context within which the document was written. For example, to understand the Constitution one must understand the political climate of the times as well as the philosophical ideas current and expressed in the Declaration of Independence whose ideas may be traced to the philosophy of John Locke some of whose ideas can be traced back to the Magna Carta and the struggle for parliamentary supremacy. Establishing the context of a period of history long gone is problematic at the very least and a speculative exercise in imaginative reconstruction, at best. In addition to understanding the external context, to understand any part of the document requires that the whole document is properly interpreted and understood and to understand the whole, one must understand the parts. This dialectical process or "hermeneutic circle" is, in part at least, a subjective process and not objectively definable because one cannot determine and be fully aware of all the presuppositions the interpreter is applying in a subconscious manner throughout the process.[295]

Moreover, the framers, like all persons, were morally and intellectually limited, and hence their views cannot be deemed infallible

---

295. D'Amico, Robert, *Contemporary Continental Philosophy*, Boulder; Westview Press, 1999, p. 155.

or unchangeable. But most importantly, to interpret the Constitution means to add greater specificity and clarity of meaning to the law and, as such, creating a new norm—which means to legislate, to some degree. In other words, to interpret is, in effect, to define and make the indeterminate Constitution more determinate, which is tantamount to the legislative act; for to give meaning to a vague statement is to change it by giving it content and making it more specific, thus eliminating other possible interpretations (at least for a time) in some way, which means to create a new law. To create a new interpretation of the Constitution is, in effect, to amend the Constitution.

If the above argument that to interpret the constitution is, de facto, to amend the Constitution, is plausible, then the interpreting function must meet the same conditions for amendment as the Constitution specifies in general. The Constitution holds that an amendment requires a 2/3 majority of both houses (and 3/4 of the states) (other conditions hold for a constitutional convention). The 6/3 rule corresponds to the 2/3 rule for Congress and since both branches of government are de facto altering the Constitution, the rule for altering should be the same, 2/3 of Congress and 2/3 of the Supreme Court or a minimum majority of six justices.

The 6/3 rule would promote what John Rawls calls the "stability" of an increasingly diverse society. A stable society according to John Rawls is a society which meets three conditions. First, a stable constitutional society is one which must "...fix, once and for all, the basic rights and liberties, and to assign them a special priority." Second, the basic structure of the society is the basis of "public reason" and the basic institutions encourage the virtues of "public life" and "fairness." By "fairness" Rawls means that institutions satisfy the two principles of justice and that one has "voluntarily accepted the benefits of the arrangement or taken advantage of the opportunities it offers to further one's interests." And third, a stable society is one where "its basic institutions should encourage the cooperative virtues of political life." These virtues are those of "reasonableness and a sense of fairness, and of a spirit of compromise and a readiness to meet others halfway."[296]

---

296. Rawls, John, *A Theory of Justice*, Cambridge: Harvard University Press, 1971, pp.

Stability implies the rule of law which requires that laws be rational, universal, impartial and consistent. Rationality of law means the law must be sufficiently justified and clear, universality means the law must apply to all persons, including those in power, impartiality means the law applies to persons only on the basis of certain valid criteria and excludes other properties, as irrelevant and consistency means that, even granted the imprecision of the notion, similar cases be treated similarly. The rule of law is a barrier against arbitrary power and sees law as the basis of social order and conflict resolution.

The 6/3 rule would enhance Rawls' ideals of stability and the rule of law for it would tend to reduce court reversals or inconsistent rulings on basic rights for the rulings would be more broadly based. The 6/3 rule would also be more consistent with Rawls' ideals of reasonableness and fairness since court rulings would likely be more in harmony with what Rawls calls the "overlapping consensus" the agreement about basic rights that are found in the various "comprehensive doctrines" which exist in a modern pluralist society.[297] This would be the case for court decisions would be more in congruence with the overlapping consensus since they would need to encompass greater ideological differences among the justices. Moreover, many issues would have to be settled by state law and other democratic processes rather than by court decision thus preserving a positive pluralism which otherwise would be in jeopardy by top-down rulings.

The Supreme Court is a pillar of federalism and of the constitutional system of checks and balances. However, in an increasingly diverse society, the legitimacy of the court and hence stability becomes more problematic especially since judicial review is not likely to be abandoned.[298] If the above arguments are plausible, then the political nature of the court appointments, the vagueness of the Constitution and conflicting theories of constitutional interpretation, the role of human limitations, the imprecise nature of legal reasoning and the importance of stability, require that the nature of the Supreme

---

454-5; *Justice as Fairness*, Cambridge: Harvard University Press, 2001, 115-7.
297. Rawls, John, *Political Liberalism*, New York: Columbia University Press, 1993, pp. 10-15,150-4.
298. For example, the *Bush v. Gore* (2000) (531 U.S. 98 ) decision.

Court's decision making structure change to the 6/3 rule. A change in the minimum number of justices for a decision would enhance its legitimacy as an instrument of the rule of law not the destabilizing rule of raw political power.

# CHAPTER 9. ABOLISH LIFETIME TENURE OF SUPREME COURT JUSTICES

> "To consider the judges as the ultimate arbiters of all constitutional questions [is] a very dangerous doctrine indeed, and one which would place us under the despotism of an oligarchy.
> — Thomas Jefferson (letter to William Jarvis)

Associate Justice William O. Douglas, appointed by FDR in 1939, refused to resign even after he had a serious stroke, was incontinent, deaf and often fell asleep while the court was in session hearing oral arguments. After he finally resigned in 1975 he had served more than 36 years on the court but even after retiring he didn't know where he was and believed he was still on the court. More recently, Justice Powell did not seem well informed while he was considering the case of gay rights, which would become the Bowers v Hardwick (1986) case, asked one of his clerks (who Powell did not know was in fact, gay himself), "Why don't homosexuals have sex with women?"[299] Powell voted with the majority in a 5/4 decision against gay rights but later admitted he probably made a mistake. Other instances of incapacitated justices include cases of mental illness, drug addiction and other problems which afflict, to various degrees, all humans such as sloth, ignorance, irrationality, envy, prejudice and the like which

---

299. Toobin, Jeffrey, *The Nine*, New York: Doubleday, 2009, p.187.

fill the pages of the history of the Supreme Court.[300]

In addition to the personal shortcomings of the judges, the Supreme Court has also made decisions throughout its history which the overwhelming majority considers serious moral and constitutional mistakes. Without mentioning more controversial decisions, the court has upheld slavery (*Dred Scott v. Sanford*, 1857), child labor (*Bailey v. Drexel Furniture Co.*, 1922), racial segregation (*Plessy v. Fergson*, 1896) and concentration camps for Japanese-Americans (*Korematsu v. US*, 1944). If the court makes mistakes just as any branch of government, why should it have special privileges, such as lifetime appointment, not given to members of the other branches of government?

Although the US Constitution does not require it, federal judges have the right to lifetime tenure unless standards of "good behavior" are violated in which case they can be impeached.[301] Good behavior has been defined as by the impeachment rule as excluding "treason, bribery or other high crimes and misdemeanors."[302] This essay will only focus on the Supreme Court, though similar but less compelling case could be made for the federal judiciary in general.

Lifetime appointment of judges has been defended as preserving the integrity of the three branches of government and the independence of the judiciary. The rationale for this tradition has been that judges should rule according to the law not from political intimidation or coercion. Secondly, lifetime appointment is seen as perpetuating an image of the judiciary and its rulings as above mere transient partisan politics thus increasing its power and legitimacy. Job security allows judges to function without distracting personal concerns relating to monetary and other irrelevant factors.

I argue here that the independence of the judiciary is important but that the practice of lifetime tenure of judges is irrational because it violates the rule of law, the ideal of meritocracy and ignores the essential political nature of the Supreme Court. Lifetime appointment of Supreme Court justices should be eliminated and replaced by appointments limited to a set number of years.

The rule of law requirement deals with the formal aspects of the

---

300. Walker, Jesse, www.reason.com July, 2005.
301. US Constitution, Article III, Section 1.
302. Ibid., Article II, Section 4.

legal system not the substantive content of law and is compatible with any number of specific legal systems with varying contents.[303] The rule of law ideal is a rejection of the practice of governance by decree, governing by issuing specific ad hoc commands and sees law as a network of norms that structure society and reflect the basic values and beliefs of society. The ideal of the rule of law understands laws as supreme rules which define how all individuals and institutions within a given society should function. It also means that no punishment is possible unless it involves a violation of some law. The rule of law stabilizes social interaction and provides for social order while setting a limit on governmental power. It promotes a social structure within which persons can pursue their goals with some security and predictability. These basic norms which define the fundamental rights and duties of persons Rawls terms the "basic structure" of that society.

The rule of law ideal has certain logical, ethical and political assumptions and implications.[304] The law must meet certain logical and formal conditions to perform the function of law. First, the laws must be well-defined, consistent and a complete nexus of rules structuring society. As well-defined laws must be clear and eschew vague and ambiguous terms to achieve their function as action guides. If laws are to determine acceptable behavior the law must be consistent for contradictory laws would make impossible demands on individuals. Laws must be understandable by the average person if they are to regulate behavior. Similarly, retroactive laws must be avoided for they cannot provide guidelines for behavior that has already happened. The set of laws ideally must be complete for laws to be action guides in all contexts, must be a sufficient number to leave no area of the domain under-determined and un-structured. Further, the rule of law means the law must be promulgated or made public since secret laws could not serve the function of guiding behavior.

Legal systems presuppose certain ethical values and exist to achieve these values and, to varying degrees, embody these values. The ethical assumptions of a legal system imply certain political

---

303. Cf. Tamanaha, Brian, *On The Rule of Law*, Cambridge: Cambridge University Press, 2004, pp. 91-101.
304. Cf. Mark Tebbitt, *Philosophy of Law*, London: Routledge, 2000, pp. 37-46.

structures and laws which will vary with differing substantive legal systems. Regardless of substantive content, the rule of law ideal must conform to the truism that "ought implies can" no law can ask the impossible of its subjects.

As political, the content of the rule of law expresses some political ideals. In the US Constitution, those ideals have traditionally taken to be some understanding of democracy, the sovereignty of the people and their welfare, liberty, equality, human rights and their various implications.

The rule of law ideal requires a judiciary consistent with the idea of the rule of law.

The adjudication process must be defined in a manner consistent with the values and beliefs embodied in the system of law and in the rule of law itself. There must be consistency in application, like cases must be treated similarly, or there is in fact no rule of law. Inconsistent implementation is a form of arbitrary rule.

The rule of law ideal also presupposes a meritocracy. A meritocracy is a social system of allocating personnel where individuals are selected for positions based on meeting criteria relevant to the maximal performance of their function, not on any other criteria. These criteria usually include intelligence, knowledge, motivation to perform the function and a sufficiently moral character to perform the function in the manner prescribed. The ideal of meritocracy is implied in the rule of law for the rule of law ideal will be most fully actualized by institutional structures and individuals who have the desired qualities of knowledge of the law, intelligence and rationality to properly apply the law and sufficient moral virtue to be motivated to act in conformity to the rule of law and their institutional function, not for purely personal gain or benefit incompatible with the role definition.

Given the above understanding of the rule of law, lifetime appointment of Supreme Court judges can be shown to violate the rule of law ideal and meritocracy. Institutional structures, individual behavior, appointments and terminations must be consistent with the values and rule of law ideal and meritocracy, leaving no aspect undefined by the law and subject to contingencies and irrelevant factors. One of these contingencies is the longevity of judges. The facts are clear that longevity in general and for judges has increased. From 1789-1970 the average supreme court justice served for 15.2 years retiring at 68.5 years of age. Since 1970 the average tenure of justices has risen to 25.5 years with the average retirement age of 78.8.[305]

Meritocracy and the rule of law dictate that longevity, good behavior and good personal health are not sufficient reasons for any person to keep a central position in government if other more qualified candidates are available. In a meritocracy, the relevant factors are the ability and willingness to perform the function in the manner prescribed and in the most efficient manner and if no one more competent is available and willing. One irrelevant factor is human longevity; individuals should not be in a position simply because they have not yet died but because they are the most qualified to perform that function. (The meaning of 'most qualified' is further explained below.) And 'good behavior' is certainly not the same standard as 'most qualified.'

Secondly, lifetime appointment of judges often motivates presidents to choose candidates for the Supreme Court on irrelevant non-meritocractic criteria. Presidents often prefer relatively young candidates to make more likely long tenure on the bench and hence perpetuate the political ideology of the president. Youthfulness becomes a more dominant criterion in some cases than qualifications and merit.[306]

Thirdly, certain practical considerations also militate against the lifetime appointment of justices. Lifetime appointment makes replacement of judges in failing mental and physical health difficult and lengthy. Failing voluntary retirement, the only alternative for removing incompetent judges is impeachment, which is a long political process often difficult to initiate and by no means necessarily resulting in the desired outcome. Moreover, evidence of judicial incompetence often takes a long time to become apparent to warrant action, during which time irreparable damage may be done to individuals and the judicial process as a whole.

---

305. Greenhouse, Linda, "How Long is Too Long For the Court's Justices," New York Times, (Week In Review) January 16, 2005, p.2. The Supreme Court has had only 17 chief justices but there have been 44 presidents.
306. Davis, Richard, *Electing Justice*, Oxford: Oxford University Press, 2005, pp. 4-6.

Political

Most importantly, the lifetime appointment of judges conflicts with the political nature of the Supreme Court. The high court is political in that, first, and most importantly, the court plays a crucial role in determining the distribution of rights and duties within society. The authority of the court to resolve disputes between states and the power of judicial review, which gives it the authority to declare a state or federal law and an act of the president unconstitutional, gives the court substantial power. The fact that the Supreme Court has the right to determine the meaning of the constitution gives it the authority to define the distribution of rights and power throughout society.

Secondly, as mentioned, the Supreme Court is political in that justices are appointed by the president for at least partly political reasons.[307] Presidential campaigns use the idea of likely Supreme Court appointments as reasons to vote for or against a candidate. The nominees are voted on by the Senate often along party lines. During the Senate review process appointees are questioned and examined to determine their judicial philosophy and overall ideology to determine their political leaning and likely future rulings once on the court.

Moreover, without an appointment with a mandatory specific end point, justices often postpone their retirement for reasons irrelevant for the performance of their function. They often refuse to retire until a president with similar political ideology is elected and nominates a replacement with like ideology, while their health and ability may dictate otherwise.

The role of the media is central and political in the nomination and review process. Supreme Court appointees are subject to intense media scrutiny as politicians are.[308] Media corporations are controlled by individuals with a certain ideology and their coverage will to some degree reflect this ideology. Special interest groups are often also active in the process and add to the political intensity.

A central feature of the political nature of the court is that it does

---

307. Epstein, Lee, & Jeffrey Segal, *Advice and Consent*, Oxford: Oxford University Press, 2005, pp. 120-127.
308. Davis, op. cit., pp.6-7.

not function in a mechanistic manner or with scientific objectivity when it interprets and applies the constitution. First, no objective standards alone, such as the results of a civil service exam, are used, required or possible in appointments to the Supreme Court. An objective exam would not be possible, first, because constitutional principles and statements, especially those concerning the bill of rights, are often abstract, indeterminate, vague, incomplete and hence difficult to interpret accurately, and the idea of "accurate" is itself problematic. Indeed, many have argued that a constitution must be vague and indeterminate in part to be relevant and useful in future unforeseen and, to the framers, unforeseeable circumstances. Historians agree that the actual drafting of the constitution was a compromise between differing ideologies and conflicting interests which necessitated vagueness as a precondition for consensus. The ambiguity, vagueness and flux of language and cultural, moral and scientific change, further exacerbates the problem of meaning and interpretation.

Some defenders of the judiciary have rejected the above argument about the difficulty of interpretation and contend that the court is not necessarily political in the negative sense. They argue that judges can and must apply the constitution according to the principles of originalism and with judicial restraint. The perspective of originalism holds that judges must base their rulings on the literal content or original meaning or "plain meaning"[309] of the Constitution and the intent of the framers of the Constitution, not on the basis of the ideology of the judges themselves.[310] They further contend the amendment provision of the Constitution exists to make changes in the constitution in a democratic process not by the decisions of the justices.[311] To abandon originalism, they add, is to give judges the power to legislate which is the function of the legislature, and as such is

---

309. O'Brien, David M., *Constitutional Law and Politics*, Vol. 2, New York: Norton, 2000, p.72.
310. Scalia, Antonin, A *Matter of Interpretation*, Princeton: Princeton University Press, 1997, pp. 5-35; Robert Bork, *The Tempting of America*, New York: The Free Press, 1990, pp. 161-190; Lee Strang, "The Clash of Rival and Incompatible Philosophical Traditions Within Constitutional Interpretation," *Harvard Journal of Law and Public Policy*, Vol. 28. Issue 3, pp. 982-998.
311. Scalia, Antonin, "Originalism: The Lesser Evil" *University of Cincinnati Law Review*, 57, 849 (1989) 57

contrary to the principles of democracy. The issue is whether this theory of originalism is a coherent and rational interpretive approach to the Constitution and whether the amendment process is a plausible alternative to constitutional interpretation.

Many questions about originalism have been raised by those defending the "living constitution" theory and similar non-originalist perspectives. The so-called living constitution adherents include Justice John Marshall who argued that the Constitution was "intended to endure for ages to come and, consequently, to be adapted to the various crises of human affairs."[312] Although certain provisions are unambiguous, such as the length of term of service for congressman, presidents, etc., the Constitution is not so clear in many other provisions. To interpret the document, originalists claim, one must first determine intent but it is not clear whose intent is deemed relevant in this process, the framers or those who voted for it. Even if this question could be answered, it is not clear how their intent could be determined since intent is not stated in the Constitution. It is also likely that whether one selects the intent of the framers or supporters, both groups often had vague, conflicting and changing intentions. In either case, critics note that many groups were excluded from the framing and the voting on the Constitution, namely, African-Americans, women, native Americans, and landless white men, thus making the entire constitutional process, given contemporary moral beliefs, immoral from its inception and contradicting the principles implicit in the document itself.

Critics of originalism claim interpreters of the Constitution must apply an evolving moral conscience and contemporary scientific beliefs to the document. Beliefs about race, gender, and society have changed and the interpretation of the constitution must conform to these new realities. After all, many of the framers believed slavery was moral and women were inferior to men and denied equal rights to both. Critics of originalism also point out that the Constitution does not itself explicitly require that original intent be used to interpret it.

Determining the meaning of vague statements requires that the

---

312. Quoted in Edgar Bodenheimer, *Jurisprudence*, Cambridge: Harvard University Press, 1974, p. 407.

intent of the author be determined but to establish the intent pre-supposes other conditions and complications. First, it requires that the context in which the document was created be understood and clarified. The context includes the cultural, philosophical and political environment within which the document was written. For example, to understand the constitution one must understand the political climate of the times as well as the philosophical ideas current and expressed in the Declaration of Independence whose ideas may be traced to the philosophy of John Locke some of whose ideas can be traced back to the Magna Carta, and the struggle for parliamentary supremacy, etc. Establishing the context of a period of history long gone is problematic at the very least and a speculative exercise in imaginative reconstruction, at best.

In addition to understanding the social context, to understand any part of the document requires that the whole document is properly interpreted and understood and to understand the whole, one must understand the parts. This dialectical process or hermeneutic circle is, in part at least, a subjective process and not objectively definable because one cannot determine and be fully aware of all the presuppositions, often unconscious, the interpreter is applying in the interpretive process.[313]

The amendment process is rejected as a substitute for interpretation by those who reject originalism for several reasons. First, the amendment process is slow and may allow unjust situations are allowed to continue for too long. Secondly, the amendment process is not a matter of a simple majority but of a supermajority (two thirds congress, three fourths of the states) vote but the constitution was designed in part to protect some rights from majority rule. Thirdly, replacing the interpretative process with the amendment process would mean too many and too frequent amendments be initiated. Additionally, when to use the amendment process and how to frame the amendment are also a matter of interpretation of the constitution and hence subject to the same uncertainties. Moreover, the amendment process would be subject to all the imperfections and distortions of the electoral process including an apathetic and uninformed

---

313. D'Amico, Robert, *Contemporary Continental Philosophy*, Boulder, CO: Westview Press, 1999,p.155.

populace, and hence cannot be expected to yield a result consistent with the principles or the overall meaning of the constitution. Finally, extensive use of the amendment process would undermine the rule of law for it would politicize all legal disputes and make legal consistency difficult to maintain.

Critics of originalism also claim that precedent is not a sufficient answer to the problem of interpretation. Precedent, the standing given past decisions of the court, do not constitute a seamless and consistent web of ideas, rules or principles and hence cannot be used to define the meaning of future disputes about the constitution. It is clear that precedents are not an absolute guide to future rulings and, indeed, precedents have been overturned by the Supreme Court more than two hundred times.[314]

Originalism, critics contend, fails to recognize certain fundamental limits framers of the constitution labored under. All persons are morally and intellectually limited and thus lack a complete and accurate understanding and cannot foresee all the consequences and future conditions which the constitution must address. The fact that they included the amendment clause is indicative of their recognition of the need for change in the years to come but the amendment process was not necessarily the only means to modify and adapt the Constitution.

However, although critics of originalism see the Constitution as a living document which must be interpreted to meet the unforeseeable exigencies of future circumstances, they do not generally adopt the view that justices have carte blanche in their understanding of the Constitution. Interpretation, the followers of the living constitution theory claim, must not become subversion, that is, an interpretation which conflicts with the underlying principles of the Constitution.[315]

To abandon originalism, critics of the living constitution claim, means inevitably that, to a degree, the legislative power is taken away from Congress and given it to the judiciary. In this defenders of originalism are partly correct. To interpret the Constitution means to add greater specificity and perhaps clarity of meaning to the law and, as

---

314. O'Brien, op. cit., thus far, the Supreme Court has reversed itself 215 times, p. 124.
315. Bodenheimer, op cit., 409-10.

such is, to various degrees, creating a new norm which means to legislate to that degree. That is, to interpret is in, in effect, to define and make the indeterminate Constitution more determinate which is tantamount to the legislative act for to give meaning to a vague statement is to change it by giving it content and making it more specific thus eliminating other possible interpretations (at least for a time) in some way which means to create a new law. However, defenders of the living constitution theory claim, this is inevitable for any constitutional court whether one follows originalism or some other theory. To interpret is to make the meaning more specific which is to change the meaning to that degree and to change meaning is to change the law. Defenders of the living constitution, however, believe this interpretation must be within the parameters defined by the underlying principles of the Constitution.

Since the interpretation of the Constitution is not a well-defined mechanistic process but is de facto, partly a legislative process, it must be to that degree, a political process. Interpretation, though constrained by the founding principles of the Constitution, cannot be complete by reliance on these principles alone. Principles are themselves often vague, abstract and open to differing interpretations.[316] Therefore, to interpret the often vague and abstract statements of the Constitution is, inevitably, whether consciously or unconsciously, to read into the lacunae of the Constitution the interpreter's own ideology, personality and beliefs. Even if the justices intend not to have their ideological views color the interpretive process, there seems to be no provable way to objectively establish this was in fact the case.

Furthermore, even if the justices were to accept the perspective of originalism, the theory is underdetermined. As suggested above, the theory cannot specify the relevant intent and how to clearly establish what the content of the intent was to interpret the Constitution. Hence even if the justices in good faith sought to apply originalism, the process could not yield a uniform or definitive (or moral) answer to matters of interpretation. Therefore, given the limitations of originalism and the purpose of the Constitution the political nature of at least some of the court's interpretation seems inescapable.

---

316. Dworkin, Ronald, A *Matter of Principle*, Cambridge: Harvard University Press, 1986, pp. 12-24.

The political nature of the court seems to conflict with the need for and relevance of meritocratic criteria argued above. However, instead of a conflict the reality is more of the nature of a tension between the conditions of meritocracy and politics. The court cannot be fully meritocratic because it is political and because of the problematic nature of the concept of meritocracy with respect to the court. Although the Constitution does not specify any necessary qualifications, a meritocractic system would institute criteria such as education, judicial experience, judicial temperament, moral integrity, intelligence, communication skills, among others.[317] Though all these criteria are clearly relevant they are difficult to define precisely and quantify. Since these criteria are to a degree themselves vague, making their meaning more concrete will allow political values to be incorporated into their definition. For example, 'judicial temperament' will be differently defined based on whether one favors the so called activist judiciary (not following originalism) or a strict constructionist view (following originalism), both politically defined.

To disguise the political nature of the process and the political ideology of nominees, judges are sometimes selected who have few or no scholarly publications on political and legal matters so that their political views remain relatively unknown. This creates a possible bias for intellectually mediocre candidates. If the political nature of the process were acknowledged, the selection process would allow nominees of higher intellectual caliber.

The conclusion of this section is that since the Supreme Court is a political institution, the court must conform more closely to political processes of democratic societies.

Procedural Justice

The political nature of the court is made more evident when compared to the idea of procedural justice. Given the above argument, the Supreme Court should approximate as much as possible what Rawls calls pure procedural justice.[318] Rawls has argued that mat-

---

317. O'Brien, David, *Storm Center*, 4e, New York: Norton, 1996, pp. 56-66.
318. Rawls, John, *A Theory of Justice*, Cambridge: Harvard University Press, 1971, pp. 85-7, *Political Liberalism*, New York: Columbia University Press, 1993, p. 192, *Justice as Fairness*, Cambridge: Harvard University Press, 2001, p. 54; James Sterba,

ters of distributive justice should be treated as an instance of pure procedural justice. Pure procedural justice can be understood by comparison with perfect and imperfect procedural justice. In perfect procedural justice there is an independent criterion for what is just and a clear procedure for achieving that end. An example would be to divide a cake equally. Here, one can geometrically divide the cake e into equal parts and the person who makes the cuts takes the last piece to ensure fairness. Imperfect procedural justice is likened to a criminal trial. The desired result is that the guilty are found guilty and the innocent, innocent but no court procedure can guarantee that result in all cases.

In pure procedural justice there is no independent criterion of the correct result but there is a correct procedure for determining the just result. An example of this is in fair games of chance where gam-blers play a game of chance, such as dice, and the results determine who wins after the dice are thrown. The goal of a just society is to design just institutions such that every person is where he or she belongs in the distribution of rights, duties and property after having pursued their plan of life within the context of the basic structure of society.

The Supreme Court is an institution which should approximate pure procedural justice. First, as interpreters of the highest law in the land, there is no higher standard which can be used to judge the interpretations and rulings of the justices. Constitutional amend-ments are not a higher standard but a change in what constitutes the standard. The sovereignty of the people is not a standard either but a process whereby the standard, the Constitution, is changed. As such, to increase the possibility of a just outcome, the structure of the court must be designed in such a manner that the results will more likely be just, i.e., consistent with the basic structure used to define the institution, once the process is complete. The structure of the supreme must be embody more fully the rule of law, meritocracy and the values of the basic structure of society if the rulings of the court are more likely to be just. Limits on the tenure of judges would be an element of this structure for it more fully reflects, as argued above, the rule of law and the political nature of the court.

*How To Make People Just*, Totowa, NJ: Rowman & Littlefield, 1988, pp. 31-35.

Conclusion

To make the Supreme Court more consistent with the ideal of the rule of law, its inevitably political nature and the requirements of meritocracy, tenure of the justices of the Supreme Court should not be determined by the lifespan of the justice. Rather, their term of service should be determined by a law which specifies the maximum number of years of service given good behavior and merit. Although an exact number of years is difficult to specify, the period of time should reflect the courts political nature which would correspond roughly to the maximum tenure of the president if reelected, and the length of the tenure of a senator, given the current practice where the president nominates candidates to the court and the Senate approves or rejects the nominee. This would mean an appointment of about eight years or, considering other factors such as bureaucratic costs, perhaps a maximum of ten years.[319]

The change from lifetime appointment to a fixed tenure would not require a constitutional amendment since, as mentioned, the constitution does not explicitly require lifetime tenure. "Good behavior" can be interpreted as a necessary condition for serving, not sufficient. There should be no right to reappointment for justices may seek to shape their decisions with a certain political point of view to please a new president with hope of reappointment.

Election of Supreme Court judges is problematic for several reasons. First, given current practices of campaign finance, there is too great a possibility of corruption and improper influence to make direct election a superior selection procedure. Moreover, the judiciary is the only branch where the ideal and maintenance of a meritocracy is necessary and possible, albeit problematic. Knowledge of the law and other criteria mentioned above are relevant and difficult for the general public to assess correctly. The demands of a campaign with its theatrical and crude aspects may attract certain personality type and reward them with success but these individuals may not be most suited for the intellectual and moral demands of the judiciary.

Although the independence of the judiciary is central to the rule of law, the independence of the judiciary does not mean indepen-

---

319. This corresponds to the custom in many foreign countries, Epstein, op. cit., p. 8.

dence of the judiciary from the democratic process and the society it serves but from the improper influence of other branches of government. In a pluralistic and dynamic democratic society and the inescapably political nature of Supreme Court judgments, social harmony and stability are enhanced when the basic structures of power reflect and are in congruence with the political and social realities which they are meant to serve.

# CHAPTER 10. ELECTING OR SELECTING STATE JUDGES

> "I never felt so much like a hooker down by the bus station...as I did in a judicial race. Everyone interested in contributing has specific interests. They mean to be buying a vote."
> — Justice Paul Pfeiffer, Ohio Supreme Court

Why would a man give more than $3 million to a judge's election campaign? Let's look at the facts: Hugh Caperton, president of Harman Mining Co., sued Massey Coal Company claiming that Massey failed to fulfill its contract with Harman Mining causing Harman to go bankrupt. In 2002 a West Virginia court agreed with Caperton and awarded his company $50 million. Massey appealed the decision to the West Virginia Supreme Court and at the same time Massey CEO Don Blankenship was involved in the judicial election campaign between incumbent Supreme Court Justice Warren McGraw and his challenger Brent Benjamin. Blankenship contributed over $3 million (more than all the other contributions together) to Benjamin's campaign; Benjamin won. When the case was about to be considered by the West Virginia Supreme Court, Caperton asked that Benjamin recuse himself because of Blankenship's contributions but Benjamin refused and voted with the majority in a 3 to 2 vote to overturn the $50 million previous award to Harman Mining. Caperton appealed to the US Supreme Court claiming that Blankenship's contribution to Benjamin created the potential for bias and required that Benjamin recuse himself. The US Supreme Court agreed that

Benjamin should have recused himself because the contribution created the appearance of an "extreme" conflict of interest.[320] This case
raises many important issues about how state judges are selected.

As we have seen in our discussion of the Supreme Court, the judicial system is essential for resolving disputes peacefully, reducing
conflict and maintaining social order. It is a system established by a
political and legal structure which, if rational and legitimate, operates in such a manner which coheres with the basic societal structure
and produces reasoned decisions by judges who apply the law to the
relevant facts of the case. A rational society, which must include a
rational judiciary, is one which must choose the most efficient means
to achieve its ends, here assumed to be that of a representative democracy similar to that outlined by John Rawls. These necessary
means to achieve these goals are the rule of law, meritocracy, stability and legitimacy.

The rule of law requirement deals with the formal dimension of
the legal system not the substantive content of law but, as will be
shown below, it has implications for that as well.[321] The ideal of the
rule of law understands laws as supreme rules which define how all
individuals and institutions within a given society should function.
The rule of law stabilizes social interaction and provides for social
order while setting a limit on governmental power. It promotes a
social structure within which persons can pursue their goals with
some security and predictability. These basic norms which define
the fundamental rights and duties of persons Rawls terms the "basic
structure" of that society.

The rule of law ideal involves certain logical and formal conditions to perform the function of law. First, the laws must be well-
defined, consistent and a complete nexus of rules structuring society. As well-defined laws must be clear and eschew vague and
ambiguous terms to achieve their function as action guides. If laws
are to determine acceptable behavior the law must be consistent for
contradictory laws would make impossible demands on individuals.
Laws must be understandable by most people if they are to regulate
behavior. Similarly, retroactive laws must be avoided for they can-

---

320. *Caperton v. A.T. Massey Coal Co.* (2009).
321. Cf. Mark Tebbitt, *Philosophy of Law*, London: Routledge, 2000, pp. 37-46.

not provide guidelines for behavior that has already happened. The set of laws ideally must be complete for laws to be action guides in all contexts and must be of sufficient number to leave no area of the domain under-determined and un-structured by law. In a rational society laws must be rational in the sense that they are based on factual evidence not falsehoods or unwarranted assumptions. Further, the rule of law means the law must be promulgated or made public since secret laws could not serve the function of guiding behavior. Finally, it means that no punishment is possible unless it involves a violation of some law.

Regardless of the substantive content, the rule of law ideal must conform to the truism that "ought to implies can" no law can ask the impossible of its subjects. In essence the rule of law ideal is a conditional of rationality as consistency itself requiring that similar cases must be treated alike.[322]

The defense of the rule of law ideal is not oblivious to the issues concerning the limits of rules and laws. It is clear that laws are, to varying degrees, vague, because language is vague and subject to change, laws cannot anticipate all circumstances but are a reaction to a problem, it is partially a matter of subjectivity which cases are sufficiently similar, etc. Further, it is clear laws do not apply themselves but human beings do so and how they are applied is, in part, a function of the persons who apply them. However, these limits of the rule of law do not negate the rule of law as an ideal of reason but merely reinforce the need for greater clarity in the formulation of laws and the need for judges of the highest level of knowledge and moral integrity.

The rule of law ideal in a rational society also presupposes a meritocracy in the sense that meritocracy will maximize the rational implementation of the rule of law. A meritocracy is a social system of allocating personnel where individuals are selected for positions based on meeting criteria relevant to the maximal performance of their function, not on any other criteria. These criteria usually include intelligence, knowledge, motivation to perform the function and a sufficiently moral character to perform the function in the prescribed manner. The ideal of meritocracy is implied in the rule of law

322. Fuller, Lon, *The Morality of Law*, New Haven: Yale UP, 1969.

for the rule of law ideal will be most fully actualized by institutional structures and individuals who have the desired qualities of knowledge of the law, intelligence and rationality to properly apply the law and sufficient moral virtue to act in conformity to the rule of law and their institutional function, not for purely personal gain or benefit incompatible with the role definition.

In addition to the rule of law and meritocracy, a rational society needs what John Rawls calls "stability."[323] A stable society is one where the social structure is consistent with human nature, its abilities and limitations, and widely accepted ethical principles such as 'ought implies can.' A stable system does not ask the impossible of persons such as is the case in utilitarianism where Rawls claims it may ask persons too much as far as contributing to the welfare of others.[324] Rawls goes on to explain that a stable constitutional society is one which must define clearly the basic structure rights and liberties to promote orderly social system and stable expectations. In addition, the basic structure of the society encourages the virtue of "fairness" understood to mean that the benefits and burdens of society are distributed consistent with the basic structure so that no one has an unfair advantage. Clearly, stability presupposes the rule of law since fairness implies that similar cases are treated similarly, which is the essence of the rule of law. The rule of law is a barrier against arbitrary power and sees law as the basis of social order and stability.

The rule of law, meritocracy and stability promote the value of legitimacy of the political system.[325] Legitimacy is the sense that the government has the moral and legal right to rule as it does. It means the political system has widespread support from the populace who see the government providing benefits and distributing them in a manner they consider fair or consistent with the basic values and beliefs they hold. A society based on the rule of law will be more ef-

---

323. Rawls, john, *A Theory of Justice*, Revised Edition, Cambridge: Harvard UP, 1999, pp. 119, 398.

324. Ibid., pp. 154-9.

325. Levasseur, Alain, "Legitimacy of Judges", The American Journal of Comparative Law, Vol. 50, 2002, pp. 43-85; Tom Campbell, *Separation of Powers in Practice*, Stanford: Stanford UP, 2004; Ran Hirschl, *Towards Juristocracy*, Cambridge: Havard UP, 2004.

---

ficient in providing benefits as a well-defined and implemented system of law will facilitate the interaction and coordination of the various institutions which must collaborate to make the political system function harmoniously and efficiently. Again, stability implies fairness which means in part that the laws are applied impartially and the rule of law will maximize legitimacy.

Given the criteria of the rule of law, meritocracy, stability and legitimacy, let's examine the alternative means for selecting state judges and whether they are consistent with these criteria. Focusing here on state courts, five methods have been suggested for determining which individuals should be judges: first, election (partisan or non-partisan), second, appointment by a governor (with or without approval of legislature), third, selection by the state legislature alone, fourth, the "Missouri Plan" consisting of a non-partisan committee recommendation to the governor who selects one (with a retention election later), and fifth, the civil service merit plan which I defend.

Let us consider reasons for the election of judges, a means still in force in many states for state judgeships.[326] In electing judges individuals would stand for various judgeship during elections, whether on a party ticket or in a nonpartisan manner. This manner of selecting judges seems most consistent with the idea of democracy which means the people are sovereign and choose individuals for government positions to fulfill certain necessary functions to serve the needs and rights of the people. Judicial decisions are political in that they affect society in general and as such in a democracy, political matters should be subject to democratic election. Elections would make the judiciary independent of the other branches of government and so enhance the rule of law. Elections give people a chance to get to know the candidates and their qualifications. It would improve public discourse and expand understanding of the law among the citizenry and it may also promote greater political participation in elections in general. It may also assure greater accountability on the

---

326. Minkow, Aaron, "Why Judges Should Be Elected", Social Policy, Fall 2010, Vol. 40, Issue 3, pp 39-42; David E. Pozen, "The Irony of Judicial Elections", Columbia Law Review, Vol. 108, No. 2, March 2008, pp. 265-330; Jed H. Shugerman, "Economic Crisis and the Rise of Judicial Elections and Judicial Review," Harvard Law Review, Vol. 123, March 2010, N. 5, pp. 1061-1150.

part of the judges to make sure they function according to the law not their own personal beliefs or ideological commitments. Finally, electing judges is superior to political appointments of judges which are open to political corruption and cronyism which are inconsistent with impartiality and the rule of law.[327]

These reasons are not sufficient to establish the election of judges as the superior means of selecting judges.[328] Democracy does require that those who serve the people must be made subject to the will of the people but how this is implemented depends on the matter in question. Even in a system where judges are not initially elected, the people could express their democratic sovereignty by removing the judge by impeachment for illegality or by a recall election.

It is also true that judicial decisions are 'political' but the term is ambiguous. 'Political' in its primary sense means something that concerns the community as a whole and as such is something that is a matter for the government and the populace as a whole to consider. However, the actions of the judiciary are political also but in a different sense, the decisions of the court may impact the community as a whole, but certainly not all decisions of the state courts do. In another sense, actions of the court are political in the sense they are a function of the political structure which means it must be consistent with democratic principles but not necessarily by a direct election. The democratic will of the people can be expressed indirectly if they approve a merit system of selecting judges.

Electing judges is one way in which the judiciary can be made independent of the other branches of government, but not the only way. Although he was speaking about federal judges, Alexander Hamilton in *Federalist Papers* #18 argued the opposite claiming that judges should not be elected since judges must be independent of the masses.[329] Selecting judges in a merit system with objective criteria

---

327. Pozen, David, "Judicial Elections as Popular Constitutionalism," Columbia Law Review, Vol. 110, pp. 2047-2134.
328. Hull, Elizabeth, "What's Wrong With Electing Judges," Social Policy, Fall 2010, Vol. 40, Issue 3, pp. 43-47; see also Pozen, op. cit., "Irony"; Ryan L.Souders, "A Gorilla at the Dinner Table: Partisan Judicial Elections in the United States," The Review of Litigation, Vol. 25:3, pp. 529-74; Steven Vago, *Law and Society*, Upper Saddle River: Prentice Hall, 2003, p.360.
329. Hamilton, Alexander, James Madison, John Jay, *The Federalist Papers*, originally published in 1788.

and with standards for their removal by impeachment or other procedures is another way of promoting independence of the judiciary.

Elections can give the people a chance to get to know the candidates and enhance public discourse of the law, but these are not the only means to achieve these goals. The credentials of the judges and their decisions can be placed online and court proceedings could be televised as well. Seminars can be held free of charge at local schools, colleges and online to educate the public. Schools could change their curriculum to reflect the need for a better informed citizenry with regards to the law. Finally, let us not forget that most elections are hardly the paradigm of political discourse but are usually a Machiavellian circus-like theatrical spectacle with sound bites, photo ops, emotional oversimplifications, hyperbole, ad hominem attacks, unwarranted vague innuendos and irrational manipulations.

Electing judges may improve political participation but again, this is not the only means of improving participation. Making election day a holiday, same day registration, internet voting, even making not voting illegal as is the case Australia, and other suggestions can do the same. Having judges on the ballot could actually decrease participation since many voters would be alienated from a process which required them to decide on matters they were not qualified.

As suggested above, accountability can also be enhanced by impeachment and by recall elections when necessary.

Traits needed to run a successful election campaign are not the traits necessary for a qualified and fair judge but, in fact, are mostly contrary to such a judge. The traits necessary to run a successful political campaign are, first, sufficient funds to run a campaign which are increasingly costly with some state supreme court campaigns costing over a million dollars. If the money is obtained through private contributions, then there is a danger of bias based on a quid pro quo.[330] In addition, acquiring contributions takes time away from judges' other duties. The potential bias was used in the case of *Caperton v. A.T. Massey Coal Co.* (2009), mentioned above, where an individual contributed over $3 million to elect a judge who he believed would be more favorable to his case. The majority of the US Supreme Court

---

330. Liptak, Adam, "Looking Anew at Campaign Cash and Elected Judges", New York Times, 1/29/2008, p. A14.

found that large contributions can create the appearance and/or the reality of bias in judges. (Unfortunately, it did not see potentially the same problem when it voted for *Citizens United v. FEC* (2010).)

If the campaign money is publicly provided, then there is a lesser danger of inappropriate influence but problems still exist. There may still be bias if the money is provided by a political party in which case there is the danger of contamination by a political ideology. If the funds are provided in a general election fund, problems still may arise. For example, some key traits needed for a successful campaign are charisma or a pleasing and outgoing personality. A pleasing personality is a good trait but not necessary for a good judge. A judge could be highly intelligent, educated and honest, yet be a poor campaigner and hence lose the election. Indeed, one would expect that those best suited with a temperament for the judiciary would not in general be well suited to the circus-like demands of the election campaign.

A recent ruling of the Supreme Court has exacerbated the problem of electing judges. The court ruled in The Republican Party of *Minnesota v. White* (2002) that the Minnesota law which required judges not to discuss political issues during the election campaign in which they were a candidate, was unconstitutional because it violated the right to free speech guaranteed by the First Amendment. Hence, judges must be allowed to discuss their political views and they must do so and articulate their ideas in a manner appealing to a sufficiently large body of voters. However, political ideology is not relevant to a judge but to the legislative branch. To politicize the judiciary is to undermine the separation of powers and more importantly, undermines the objectivity of the judge and the rule of law.

More than the politicization of the judiciary, there is the problem of what John S. Mill called "the tyranny of the majority."[331] Since elections are won or lost based on whether or not a majority of the electorate (in a two candidate race), the minorities and individuals may be overlooked or denied their fair chance in a court of law. There is evidence that judges apply tougher sentences during election years including applying the death penalty.[332] This politicization of the ju-

---

331. Mill, John Stuart, *On Liberty*.
332. Brace, Paul, "State Public Opinion, The Death Penalty, and the Practice of Elect-

dicial system raises the real potential of the violation of the rule of law since the rule of law requires that the law be applied to the facts without consideration of the political implications or whether one is in a majority or minority or whether one is going to be re-elected or not.

If it is a nonpartisan election, the judge must still explain his or her views on certain issues. This will again politicize the process in an ideological manner to appeal to the majority and other issues with elections mentioned above.

Finally, the general citizenry does not have the knowledge to make judgments about the qualifications of the candidates for judgeships. Assessing the education and prior experience of the judicial candidates is generally beyond the scope of most people who are not lawyers or judges and some who do not even have a high school or college degree or the time and interest to become educated about these matters. Judges can be made accountable to the people in several ways, not just by elections; corrupt and/or incompetent judges can be impeached and removed by a trial.

Selecting judges by the governor alone has obvious advantages and disadvantages. This method is quicker and less expensive then electing judges and, as mentioned above, Alexander Hamilton saw it as safeguarding the independence of the judiciary from the ignorant masses. There are also fundamental problems with the appointment method as well. Appointed judges are not necessarily the most qualified and there is the danger of the corrupting influences of money, cronyism, and inappropriate political influences. This method of selection is most prone to a violation of the rule of law due to political influence which weakens legitimacy and stability.

Obviously, selection by the legislature alone has the same problem mentioned above, i.e., politicization, lack of a merit based approach, cronyism, bribery, etc.

The Missouri Plan was developed as a merit selection process to respond to the weaknesses of the election and the appointment models of selection. This plan was created in 1940 and about a dozen states use it currently. It involves the bar association selecting the

ing Judges," American Journal of Political Science, Vol. 52, No. 2, April 2008, pp. 360-372.

selection committee which consists of three lawyers, three citizens selected by the governor and the state chief justice as chair of the committee. The committee considers various candidates and decides on three it considers best and submits their names to the governor, who selects one. The judge then faces a retention election in the first state general election.

Former Justice Sandra D. O'Connor has proposed a similar method.[333] She has been outspoken against the election of state judges and supports a nonpartisan nomination commission which interviews and selects top candidates whose CV is posted online. This commission would hold open meetings and would include not just lawyers but past judges, experts on the law and the like. The commission would select three names as qualified and send them to the governor who would select one as judge for a limited number of years. After the term of office is over the judge could stand for election to retain or terminate.

This method, which we can call the Missouri–O'Connor method, is clearly superior to the  election and appointment methods but clearly also has serious limitations.[334] The superiority lies in that it eliminates, at least for the initial appointment, the potentially corrupting effect of private monetary contributions to election campaigns, but this problem could reoccur for the retention election. Merit can clearly play a large role in this selection method, but, again, not sufficiently since there are members of the committee who may not be qualified to judge the merits of candidates. The additional weaknesses of the Missouri–O'Connor plan are that there is a question of how and who selects the nominating commission and what criteria are used to choose members of the commission. The role of the governor obviously leaves additional room for the influence of politics and other extraneous factors. The retention election, again, introduces all problems associated with elections.

---

333. O'Connor, Sandra Day, "Take Justice off the Ballot" New York Times, 5/22/10, "Stop Electing Judges", www.HuffingtonPost.org, 9/14/09; Michael S. Greco & Stephen J. Wermiel,  "Sandra Day O'Connor," Human Rights, Vol. 36, Issue 1, pp. 25-6; Sandra Day O'Connor, *The Majesty of the Law*, New York: Random House, 2003.

334. Carp, Robert A., & Ronald Stidham, & Kenneth L. Manning, *Judicial Process in America*, 7e, Washington. DC: Congressional Quarterly Press, 2007, pp. 99-108.

The fifth method for selecting judges is the fully merit based method where judges are part of the civil service system. The civil service method of selecting government officials was established in the US in the 19th century to replace the spoils system where individuals were appointed to non-elective government positions based on political allegiance, campaign contributions, and the like, not merit. In the federal government, all such persons served at the pleasure of the president and could be fired for any reason. When a new administration came into power, many of these persons were terminated and replaced by those loyal to the new administration.

The civil service system must be extended to the judiciary if the values of the rule of law, stability, legitimacy and meritocracy are to be more fully part of the process of selecting judges. Individuals who graduate from professional institutes or universities with degrees in law and judging would be appointed as judges based on their professional competence, objective examinations and experience, not by elections, political appointments or quasi-political appointments by committees. This method exists in many parts of Europe and whereas the current American system at the state and federal levels does not have specific training for judges and some lower level courts do not even require a law degree.[335]

In this more meritocratic expanded civil service system, judges would be assigned to various positions based on objective merit-based criteria. These criteria, as mentioned above, are intelligence, education, knowledge, experience, and moral character. To be sure, the last category of moral character is somewhat subjective but the system proposed here would require that this criterion be based on factual grounds of legal convictions for felonies or misdemeanors and other factors based on empirical evidence, not rumor or innuendo. The appointment of judges would be based on knowledge, experience and character not political ideology, money, political party, personality, looks, height, skill in using TV, charisma or other irrelevant factors. In this merit system, judges would be assigned positions as

---

335. Abraham, Henry J., *The Judicial Process*, 7e, New York: Oxford UP, 1998, pp.34-5; Stanley Anderson, "Judicial Accountability: Scandinavia, California & the USA", The American Journal of Comparative Law, Vol. 28, 1980, pp. 393-422; C. Neal Tate, & Torbjorn Vallinder, eds., *The Global Expansion of Judicial Power*, New York: NYU Press, 1995, pp.289-323.

judges based on standards which would enhance the values of the rule of law, stability, legitimacy and meritocracy.

The appointment in the civil service system would not be for life but for a set number of years. Tenure would be renewable and promotion achieved based on competitive examinations and overall performance evaluation. Of course, impeachment would always be an option for criminality and other valid reasons.

As Rawls states in the beginning of his *A Theory of Justice*, "Justice is the first virtue of social institutions, as truth is of the system of thought."[336] This means that the conditions which maximize truth would also apply to the maximization of justice, which is allegiance to the facts, logic and an impartiality based on the love of truth and justice.

---

336. Rawls, op. cit., p.3.

# CHAPTER 11. REDUCE PRIVATE MONEY IN ELECTION CAMPAIGNS

> "There are two things that are important in politics. The first is money and I can't remember what the second one is."
> — Mark Hanna

They say money talks and if it does, what does it say? One thing it says is that free speech is not necessarily free, especially if it is to count. Leon Panetta, who served in the Clinton administration and later became President's Obama's Director of the CIA (now Defense Secretary) has called campaign contributions "legalized bribery."[337] Panetta goes on to say that members of the House and Senate "rarely legislate; they basically follow the money...They're spending more and more time dialing for dollars...The only place they have to turn is the lobbyists...It has become an addiction they can't break."

Although several campaign reform laws have been enacted, because of loopholes and other limitations in the law, the role of money still being contributed overwhelmingly by the affluent to political campaigns is a concern to many. As Senator Bob Dole remarked, "Poor people don't make campaign contributions. You might get a different result if there were a 'Poor PAC' [Political Action Committee] up here."[338] Research shows that in overwhelming number of cases, the

---

337. Kaiser, Robert G., *So Damn Much Money*, New York: Vintage, 2010, p. 19.
338. Ibid., p. 148.

candidate who spends more in the campaign usually wins.[339] This is not a view just held by Democrats for even Newt Gingrich, before he was Speaker of the House, said "Congress is increasingly a system of corruption in which money politics is defeating and driving out citizen politics."[340] Republican candidate for president Senator John McCain agrees saying that American politics is "an influence peddling scheme in which both parties conspire to stay in office by selling the country to the highest bidder."[341] Even more recently Sen. Dick Durbin (D., Il.) said: "And the banks are still the most powerful lobby on Capitol Hill, and they, frankly, own the place."[342]

Rawls has expressed concerns about the role of economic inequality and private funds in election campaigns in connection with political equality but his suggestions are incomplete and lack sufficient analysis and grounding in his theory.[343] The conflict between political equality and the funding of election campaigns concerns several problems. The first concerns the fact of a class divided society where not all persons have sufficient funds to have a fair chance to run for public office. The second problem is that the current campaign funding system is open to the possibility of bias of those who receive private funds and successfully run for public office. These problems create a conflict between Rawls' theory of justice and the current campaign funding system. To reconcile this conflict and achieve fair elections and an impartial government require at least two conditions: 1) virtual elimination of private monetary contributions to the campaigns of candidates for public office, and 2) government funding to provide a necessary minimum of financial resources to all candidates for public office.

Problems exist in the current election campaign system because of three prevalent circumstances. The first problem is the high and increasing costs of federal and state election campaigns. The second

---

339. Goidel, Robert K., Donald A. Gross, Todd G. Shields, *Money Matters*, New York: Rowman & Littlefield, 1999.

340. Moyers, Bill, *Moyers on Democracy*, New York: Doubleday, 2008, p. 184.

341. Alperovitz, Gar, *America Beyond Capitalism*, New York: Wiley, 2006, p. 11.

342. www.huffingtonpost, accessed 4/29/09.

343. Rawls, John, *Political Liberalism*, New York: Columbia Up, 1993, p. 328; Samuel Freeman, ed., *John Rawls: Collected Papers*, Cambridge: Harvard UP, 1999, p. 580; Ronald Dworkin, *Is Democracy Even Possible Here?*, Princeton: Princeton UP, 2006, p. 128.

problem is the unequal distribution of wealth, income, and educational opportunities among citizens which give some individuals greater access to funds to run an effective election campaign. Thirdly, human moral limitations and weakness have the potential to lead some politicians to compromise their impartiality and oath of office and favor a special interest in legislation or some governmental action even if it conflicts with the general interest, what Rawls would call the basic structure of rights, as a quid pro quo for campaign contributions. These special favors have included, in addition to the shaping of legislation to suit and favor special interests, appointments to ambassadorships, awarding of government contracts, promise of future employment, lessening of oversight by federal and state agencies, etc. If one defines 'bribery' as the offering of money, or something of value for the intended purpose of getting some public official to oppose or support a bill he or she would not otherwise support, then the public official who acts in such a manner is in fact being bribed and is acting in violation of his role obligations. However, not all agree that this alleged bribery necessarily exists in practice and if it does not exist, then there is no need to replace it with public financing or to drastically limit private contributions. Let us first consider some arguments against public financing of election campaigns.[344]

First, it has been argued that public financing of election campaigns would unnecessarily enlarge government and increase taxes. A second argument against public financing is that there is no proof that money influences legislation or buys the votes of politicians. Monetary contributions, it is argued, are not instances of legal bribery but a reflection of support for the existing ideology of the candidate and do not influence the actual legislative process.

Thirdly, it has been argued, as in the *Buckley v. Valeo* case (see below), that campaign contributions are a form of free speech and as

---

344. Goidel, Robert, Donald A. Gross, Todd G. Shields, *Money Matters*, Lanham: Rowman & Littlefield, 1999, pp. 37-54; John R. Lott, "Empirical Evidence in the Debate on Campaign Finance Reform," *Harvard Journal of Law and Public Policy*, Fall 2000, V.24. 1, p9-16: Donald Gross & Robert Goidel, *The States of Campaign Finance Reform*, Columbus: Ohio State University Press, 2003; Bradley A. Smith, *Unfree Speech: The Folly of Campaign Finance Reform*, Princeton: Princeton Univ. Press, 2001, pp. 44-56; David Lowery & Holly Brasher, *Organized Interests and American Government*, New York: McGraw Hill, 2004; Floyd Abrams, *Speaking Freely*, New York: Viking, 2005.

such protected by the First Amendment. To limit contributions to campaigns is to limit free speech without sufficient justification.

As for the first claim, it's possible that government may have to expand and taxes may be raised but, it will be argued below, on balance, these are small inconveniences when one considers what is at stake. Furthermore, the virtual removal of private money from government would lead to fairer legislation and more impartial and efficient government. This, in turn, would reduce government waste which means taxes would probably be generally lower for the vast majority of the population who are not among the affluent elite and current large contributors to election campaigns.

The second claim that there is no proof of corruption from campaign contributions is a more complex argument. The argument claims that there is no empirical proof of any candidate receiving money from a contributor voted in favor of the contributor just because they received money from the contributor. To be sure, there have been cases where lawmakers and other government officials have been convicted of bribery, but this is distinct from a proof of a general connection between campaign contributions and the content of legislation.[345] There is anecdotal evidence of politicians complaining about the current system of campaign finance but nothing that could be considered scientific proof of political bias caused by monetary donations.[346] Several responses can be made to this claim.

It is true that, from a methodological perspective, it would be impossible to prove a case which involved the private mind state and intentions of lawmakers. In the absence of proof of a cause/effect relationship between money and legislative actions, one must consider what is reasonable to believe in the realm of uncertainty.

First, the argument against private contributions does not necessarily assume that monetary contributions alone determine legislation. Lawmaking is a complex process with many elements and many theories how these elements interact and produce legislation. Legislation may be the result of public opinion, the need to protect society from perceived harm, to institutionalize custom and moral

---

345. Dilanian, Ken, "Senators Who Weakened Drug Law Received Millions from Industry" USA Today, 5/12/07, p.14.
346. Green, Mark, *Losing Our Democracy*, Naperville, IL: Sourcebooks, 2006, pp. 21, 89.

beliefs, to regulate social processes, a way the elite protects its own privileges, and, to be sure, special interests.[347]

Second, if it is reasonable to assume that the contributors to election campaigns are rational, then they must be giving money for what they believe are good reasons. One reason that is not in dispute is that money gives the contributor access to the candidate and legislator and allows him or her to explain their needs to the government official.[348] The opportunity to explain and attempt to persuade the government official of one's needs, although not necessarily implying that legislation will reflect these needs, is a substantial advantage in the lawmaking process. If nothing else, it can be agenda setting and frame the debate in a certain manner advantageous to some group and so improperly influence the legislative process. If this happens, certain problems get addressed and others, perhaps of equal or greater urgency, do not and the problems that are addressed are conceptualized in a tendentious manner.

An additional claim made by defenders of private funding is that contributions are support for those who already share the same political views. They claim that the candidate's ideology and political party already support the interests of the contributor and so the contribution does not influence legislative actions in the negative sense since the government official is already inclined to vote in support of the contributor's interests. First, an ideology may itself be unjust and therefore not merit support. Second, political ideologies, being general belief systems of varying levels of completeness, complexity and clarity are usually not specific or complete enough to clearly indicate which way the candidate would vote. (This vagueness is, of course, often intentional to facilitate the maximum appeal of the ideology to the target electorate.) Finally, a candidate may vote in contradiction to their ideology or claim he or she changed their ideology to some degree and vote in favor of the contributor's interest even if in conflict with their original ideology or the common interest.

Finally, if, as private contributor claim, that private monetary contributions are not made to influence the lawmaker but only to sup-

---

347. Vago, Steven *Law and Society*, Upper Saddle River; Prentice Hall, 2003, pp. 152-160.
348. Lowery, op. cit., p. 171; Goidel, op. cit., p.52.

port someone who already shares the same ideology, then a dilemma follows. The dilemma is that if the private contributor sincerely believes that to be the case, then they should be willing to make the contribution anonymously. An anonymous contribution cannot bias a lawmaker but it can help their election chances. If the contributor refuses to make his or her gift anonymously, then they are indirectly admitting that they believe there is a connection between the money and the acts of the government official. Most contributors would likely not be willing to make anonymous contributions which suggests that contributors give money because they think they will receive special treatment in the governmental process not assured to them otherwise.

Even if the cause/effect connection between money and legislation cannot be proven, there is still the problem of the appearance of corruption even if there is none in fact. Here Rawls' idea of the "burdens of judgment" is relevant.[349] The fact that all persons are morally and intellectually limited is part of Rawls' idea of the burdens of judgment. These burdens are due to the fact that evidence about ethical and philosophical matter is often conflicting, complex and difficult to assess. Further, Rawls adds, concepts are vague and peoples' different life experience and worldview yield different interpretations of the evidence. Given the burdens of judgment, people tend to make judgments based on impressions, anecdotal evidence, feelings and other factors. These psychological factors and the occasional scandals concerning lobbyists contribute to the perception on the part of the general populace that private contributions to campaigns do lead to a government that is biased.[350]

The appearance of corruption has negative consequences beyond mere cynicism. Perceived corruption is a factor in low voter turnout in elections and a general lack of participation in politics among many. As will be argued below, this perception is relevant to the belief in the legitimacy of the political structure.[351]

What these arguments suggest is that, in the realm of uncertainty, one must consider the question of whether to make a decision

---

349. Rawls, John, *Justice as Fairness*, Cambridge: Harvard Univ. Press, 2001, pp.35-6.
350. Green, op. cit, for scandals such as that of Jack Abramoff, p. 321.
351. Goidel, op. cit., pp. 89-95.

and if so, how to make a decision. Not to decide, as William James explained, is to make a decision, a decision to maintain the status quo.[352] Since we must decide, under uncertainty we must choose the lesser of two evils or the lesser of two possible evil consequences. If there is a causal connection between money and legislative behavior in some cases and we assume there is no such connection, then more harmful consequences for the integrity of the basic structure of society are possible than if there is no such connection and we assume there is. If there is no connection between private money and governmental actions, and we assume there is, then public funding of campaigns, properly structured, will allow democratic elections to continue with a possible minor drawback of some additional governmental bureaucracy. Most would see the latter as a risk one should take given what is at stake, except, of course, those who believe that what is at stake is free speech-let us consider that claim next.

The most compelling argument against public financing of campaigns is the free speech argument. The claim is that one can speak with words or with actions and that contributing money is supporting someone and is a form of free speech and therefore constitutionally protected. This was one of the main reasons that in *Buckley v. Valeo* (1976) the Supreme Court overturned many provisions of campaign financing law as existed then. The Federal Election Campaign Act of 1971 was a significant attempt to regulate the various sources of funding. Among its main provisions were: 1.) limits on media expenditures for candidates for federal positions, including primary and general elections; 2.) an upper limit on contributions by the candidate or his immediate family to his or her own campaign; 3.) provision for a federal bureaucracy (Federal Election Commission) to monitor campaign practices, including reporting and public disclosure of contributions over $100; 4.) a requirement that each candidate and political committee report total expenditures. In 1974, several amendments were added to the bill including: 1.) public funding for presidential conventions and elections; 2.) contribution limit of $1,000 per individual for each election; 3.) independent expenditures by political action committees (PAC's) for a specific candidate are

---

352. James, William, *The Will To Believe*, New York: Dover, 1956, p. 14.

limited to $5,000 per election.[353]

Among other claims, the plaintiffs in Buckley contended that the legislation violated the First Amendment right to freedom of speech. The court upheld public funding of presidential campaigns and the contribution limits which individuals can make to a campaign because of the possibility of improper influence. However, limits on personal spending by the candidates and independent spending by others on behalf of a candidate were declared unconstitutional because it "necessarily reduces the quantity of expression by restricting the number of issues discussed, the depth of exploration and the size of the audience reached."[354] However, this was not the end of the story.

Almost thirty years later, the Bipartisan Campaign Reform Act of 2002 (also known as the McCain-Feingold Bill or BCRA) was another attempt at campaign finance reform. In addition to requiring public disclosure at the federal level by candidate committees, party committees and PACs of contributions made and spent, the bill: 1.) outlawed all soft money (money not earmarked for a specific candidate) contributions from corporations, unions and individuals to national party organizations and state and local parties, (state and local parties can accept up to $10,000 per individual each year for get-out-the-vote and voter registration efforts; 2.) raised the hard money allowed (to specific candidates) from $1,000 to $2,000 for each election (with change for inflation); 3.) individual contributions to national party committees raised from $20, 000 to $25, 000 per year; 4.) Individual donations to state and local party committees raised from $5,000 to $10, 000; 5.) no monetary limit on independent expenditures by PACs, the "527 groups," which are expenditures made in support of a candidate but made independently of the candidates' campaign, but placed a time limit limited "issue ads" from third parties which mention a candidate to stop 30 days before the primary election and 60 days before the general election; 6.) minors prohibited from making any contributions; 7.) public funding continued to

---

353. Hall, Kermit, ed., *The Supreme Court of The United States*, New York: Oxford Univ. Press, 1992, pp. 851-2.
354. Fein, Bruce, E., *Significant Decisions of the Supreme Court*, Washington, DC: American Enterprise Institute, 1977; Herbert Alexander, *Financing Politics*, Washington, DC: Congressional Quarterly Press, 1976, p. 138.

be available to presidential candidates for primaries and general elections if they chose to use it; 8.) a ban on all foreign contributions; 9.) house and senate candidates (and presidential candidates if they opt out of federal funding) may spend unlimited amount of their own money. In sum, the bill increased the total amount individuals can contribute to each 2 year election cycle to all federal candidates, parties and PACs from $50,000 to $95,000.[355]

The McCain-Feingold law was challenged and debated in the Supreme Court in *McConnell v. Federal Election Commission* (2003). A 5/4 vote upheld most of the provisions of the law as constitutional but it struck down the provision which prohibited minors from making contributions (and some other restrictions). Most importantly, the court held that some restrictions on contributions were acceptable because of the state's legitimate interest in preventing corruption and the appearance of corruption which could result in the loss of confidence in the integrity of the election process.[356] However, the court did not take as seriously this possible corrupting influence as is taken here.

In 2010 the Supreme Court ruled again on campaign finance in the case of *Citizens United v. FEC*. Based on the idea that money is speech, the ruling removed limits on independent expenditures by corporations, profit and non-profit as well as unions.

Although these Supreme Court cases are central to the constitutionality of campaign financing, they did not definitively resolve the question of how money relates to speech. To do this, one needs to look at the concept of speech more closely and its relation to other rights. First, free speech, in the abstract, means that there are no legal restrictions on the content of the speech. That is, no point of view or subject matter is forbidden by law. Further, free speech may mean no legal limit on the scope of one's speaking, i.e., no restriction to the extent, timing or location of the potential audience. In addition, speech or self-expression can be direct or indirect. In direct speech, the individual expresses his or her views; while in indirect speech, the individual gives some form of support to someone else's speech.

---

355. Mitchell, Alison, "Campaign Finance Bill Approved 60-40," New York Times, 3/21/02, pp. 1, 30.
356. McConnell v. FEC (2003); www.findlaw.com.

There is also what the courts have termed "symbolic speech" which is meaningful nonverbal expression such as flag burning.[357] Finally, the courts have also made a distinction between commercial speech and political speech arguing that commercial speech does not have the same level of protection.[358]

There are several points relevant to free speech and campaign money in the above distinctions. First, it seems fairly clear that the sense of free speech which the constitution primarily protects is that of free debate about political and public matters.[359] From this follows that the primary sense of speech must be that of meaningful linguistic utterances directed at others or society in general, not contributing money to someone or some group. The meaning of contributing money is parasitic on the meaning of linguistic utterances and cannot be the central meaning of speech.

Second, the Supreme Court has ruled that free speech, even as linguistic utterances, is not absolute. The court has accepted as constitutional the limitations on free speech in against pornography, falsely yelling 'fire' in a theater, libel, fighting words, etc.[360]

Third, in other cases, the court has ruled that speech can be limited if a legitimate state interest is involved. Even if donating money is construed as symbolic speech as was the draft card burning case of *US v. O'Brien* (1968), nevertheless the court ruled that the First Amendment did not protect absolutely such symbolic speech because burning draft cards violated a legitimate government interest in record keeping and implementing the draft. Given this ruling, money contributed to a campaign, even if interpreted as symbolic speech, would not necessarily be unlimited if there was a legitimate governmental interest to restrict it.

Fourth, if contributing money is construed as commercial speech since money is involved, the defense of private contributions is even more precarious. Commercial speech does not have the same kind of constitutional guarantee because it does not play an equally impor-

---

357. *Texas v. Johnson* (491 US 397, 109 S. Ct. 2533) (1989) in David O'Brien, *Constitutional Law and Politics*, 4e., Vol. 2, New York: Norton, 2000, pp. 629-32.
358. Hall, Kermit, ed., *The Supreme Court of The United States*, New York: Oxford Univ. Press, 1992, pp. 852-3.
359. Hall, op.cit., p. 808.
360. *Schenk v. US* (249 US 47, 39 S. Ct. 247) (1919) see O'Brien, op.cit., pp. 389-41.

tant political role as does noncommercial speech.

It seems clear from these considerations that speech is limited by other rights and legitimate government functions. Rawls' theory of the "worth of liberty," the "scheme of liberties" and other concepts gives a theoretical justification and explanation why limiting or eliminating private funds from campaigns is not a violation of free speech or any other legitimate right but, in fact, will expand rights and opportunities.

Rawls says that his theory of justice, justice as fairness, is defined by his two principles of justice. These principles state: "First: each person is to have an equal right to the most extensive scheme of equal basic liberties compatible with a similar scheme of liberties for others. Second: social and economic inequalities are to be arranged so that they are both (a) reasonably expected to be to everyone's advantage, and (b) attached to positions and offices open to all."[361] Given this definition of justice, the basic problem of justice as Rawls sees it is that the social structure into which one is born "contains various social positions and that men born into different positions have different expectations of life determined in part by the political system as well as by economic and social circumstances. In this way the institutions of society favor certain starting places over others."[362]

Rawls goes on to explain that the liberties of the basic structure must be protected "by including in the first principle of justice the guarantee that the political liberties, and only these liberties, are secured by what I have called their fair value." Further, "this guarantee means that the worth of the political liberties to all citizens, whatever their social or economic position, must be approximately equal, or at least sufficiently equal, in the sense that everyone has a fair opportunity to hold public office and to influence the outcome of political decisions."[363]

Rawls is distinguishing between formal and real equality. Although the constitution may state formally that all persons have equal rights, the actual worth of these rights is not equal since not

---

361. Rawls, John, A *Theory of Justice*, rev. ed., Cambridge: Harvard Univ. Press, 1999, p. 53.
362. Rawls, *Liberalism*, op. cit., p. 326.
363. Ibid., p. 327

all have the same opportunities to exercise them or exercise them equally due to socioeconomic factors. This is obviously true of the right to run for public office which fundamentally impacts on the basic structure and citizens as free and equal.

Rawls' next point about liberties relevant to the free speech issue is his conception of the "coherent scheme of liberties." Rawls claims that no liberty is absolute since liberties can and do conflict with each other. A just society, as he envisions it, needs a coherent scheme of liberties where no one liberty can undermine the others.[364] In a sense, the scheme of liberties is analogous to the parliamentary rules of order where speech is limited to enhance meaningful speech and help achieve the purpose of speech, rational understanding and consensus. Rawls is clear that the manner that these liberties are structure must be guided by the conception of citizens as free and equal. "The final scheme [of liberties] is to be secured equally for all citizens."[365]

Rawls' view of liberties as a coherent scheme implies that no liberty can be implemented in such a manner that it would undermine the total scheme of liberties and compromise Rawls' conception of citizens as free and equal. Hence, if free speech is interpreted to mean unlimited right to contribute to election campaigns, then it would potentially undermine the system of liberties since the process would potentially bias election winners to favor those who enable them financially to become elected and potentially produce legislation and governmental actions consistent with that bias. Hence, from a Rawlsian perspective, whether money is considered speech or property, it cannot be exercised in such a manner that it would contaminate the full scheme of liberties and contradict the idea of citizens as free and equal.

This argument is analogous to John S. Mill's argument about speech and the harm principle. Mill argued that speech can only be limited by the harm principle, which holds that "the only purpose for which power can be rightfully exercised over any member of a

---

364. Rawls, John, *Justice as Fairness*, Cambridge: Harvard Univ. Press, 2001, pp. 111-2, A *Theory of Justice*, op. cit., p. 203.
365. Rawls, *Fairness*, op. cit., p. 112.

civilized community, against his will, is to prevent harm to others."[366] The difference here is, that the harm from interpreting money as speech and placing no limit on this type of speech would 'harm' the totality or scheme of liberties and rights which constitute the basic structure.

Rawls' arguments about speech in relation to citizens as free and equal are found in another form in US constitution as the equal protection clause of the Fourteenth Amendment.[367] This clause was instituted to deal with the aftermath of the abolition of slavery and intended to exclude racial classification of persons. The basic idea of the equal protection of the laws has evolved reflecting changing conceptions of human nature and equality. In essence, it is a requirement that the law be written and applied consistently without respect to characteristics that are irrelevant to the purpose of the law, the determination of rights and duties, penalties and opportunities. Increasingly the courts have excluded property, race and sex, and more recently sexual orientation, as irrelevant in assigning rights and duties based on the equal protection clause.

The implicit logic of the equal protection clause points to factors beyond that of race and sex as irrelevant in the application of the law. The inherent values of the concept of the equal protection of the laws extend to exclude matters of social class and wealth. One's wealth, campaign contributions or social position should have no role in determining who is elected as public official or how legislation is drafted or implemented.

If the above rationale for public funding of campaigns is cogent, its implementation would require two conditions. Rawls' principle of fair equality of opportunity requires that all should have "same prospects of success regardless of their social class of origin."[368] This implies that all citizens, especially the least advantaged, must have equal access to government provided funds necessary to run for public office. This view is further supported by Rawls' ideas of a well-ordered and stable society and public reason.

The most basic idea of this theory of justice is that a just society

366. Mill, John S., *On Liberty*, Indianapolis: Hacket, 1978, p. 9.
367. US Constitution, Amendment 14.
368. *Rawls*, Fairness, op. cit., p. 44.

is a fair system of cooperation. This idea includes for Rawls, the idea of citizens as free and equal persons and the idea of a "well-ordered" society. A well-ordered society is an ideal society "effectively regulated by a public conception of justice" by which Rawls means three things: 1.) "a society in which everyone accepts and knows that everyone else accepts, the very same political conception of justice." 2.) "Society's basic structure-that is, its main political and social institutions and the way they hang together as one system of cooperation-is publicly known, or with good reason believed, to satisfy those principles of justice." 3.) "Citizens have a normally effective sense of justice, that is, one that enables them to understand and apply the publicly recognized principles of justice, and for the most part, to act accordingly as their position in society...requires."[369]

A well-ordered society will also be a stable society according to Rawls. For Rawls, a stable society is a society where there is a harmony between the political theory of justice and human nature and the "normal conditions of human life."[370] It is a society which must meet three conditions: First, a stable constitutional society is one which must define the basic rights and liberties and assign them a special priority. Second, the basic structure of the society is the basis of "public reason." Rawls explains that public reason is public in three ways: 1.) it pertains to the reasoning of citizens as free and equal; 2.) it is open and public discourse is about the general good and social justice; 3.) the content of the discourse is given by a public conception of justice and the basic structure.[371] And third, a stable society is one where the basic institutions encourage the virtues of public life. These virtues are implied in the conception of citizens as free and equal and include, reciprocity, trust, compromise, reasonableness and fairness.[372]

Private money in campaigns clearly contradicts the Rawlsian ideal of a well-ordered and stable society in several ways. As suggested above, private monetary contributions place in jeopardy the basic rights and liberties since there is the possibility that money

---

369. Ibid., pp. 8-9.
370. Ibid., p. 185.
371. Freeman, *Papers*, op. cit., pp. 573-86.
372. *Theory*, op. cit., pp. 111-2; *Fairness*, op. cit., pp. 116-8.

does influence legislation which will be in contradiction with the equal basic rights of the basic structure.

Second private contributions may be in conflict with the idea of public reason. As mentioned, public reason is an ideal of democratic citizenship and fairness where citizens agree that political discourse in a just society will be open and public and in terms of the basic rights and duties embodied in the mutually acknowledge principles defining the basic structure. The content of public reason involves constitutional essentials and basic justice to be settled by political values alone. The legitimacy of public reason is based on whether or not it uses concepts and principles constitutive of the overlapping consensus. This consensus is the conceptual space where the various philosophies and religions, what Rawls terms "comprehensive doctrines," have in common and which makes possible a basic structure most would consent to. Public reason does not apply to private deliberations about comprehensive doctrines but only to constitutional essentials of the basic structure.

To see the contradiction between public reason and monetary incentives, one must distinguish between reasons and causes. In the case of campaigns and elections, the basic structure determines what is relevant or irrelevant evidence in public discourse. The basic structure does not recognize financial contributions as a relevant factor in drafting or deciding legislative proposals or governmental actions in general. And, as suggested above, even if monetary factors are not directly influential in the vote on legislation, it may be a factor in agenda setting and in framing the issues. Money, if influential in any sense, is a cause, not a reason, in the legislative process as defined by the basic structure, and has no legitimate role in the public political dialogue.

Rationality requires a mind open to public debate and dialogue. Legislative decisions based on personal monetary gain would not meet this criterion for one certainly could not claim publicly that receiving financial contributions was a reason for voting in a certain way. Though contributions themselves, as suggested above, do not necessitate bias in legislation, they introduce an element into public discourse, directly or indirectly, which are inconsistent with the ideal of public reason. As mentioned above, what seems not to be in dispute is the access (and influence over agenda and framing) money gives to the giver and, this in itself is a sufficient indication that money is incompatible with public reason.

Private money also conflicts with the third element of a stable society, that basic institutions encourage the virtues of public life, especially reasonableness and trust. To be reasonable means to honor the principles one has agreed to accept and to follow the "even at the expense of their own interests"[373] However, the problem is that private funding of campaigns makes the lawmaker's own interests in being re-elected potentially a factor in their vote. Certainly the virtue of trust, given just the appearance of corruption, would be weakened.

According to Rawls, a just legal system must be consistent with the basic principles of the basic structure and conforms to the rule of law if.[374] The rule of law ideal sees laws as specific norms generated by the basic principles of justice as applied in a given domain. The laws must be clear, public, complete, consistent and possible for most to implement.

Private campaign contributions have the potential to contradict the rule of law ideal by making the legal system inconsistent. If a monetary contribution is used as a factor in drafting and approving legislation, not the existing body of law and the basic structure, then the result could clearly be inconsistent and anomalous laws in conflict with the basic structure.

The contradictions between the current campaign laws and the rule of law raise the issue of the legitimacy of the political system. In general, the legitimacy of political power is determined by whether the political system functions consistently with the moral and legal parameters of the society within which it exists. Rawls understands the legitimacy of political power as existing, "only when it [political power] is exercised in accordance with a constitution the essentials of which all citizens as free and equal may reasonably expected to endorse in the light of principles and ideals acceptable to their common human reason."[375] One need not subscribe to every nuance of Rawls' idea of legitimacy to see that money can be a corrupting influence

---

373. Rawls, *Fairness*, op.cit., p. 7.
374. Rawls, *Theory*, op. cit., p. 208.
375. Rawls, *Liberalism*, p. 136.

which undermines the common good. Monetary contributions either create corruption or the appearance of corruption and so undermine legitimacy. Society as a fair system of cooperation is weakened when the process of elections is incompatible with the required function of lawmakers.[376]

Rawls' ideas of a stable legitimate society governed by public reason and the two principles of justice presuppose the importance of rationality. For a society to continue to be rational and stable the election process must also be rationally structured. A rational election, just as a rational act, must act towards a rationally assessed goal on the basis of all relevant available information. Secondly, rationality requires we consider available alternative means and choose the means that are most consistent and that maximize the overall goals(s) sought. The optimal means are the most efficient (least costly in time and resources) and have the highest likelihood of success to bring about the desired end.[377] From a Rawlsian perspective, the goal is the support and proper implementation of the basic structure, the two principles of justice.

If the election process is to achieve its goal it must select individuals who are the most willing and able to perform their function. Ideally, then, the election process must select the most morally virtuous (act consistently according to their function elected for) and competent (sufficiently intelligent and knowledgeable) individuals who will protect the basic structure and consistently apply it to new problems, it must consist of several components. In other words, the chosen candidate should have a program or policy consistent with the basic structure, and be willing, i.e., has the moral character or proper virtues to act on this program consistently. Without a character of sufficient integrity to withstand the temptation of self-interest (when incompatible with the general interest) or favoritism of special interests (again, when incompatible with the general inter-

---

376. Looking at the debate from the point of view of members of the original position, supports the argument for public funding. Since they have general information about society, they would know that they are more likely not in the very affluent and so not in a position to contribute money to campaigns. Second, knowing human nature and the limitations on moral virtue, they would decide to keep private money out of the election due to the possibility of bias and corruption of the basic structure.

377. Rawls, *Theory*, op. cit., p. 45.

est) to those who may offer various inducements (financing of campaign, gifts, jobs, etc.), the representative is not truly representing *all* of his constituents for which he was elected, and is therefore violating his contractual obligation. Bribery, for example, if successful, is the alienation of function, and so is incompatible with any political system for in not performing his or her function, he or she is damaging the common good as defined by Rawls' basic structure of the two principles of justice.

Public funding allows for a more rational election in several ways. First, it expands the spectrum of potential candidates by neutralizing the effects of socio-economic class. By increasing the pool of potential candidates, it increases the possibility of superior candidates.[378] Second, public funding reduces the time spent on the pursuit of private funds. Some estimate that as much as half of a congresspersons time in campaign solicitation and planning. This is time that can be spent more effectively with activities relevant to the function chosen for not to secure the means to keep one's employment. Third, many candidates find asking for funds unpleasant and many potential candidates who have the talent and personality to be effective legislators may not have the personality that makes for a successful fundraiser. Fourth, under public funding those elected are more likely to be faithful to their function, ceteris paribus, since the potential for bias in favor of contributors is eliminated. Fifth, the confidence of the citizenry in the governmental process will be increased, the belief in the legitimacy of political power is enhanced from which greater overall participation in the political process is likely. In sum, a rational society must be a meritocracy (given that the two principles have been implemented), a social system where individuals are allocated positions based solely on relevant ability and willingness to perform their function. The reforms argued for here are meant to be perfectly general and apply to federal and state as well as local primary and general elections.

Some clarifications are necessary about the current proposals. First, independent expenditures by those not affiliated with the cam-

---

378. Evidence shows that at least one third of the current members of the Senate are millionaires and 123 out of 435 members of the House are also, whereas the total number of millionaires in the US is less than one percent.(*Losing*, op. cit., p. 23.)

paign are a form of free speech and must be allowed. However, if the opposing candidates do not have sufficient funds to respond to these independent messages, then the government must ensure that sufficient funds are provided to respond to such ads. An election committee would make these decisions in an impartial manner. Funds could go to political parties or to individuals not affiliated with a party. (Contributions other than monetary, such as contributing time and labor, can be translated into their monetary equivalent.) To eliminate promises of lucrative future employment from lobbyists in exchange for favors, government employees should not be allowed to work for a lobbyist for at least ten years after leaving government service.

Second, individuals should be allowed to use their own funds since one's personal funds are not in themselves a source of potential inappropriate influence. However, personal funds can be problematic if the opposing candidates have significantly lower funds. Two suggestions should be made here. There should be an upper limit placed on self-funding so that individuals of massive wealth do not receive an unfair advantage, i.e., an advantage simply because of superior financial resources. Second, the government must ensure that the opposing candidates have roughly equal funds to compete effectively with the self-funded affluent opponent. If this were to be implemented, many wealthy individuals would likely not choose to self fund. Access to free mass media would be part of this reform as well.

The above argument has been that private donations must be virtually eliminated from election campaigns, but not totally for the following reasons. First, in a democratic system, the citizens must have legal options to initiate political change from below. Second, to ban all individual contributions would likely be an obstacle to third parties and other emerging political groups. What is necessary is that the contribution be of such limited quantity (such as, say, a maximum contribution of $100 per candidate) that almost all members of society can contribute such an amount. And, second, such small amounts would not bias the governmental processes and so should be allowed.

Political power, Rawls remarks at one point, is based on wealth, education and organization.[379] The problem is that not all citizens

---

379. Rawls, *Fairness*, op. cit., p. 131.

have an equal chance to acquire the elements of power. The argument presented here is that the process of elections must be consistent with the function of elections, to defend and apply fairly the basic structure of rights. If citizens are free and equal, then class origins and money should not determine who runs and who wins public office. Those who win should be dedicated to perform their function of serving the common good not the good of groups or individuals who contributed money to their campaign.[380]

---

380. The elections reforms made at the state level in Arizona, Maine and elsewhere known as "clean elections" is an interesting attempt to make reforms at the state level. (See www.commoncause.org.)

## Chapter 12. Expand the Right to Run for Political Office

> "... [T]here is a natural aristocracy among men...[of]... virtue and talents... There is also an artificial aristocracy founded on wealth and birth, without either virtue or talents...a mischievous ingredient in government, and provision should be made to prevent its ascendancy."
> — Thomas Jefferson (Letter to John Adams)

Billionaire Mike Bloomberg (net worth estimated at $16 billion) spent nearly $250 million of his own money when he ran for mayor of New York City in 2009 and won. Governor Jon Corzine (received $400 million when he left Goldman Sachs) spent over $100 million of his own money and won when he ran for the Senate in 2000 and later for governor of New Jersey.[381] Lawyers make up 43% of Congress while 2/3 of senators and 39% of representatives are millionaires and both houses are overwhelmingly white and male?[382] Primarily because of gerrymandering where voting districts are designed to favor a party, only 10% of the 435 seats of the House of Representatives are truly competitive. The cost of national campaign elections have skyrocketed so that the average winning House campaign costs $1.1 million and the Senate campaign estimates at about $10

---

381. Kocieniewski, David, "Corzine's Wall Street Resume Loses Value for Voters", The New York Times, 10/5/09, pp. A17-18.
382. Seelye, K., www.newyorktimes.com, 4/7/95 ; R.Cohen 8/5/09.

million. The 2008 election saw a record spending of almost $1 billion (primary and general elections) with the Obama campaign spending $712 million (raised $742) and Senator McCain $326 million (raised $357 million). Most of these monies were collected from private citizens who constitute less than 1% of the population who gave $200 or more and half the donors have incomes of $250,000 or more.[383] How can an ordinary citizen who is not a lawyer or a millionaire but has a job and a family supposed to run for public office? Do we have a democracy or a moneyocracy and a lawyerocracy?

Democracy is based on the values of the liberty, equality and sovereignty of the people. Democracy means the people rule themselves but in a large society, given current technological and social conditions, democracy cannot be direct but must be implemented as representative democracy. Representatives are, in theory, voted into office by the citizenry to serve the needs, beliefs and interests of the people whom they are said to represent.

We know that our society has millionaires (and billionaires) and people born into these classes have greater power, the right social contacts and opportunities others do not. This unequal social starting points leads to what John Rawls calls inequality of the value or "worth of liberty." Simply put, the wealthy have the economic resources, educational opportunities, professional training, and social contacts to expand the power of their rights, such as running for public office, to a far greater extent than those with far lesser educational, social, and economic means. Can we have a representative democracy if the vast majority is excluded from even the chance of running for office? Rawls attempted to answer this question in his *A Theory of Justice* and *Political Liberalism,* but his proposals are weak and insufficient.

Rawls believes that political parties must be kept independent of large private economic and social power which means that society as a whole must bear at least a large part of the cost of carrying out

---

383. www.opensecrets.org, 2/8/09; Chuck Todd & Sheldon Gawiser, *How Barack Obama Won,* New York: Vintage Books, 2009, pp. 9-30; Kuttner, Robert, *The Squandering of America,* New York: Vintage Books, 2008, pp. 268-70; Bradley Bill, *The New American Story,* New York: Random House, 2008, p. 203; Thomas E. Mann & Norman J. Ornstein, *The Broken Branch,* Oxford: Oxford Univ. Press, 2006, pp. 229-30.

the electoral process. Here he is somewhat vague but he seems to be alluding to public financing of political campaigns. The thesis argued here is that these measures, to the degree they are clear, are inadequate and incomplete in providing for the equal worth of liberty.

I argue that, among other reforms, what is needed is the implementation of the right to what I call "political leave." This is the right to be a candidate for public office, the right to have the campaign publicly funded and the right to return to one's place of employment at the end of the campaign or term in office. The need for these more fundamental reforms is even more urgent given Rawls' current focus on what he calls the pluralism of comprehensive doctrines.

Democracy is a political structure where citizens freely decide who has political power and how they are to exercise that power. Clearly then, political participation and elections are central to legitimate democratic systems for without the right to elect and remove individuals who control the power of government, not only is our right to development of our moral powers as free and equal denied but, even more importantly, all of our other basic liberties and rights listed in the first principle are in jeopardy because those who have political power control the rights people have and what these rights mean. The problem is that the right to political participation is more complex than at first sight.

Political participation can be understood negatively or positively. In the negative sense, it has usually been defined as the absence of legal impediments in voting and declaring one's candidacy for some office. This idea has been justified by Rawls and others in the following ways: First, as based on what Rawls calls the moral conception of the person as free and equal; as autonomous in having the right to control his or her own life and personality within the parameters of the equal rights of others to the same. Second, as self-protection; controlling the powerful political structure enables one to more fully protect one's rights and interests. Thirdly, the equal rights of persons to what Rawls calls self-respect; to actualize their human potential by participating in various activities and functions including political processes. Fourth, it is an efficient means to receive information about the state of the populace thus enabling more adequate policies to address problems. And finally, the right to political participation is based on the assumption that human beings have sufficient rationality, ability and interest to determine their form of government.

Rawls realizes that the negative sense of political participation is inadequate. It is inadequate because it overlooks the social and economic obstacles to participation; the poor face many obstacles not faced by the rich. This is why Rawls calls for "fair equality of opportunity." This equality of opportunity is again, not merely "formal" or one where the laws do not keep one from pursuing an education or some opportunity, but a real one in terms of equal social and economic conditions. He elaborates on this in *Theory* as requiring that "The expectations of those with the same abilities and aspirations should not be affected by their social class." This means Rawls adds that "The importance of preventing excessive accumulations of property and wealth and maintaining equal opportunities of education for all."[384] What Rawls calls background institutions are such institutions as the family, economic, educational, and communication institutions, among others which exist within the larger basic framework. The function of these background institutions is to help develop the potential needed to participate and guarantee the values of democracy. This implies, in addition to the right to an education, the right to participate in the political process. Moreover, it means more than this, it will be argued, it implies the right to what is here termed positive political participation, i.e. the right to the necessary means to be a candidate for political office.

It should be apparent that the above argument implies that all citizens must have the right to positive participation in the political process. This means going beyond the mere right to speak and vote; it means the *positive* right to run for office oneself. Of course the right to run for political office is already provided in democratic systems in its *negative* or what Rawls calls formal sense as the absence of legal impediments to run; what is not provided are the necessary means by which to do this. In the past, obstacles to full political participation have included legal impediments which have excluded the without property, women, racial and religious minorities. Today, legal and other obstacles have disappeared for the most part but economic impediments remain; although property ownership is not a legal condi-

---

384. Rawls, John, *A Theory of Justice*, Cambridge: Harvard Univ. Press, 1971, p. 73.

tion for voting, lack of economic means is an overwhelming practical obstacle nevertheless. The facts are simple enough; most persons lack the time, money and an adequate education to run for public office. The demands of earning a living, employment and sufficient funds to run a viable campaign limit full political participation to an elite wealthy few.

By elite is meant those individuals who share certain privileges. They have attended and benefitted from prestigious or highly selective colleges and universities and either control wealth of sufficient magnitude or are members of a lucrative profession which allows them self-employment (e.g., lawyers, entrepreneurs, etc.). These persons have the educational background and/or rhetorical skills, time and money to run a political campaign without any significant decrease in their standard of living.[385] This economic dependency and exclusion of the non-elite is incompatible with the Rawlsian basic moral structure of fair equality of opportunity and the equal worth of liberty of citizens to participate in the political process not just as voters but as candidates.

The right to full or *positive* political participation is based on the same Rawlsian reasons for equal value of political liberties and fair equality of opportunity. He states that the equal value of political liberties is so important and must be protected by including in the first principle of justice the guarantee that the political liberties, and only these liberties, are secured by what I have called their "fair value." He goes on to explain "this guarantee means that the worth of the political liberties to all citizens, whatever their social or economic position, must be approximately equal, or at least sufficiently equal, in the sense that everyone has a *fair opportunity to hold public office* and to influence the outcome of political decisions."[386] But Rawls does not provide for the implementation of this fair value to hold public office nor does he realize what not having fair value implies for the first principle of political liberties.

The lack of provision for positive political participation is in-

---

385. Ibid., p. 75.
386. Rawls, John, *Political Liberalism*, New York: Columbia Univ. Press, p.327.6. Ibid., p. 297. 5. This must include the right to a salary equal to what one would be earning if employed (paid as part of public financing) if the campaigning is full time as may be the case in federal elections.

consistent with several central Rawlsian ideas. First, it denies what Rawls terms the equal right to "adequate development and full exercise of the two moral powers of citizens as free and equal persons."[387] Political elites are free to set the agenda and parameters of political debate leaving voters only the limited choice of reacting to a predetermined set of options. The current privately financed economic structure of the media is incapable of rectifying this problem fully for it is itself part of the economic nexus of the elite since it is owned by members of the elite and depends on that elite for financing through advertising. Consequently, it is not presently structured to provide complete and impartial information about the political or economic systems. It denies the non-elite the equal right to full self-development in being excluded for economic reasons from full participation in the electoral process.

Lack of the right to positive political participation also undermines Rawls' idea of social stability. His conception of stability means two things. First, it means citizens have a sufficient sense of justice so that they generally comply with and have an allegiance to the basic political institutions. Second, stability means citizens generally endorse the political system from their own respective comprehensive doctrines albeit for different reasons. Rawls specifies that allegiance requires at least two conditions: a recognition of the right to pursue our conception of the good; and second, protection of our self-respect.

Self-respect, Rawls explains, is protected by upholding the priority of the first principle over the second. To Rawls self-respect means having "self-confidence as a fully cooperating member of society capable of pursuing a worthwhile conception of the good over a complete life;" it provides a "secure sense of our own value."[388] Without self-respect, Rawls states, nothing seems worth doing. Can allegiance be maintained if the vast majority are excluded from active political participation? Can one's self-respect be maintained without positive political participation? Can one pursue one's conception of the good when one is denied positive access to the machinery of power? No, exactly because what Rawls concedes is a fact of contemporary soci-

---

387. Rawls, John, A Theory of Justice, op. cit., pp. 60, 102-7.
388. Ibid., p. 105.

ety, a pluralism of comprehensive doctrines.

The reality of pluralism of reasonable doctrines explains the urgency for positive political participation. That is, if we all shared essentially the same comprehensive doctrine or worldview, lack of equal political participation would not be a substantive political issue for judgments of those who had the power would flow from basically the same moral, religious and other fundamental assumptions. But since there is no shared comprehensive conception of the good, no shared religion, no shared overall philosophy, then a systematic lack of access to political decision-making puts in jeopardy one's own conception of the good and status as a free and equal member of society.

The fact of philosophical pluralism is exacerbated by human moral limitations. When the fact that only the social and economic elite have the resources to run for political office is combined with the given fact of human self-interest and moral limitation, then the resulting possibility of the lack of equal consideration of the rights, self-respect and conceptions of the good of the non-elite are obvious. It may also be a fact, as many have argued, that the elite generally share a comprehensive worldview that is distinct from the worldview of the less educated and economically disadvantaged. It should also be clear that the elite generally have an interest in maintaining the status quo and thus excluding significant change that may enhance the welfare of the non-elite at the cost of the elite. This, of course, contradicts the Rawlsian idea of equal worth of liberty, fair equality of opportunity and stability and thus undermines the basic structure of the liberal democracy.

This weakens another idea of Rawls, that of "social union." Social union is fostered when citizens see themselves as part of a fair system of cooperation, when everyone participates in this good of social cooperation. Social union also includes the idea of "reciprocity"[389] of everyone contributing to society what they can and benefitting from the contribution of others. Clearly Rawls' idea social union implies participation at every level of the basic structure for to exclude some from contributing at any level is to abandon fairness and cooperation. Lack of participation by the non-elite also denies the political

---

389. Rawls, *Political*, op. cit., p.321.

system adequate information feedback to enable the formulation of policies with the complete set of relevant facts in at least three ways. First, direct positive political participation by all socio-economic levels is the best way of ensuring that the circumstances of the non-elite are accurately represented since it would eliminate intermediaries from the elite class who may distort or simply be oblivious of the true interests of those whom they claim to represent. Second, if rationality is defined as choosing the best means to achieve some goal, then full considerations of all possible means is necessary. Positive political involvement enables greater access to the political debate by all strata of society thus expanding the pool of ideas, professions, approaches and policies thereby enhancing the rationality of the electoral process. Third, by expanding the pool of candidates, the likelihood of the most qualified emerging from the contest for power is increased.

Finally, inability to participate fully in the electoral process increases the alienation of vast numbers who sense the de facto system is designed to exclude full consideration of their rights by favoring the interests of the ruling elite. This sense of exclusion is made even more acute when combined with an ideological socialization which promises equality. As Rawls himself states, "for without the public recognition that background justice is maintained, citizens tend to become resentful, cynical and apathetic."[390] The awareness of inconsistency between ideology and reality exacerbates alienation and reduces general loyalty for the system thereby increasing the possibility of social conflict and instability thus endangering the rights of all.

It follows, that the present structures of democracy must change in the following manner. First, as discussed in a previous chapter, all political campaigns must be publicly funded to the degree of allowing an adequate campaign. Second, private contributions to campaigns are allowed as long as they are anonymous. Third, contributions of one's own resources are allowed as long as matching funds are then contributed to opponents from the public funds. This will effectively limit contributions from one's own resources to a manageable limit. To this must be added the crucial component that employees must have the right to what one may call political leave: the right to paid

---

390. Ibid., p. 363.

leave from place of employment and the right to return to the same or equivalent at the former employer or similar job after the campaign or after one's term of office is over. This could be implemented as a kind of affirmative action for former public servants.

Political leave is necessary for the implementation and realization of the equal values of liberty. How can an ordinary worker launch campaign with all the uncertainty this entails without the guarantee of re-employment if he or she loses or after the term of office is over? Without this provision, only the wealthy or self-employed could have the luxury of taking the risk of running for office. Just as family leave reflects the value of the family, so political leave reflects the value of political participation.

Property rights cannot override this right to political leave and the right to an equivalent job after public office. Rawls himself believes only in the right to what he calls "personal property "not the right to own the means of production of natural resources.[391] The right to private property cannot be used to deny this expansion of the value of political rights and employee rights. As argued above, the right to property cannot be absolute because to maintain that is to contradict what Rawls calls the basic structure of liberal democracy providing for equal or fair value of rights. To hold that the right to private property is absolute to the degree of denying the right to political leave and the necessary resources to do so would indefinitely exclude most members from full political participation thereby jeopardizing their basic rights which democracy promises. That is, rights that cannot be defended through participation in the process that defines and enforces them are obviously not real but merely formal or paper rights. This would be analogous to arguing that the right to property precludes taxation of any sort; but without taxes government and all rights would not exist or be in the insecurity of state of nature. This means that the right to private property is not basic or

---

391. Ibid., p. 298.   The implementation of this right may require the exemption for some small businesses which may not be able to economically sustain the burden of re-hiring employees who, having won an election requiring full time service, were long absent.  To ensure no serious economic hardships ensue former public servants, alternatives such as preferential treatment for former public officials would have to be given serious consideration.  To be sure, there will have to be a procedure to eliminate frivolous candidates.

absolute but instrumental in that it is a form of social ordering of resources which, thus far, has been found to be, when properly limited,
the best means to enhance the welfare and protect the basic rights
of persons as defined in the democratic framework. If the above argument is persuasive, there is no alternative means to safeguard the
basic rights of persons except through full access to the political process. This must mean the right to political leave as defined. Rawls'
concept of fair equality of opportunity also implies more than the
equal right to participate in the political process. Money and time are
not all that is needed to compete, other social institutions must also
be equalized. This means equality of educational facilities. Schools
must be equally good regardless of the social class one happens to
fall into due to what Rawls calls the "lottery of birth." This would
actually necessitate greater funds be allotted to the least advantaged
to compensate for the advantages of the well to do have on the basis
of the family they were born into. This also means programs for re-
training later in life to meet new economic conditions in a dynamic
economy.

These measures can also be seen as specifying the meaning of
Rawls' difference principle more fully. The difference principle, you
recall, states that social and economic inequalities must benefit the
least advantaged. Rawls never fully explains what this means. Part
of its meaning surely involves social welfare programs such as unemployment insurance and the like. But the measures Rawls has in
mind here are more distributive rather than political. To benefit the
least advantaged in a more lasting way is to provide for the social
and economic conditions for them to rise above their conditions and
avoid these conditions. As the old saying goes, one can help the poor
by giving them a fish or teaching them to fish; teaching them to fish
is more in harmony with the Rawlsian conception of persons as free
and equal.

There are some objections to this expansion of equality that
should be mentioned. Rawls might argue that greater economic
equality reduces incentives for investment, production and thus
harms all. What Rawls does not seem to be aware is that one must
distinguish between temporary and permanent lesser value of liberties. The least advantaged might well agree to a temporary lesser val-

ue of liberties with reasonable assurance for long term gains. There may be some reduction in economic production but at the long term gain to the least advantaged of equal citizenship. The kind of equality argued for here is not that of results but of opportunity. Indeed, the proposal here defended would increase the pool of talent from which greater excellence and economic efficiency could flow.

John Rawls' theory is based on the central value of the rights of persons as free and equal. Rawls views his principles of justice as an attempt to rectify what he calls in *Theory* the "lottery of birth," the undeserved social circumstances of birth that restrict autonomy and equal opportunity of the lowest socio-economic strata of society.[392] Positive political participation is a step in the direction Rawls envisioned and one that is implied in the full realization of the democratic ideal of equal autonomy and right to self-development. When Rawls speaks of the priority of liberty, he means the moral priority of liberty over economic conditions. What Rawls seems to have overlooked is what Marx saw more clearly, at least in this instance, the economic forces have a practical priority in history and society over political structures. To mitigate this practical and political priority, Rawls' ideas of fair equality of liberty and fair equality of opportunity necessitate greater political and economic reforms than he seems to be aware. Without direct access to the decision-making loci of power, the basic structure becomes the structure that serves the interests of those that do have that access. The connection between economic power and political participation must be severed if political equality is to be preserved. Without the equal fair value of liberty, liberty becomes just words on paper.

---

392. Ibid., p. 324.

# CHAPTER 13. EXPAND EMPLOYEE RIGHTS

> "Labor is prior to, and independent of, capital. Capital is only the fruit of labor, and could never have existed if Labor had not first existed. Labor is superior to capital, and deserves much the higher consideration."
> — Abraham Lincoln

In the middle of the night a mysterious deadly cloud spread quietly from the Union Carbide plant in Bhopal, India. As the cloud of pesticide permeated the city, people who breathed it were overtaken with severe coughing, vomiting and suffocation leading to the immediate death of 8–10,000 and eventually to 25,000 dead and injury to about 500,000 residents. The leaves fell off trees days later in the area of the cloud, and thousands of farm animals died as well. Soon the next morning, bands of thieves wandered among the dead lying in the streets and in abandoned houses and took any item of value they could find before the police and soldiers arrived. Whether due to poor design, inadequate language skills, incompetent management, poorly trained workers, corruption, sabotage, or something else, on Dec. 3, 1984, the worst industrial accident, so far, became history.[393]

---

393. Lapierre, Dominique & Javier Moro, *Five Past Midnight in Bhopal*, New York: Warner Books, 2002, pp. 3-15, 173-9; Ward Morehouse & M. Arun Subramanian, *The Bhopal Tragedy*, New York: The Council on International and Public Affairs, 1986, pp. 1-22,107-15.

Although the Bhopal tragedy was horrific, it was surely not the only corporate disaster. In 1911 the Triangle Shirtwaist factory fire in New York was pivotal in the development of new regulations. Locked doors that should have been open, a fire escape poorly made collapsed from the escaping workers and spilled them on to the street, fire trucks with ladders that could only reach the sixth floor and other factors all contributed to the death of 146 poor immigrant young ladies (out of about 600 workers). These workers who labored between 60-72 hours a week for about $6 a week either burned to death or jumped to their demise to avoid the flames to the horror of the people helplessly watching on the street.[394]

In the 1970s, The Ford Motor company engineers were developing a new subcompact car, the Pinto. The problem was that in the event of a rear end collision, its fuel tank tended to rupture, creating a likelihood of a deadly fire. Although some of the facts are in dispute, it seems fairly clear that, instead of improving the tank, which would have cost about $11, Ford did a cost/benefit analysis and decided to risk lawsuits that would emerge due to accidents and deaths, which it believed would be cheaper. Twenty-seven people died in Pinto fires resulting in the loss of millions of dollars to Ford from lawsuits, giving the car the nickname "the barbecue that seats four."[395] Other more recent scandals including outright fraud, theft, bribery, the death of workers, lost jobs and pensions and other side effects of the recent financial crisis are too many to list here.[396]

These disasters are not mentioned to assign responsibility and blame or to tar with the same brush all corporations. On the contrary, history shows that the corporation was an innovation that enabled large scale economic activity which produced vast goods and services never before seen in history. The examples of corporate crimes and mistakes mentioned must be put into this historical context, including the current financial crisis. With issues such as subprime mortgages, bad loans, failed banks, foreclosures, rising unemployment coupled with huge bonuses for incompetent executives

---

394. Drehle, David von, *Triangle*, New York: Atlantic Monthly Press,2003, pp. 23-54.
395. Spence, Gerry, *With Justice for None*, New York: TimesBooks, 1989, pp.200-1.
396. Richardson, John, ed., *Business Ethics*, 03/04/, Guilford, Ct: McGraw-Hill/Dushkin, 2003, pp.71-2.

and crimes such as the Madoff $65 billion Ponzi scheme (sentenced to 150 years of prison), continue to raise profound questions about the nature and viability of the modern corporation and the future of capitalism itself.

Although the modern firm is legally owned by the stockholders who elect (or allow the management to do so by proxy vote) the board of directors to oversee and control its operation, the corporation's day to day running is handled by the managers or executives who are chosen by the board and answerable to the board who, in turn, are responsible to the stockholders. In reality, since the ownership of the large public corporation is so widely dispersed among possibly millions of stockholders, the managers, who may own little or no stocks, actually often exercise most of the control of the firm to the degree that the board members are often indirectly chosen by the managers. The board of directors is typically not familiar with the details of the management of the firm and often become a rubber stamp for the decisions of management.

This managerial revolution, as it often referred to, which is the separation of ownership and control, raises many issues about who is in control of the firm and how the control is exercised and the transparency or lack thereof, of this control. This problematic nature of control raises issues about responsibility which obviously can have serious ethical ramifications.

Many agree that the unethical behavior of firms is partly the failure of government, the structure of the corporation and partly the greed and immorality or amorality of individuals.[397] For illegality and immorality to occur all that is needed is a weak or nonexistent conscience, secrecy and an opportunity for illicit gain. A weak conscience allows one to act contrary to basic moral values and to violate core laws and secrecy makes getting away with one's criminality more likely. It follows that to eliminate or limit one these preconditions for immoral/illegal actions would greatly reduce the scope of corporate crime. The goal is to show how that can be done consistent with the evolving structure of capitalism and Rawls' theory of justice.

To address this problem, we must look at what a conscience is,

---

397. Lanman, Scott, Steve Matthews, "Greenspan Conceded a 'Flaw' in his Market Ideology," *www.bloomberg.com*, 8/23/2009.

its origin and function. A conscience is a part of the mind which consists of cognitive and emotive elements. As cognitive it presupposes knowledge of concepts of right, wrong, duty, whereas the emotive element includes the feelings of guilt or shame for falling short of one's sense of duty. One's conscience involves a sense of responsibility for past actions and an awareness of obligations with respect to anticipated future actions. It consists in the capacity for self-observation, and criticism by comparing our actions with values, ideals and group-norms one accepts as correct.

A conscience is formed by the process of socialization when the individual internalizes the customs, beliefs and moral rules of his or her society as taught by parents, teachers and peers. These customs, values and moral norms are believed by the society to preserve and promote the common good. To be sure, having a conscience does not make one morally perfect for the conscience is as mentioned, a product of socialization which is a product of the society one happens to be born into whose moral system may not be perfect. Hence, one's conscience must be subjected to critical reflection, what Rawls includes in his theory of reflective equilibrium, to expose problematic beliefs and values, difficult this is to be sure. Let us call such a conscience a well-formed conscience which will generally control selfish and immoral tendencies and promote, or at least not grossly violate, the common good of the community.[398]

The advantages of conscience to mere external monitoring and attempted control of behavior are clear. The judgment of a properly formed conscience is ever-present, whereas external authority and punishment may be more easily avoided, is more uncertain, and may be more often mistaken. It follows that a society where individuals and basic institutions have something like a conscience will tend to act in harmony with social norms and the prevailing conception of justice then those institutions which lack internalization of moral norms and thus would tend to a more amoral, immoral and conflict-ridden society. Since a corporation is a legal person not a biological person it cannot have a conscience in the same sense, but it can have an objective structural correlative of a conscience.

However, a conscience is not sufficient for moral behavior be-

---

398. Loevinger, Jane, *Ego Development*, London: Jossey-Bass, 1976, pp. 397-8.

cause socialization is always more or less incomplete and defective and because the self-interest of individuals is rarely fully controlled by socialization. What is also needed to maximize (but still not perfect) moral behavior is an environment of norms and laws which will provide the necessary 'carrots and sticks' to encourage ethical actions and discourage unethical conduct. Hence, a conscience is a necessary but not a sufficient condition for moral action.

To create a structural correlative of a conscience in a corporation means to establish a form of control of the corporation which will produce the same results as a well-formed conscience. This means installing in controlling positions in the corporate hierarchy individuals who represent those social concerns which constitute the common good of society.[399]

One group of these individuals would be the workers. Workers are a necessary part of any firm and have contributed their labor, time and often their health and lives to their work. Moreover, workers and their wellbeing are part of the common good can be harmed and, of course, benefitted, by the actions of the corporation and as such must be protected by having worker representatives on the board of directors of the firm. Workers could then speak and act directly to protect their interests especially since they would have more complete information about the actions of the corporation. Workers would have the right to vote on any proposed action of the firm if their legitimate interests would be impacted negatively.

However, worker representation alone on the board of directors is not sufficient for the creation of an ethical firm. This is so because the interests of workers are not always consistent with the common good. For example, workers may want higher wages but wages that are too high could make the firm less competitive and could ultimately bankrupt the firm. This means that the interests of the stockholders would also have to be represented on the board of directors. Stockholders, in addition to being part of the community and in part constituting the common good, have contributed their capital and as such have a legitimate interest in the performance of the firm.

---

399. Similar claims for different reasons have been made by R. Edward Freeman, *Strategic Management: A Stakeholder Approach*, Boston: Pitman, 1984; Norman E. Bowie, ed, *Business Ethics*, Mass. Blackwell, p. 2002, pp. 19-37.

However, the workers and the stockholders are not the only group that can be harmed by the corporation. The general community would also have to be represented for they too can be harmed by pollution of the environment, poorly designed products and similar problems.

This means that to make the corporation a more moral entity, there must be equal participation of workers, investors and members of the community in general, on the board of directors of the corporation. Management would also be represented since they may be stockholders and are members of the community as well as sources of information about the corporation to help the entire board make rational decisions.

This type of democratic representation would be the institutional correlative to a person's conscience for it will more effectively protect those groups and interest the corporation is most likely to offend. It will be present to protect their interest and at the same time, the general interest for the general interest is constituted, to a large degree, by these three stakeholders.

This democratization of the firm can also be part of a solution to the agent/principal problem. The agent/principal problem is the problem of how to ensure that agents act in the interest of the principal who hired and pays them to do just that. The problem exists because of three other main problems. First, there is the problem of asymmetrical information and knowledge-the agents, the corporate executives, have knowledge and information which the principals (stockholders under the current model) usually do not and as such the employee is in a superior position to his or her employer. Secondly, the agent and principal do not necessarily have the same interests, the agent wants to maximize his or her income while the principal wishes to minimize costs and maximize long term profits and viability. Finally, the entire scenario is in a domain of market and economic uncertainty which exacerbates all variables.[400]

Democratizing the firm minimizes these problems. A democratized firm reduces the information asymmetry which is key to the enabling of the other problems. Most importantly, executive overactive

---

400. Bernstein, Peter L., "The Moral Hazard Economy", Harvard Business Review, pp. 101-3.

self-interest cannot be given the same room to operate in a structure where there is more publicity and transparency of corporate decisions and actions.

This argument for a more democratic corporation is supported by key ethical elements of Rawls' theory of justice, namely his ideas of stability, self-respect and social union. Stability is a basic value for Rawls and deals with the relationship between the theory of justice, human nature and social institutions. A theory of justice is stable according to Rawls if its realization by the society tends to bring about the corresponding sense of justice in people. If we accept as a psychological law that persons tend to support whatever affirms their own good, and Rawls believes his two principles do this, then all will be inclined to support the institutions defined by justice as fairness.[401]

In other words, a stable society is perceived as legitimate by the populace. As such it generates its own support because the basic structure is consistent with human psychology and individuals have internalized the basic values and principles which define the social system.[402] In such a society the members of the community have a conscience which controls individual actions so that their actions do not override common good (as understood by the community.).[403]

Self-respect, according to Rawls, is the most important primary good which he defines as having two aspects. Self-respect includes a person's sense of his own value and that his or her life is worth pursing and that one has confidence in one's ability to fulfill his or her intentions. According to Rawls, without self-respect, nothing will seem worth doing and we sink into apathy. Self-respect contributes to self-esteem, to value oneself as good and competent.

Rawls is clear that persons in the original position would choose the two principles primarily on the basis that it guarantees self-respect, among the other primary goods. Self-respect, therefore, presupposes certain liberties and rights guaranteed by Rawls' first principle.

---

401. Rawls, John, *A Theory of Justice*, rev., Cambridge: Harvard University Press, 1999, pp. 119, 398.
402. Rawls, John, *Collected Papers*, Cambridge: Harvard University Press, 1999, p. 171.
403. Bell, Daniel, *The Coming of the Post-Industrial Society*, New York: Basic Books, 1973, pp. 270-98.

A component of self-respect is the acknowledgment by others that one's life and work are worthwhile. Our beliefs and judgments about ourselves are predominantly determined by how others view and judge us. They admire us more if our activity is complex and requires talent and is for a good purpose. This admiration is enhanced to the degree the activity is of our own choosing because merit or praise, just as blame, presupposes free-choice in some sense.

Rawls takes it as general fact that "other things equal, human beings enjoy the exercise of their realized capacities...and this enjoyment increases the more the capacity is realized, or the greater its complexity."[404] That is, ceteris paribus, people would generally prefer to play chess over checkers. The Aristotelian Principle is related to Rawls' conception of self-respect in that the Aristotelian principle can contribute to the sense of competence. To be sure, the ceteris paribus clause is important since if one failed at chess more than at checkers one would tend to prefer checkers. According to Rawls, complex activities are more enjoyable because they satisfy the desire for variety of experience. Some have questioned whether the Aristotelian principle is generally true, but if it is true in, when successfully applied, be seen as specifying two conditions for fully human activity, complexity and diversity.

Given the above understanding of self-respect, then clearly one's confidence in one's self-worth is diminished if the work activity is imposed on one from the outside by persons and forces one has little or no control over. But this is the condition of most employees in most corporations where the employee has no direct say in the policy decisions of his or her firm, nor about the nature and conditions of their role in the corporation. Though the worker invests a large share of his or her life in the company, they have almost no direct decision making power over the conditions upon which their happiness in work depends, he or she has no direct access to the management which affects him as a worker and consumer. To the managers and stockholders, the worker is just one more element in the assembly line.

Hence, self-respect and the Aristotelian principle are consistent with the idea of worker participation in the running of the firm. The

---

404. Rawls, *Theory*, op. cit., p. 374.

empowerment of workers adds meaningful complexity into the life of work as demanded by the Aristotelian principle and so enhanced the self-respect of workers.

The next concept in Rawls for employee rights is based on the Rawlsian idea of social union. This idea of mutual support of the just individual and the just society Rawls' calls "social union."[405] For Rawls, a society which fully implements justice as fairness will be a well-ordered society which would be conducive to a genuine community or social union. Such a society would be seen as a voluntary association among free persons for mutual advantage and where the basic structure is seen as embodying these values. It is a community where individuals have shared goals and enjoy one another's abilities and individuality. Rawls adds that when persons are secure in the exercise of their own powers, they are disposed to appreciate the contribution of others. Hence social union would obviously imply the implementation of the Aristotelian Principle and exemplify the Kantian ideal of autonomy where persons can express their nature as free and equal moral persons.

By contrast, a society where individuals try to maximize their wealth and see others and institutions as merely means to personal affluence, Rawls terms a "private society." In such a society, "each person assesses social arrangements solely as a means to his private aims. No one takes account of the good of others (and) institutions are not thought to have any value in themselves"[406] Such a society would be unstable and one of increased conflict and would be the antithesis of social union.

Given the current system of corporate ownership and management, Rawls ideal of social union seems impossible. Even in a well-ordered society where the two principles are fully implemented, the current world of economic activity and corporations would seem to be closer to what Rawls calls a private society.

There is also empirical support that contemporary workers are interested in more than only wages. Research shows that workers are more productive when they are consulted and treated with re-

---

405. Ibid., pp. 456-7.
406. Ibid., p. 457.

spect.[407]

In the interest of clarity, we need to consider other alternatives for making the firm more ethical and law binding.

Another proposal for improving corporate behavior is through outside public directors.[408] The role of these public directors is to be an ethical watchdog on the affairs of the firm and be available for consultation with employees.

The strength of this idea lies in that the public director has no financial interest in the corporation and can be, in theory, an objective watchdog of corporate activities. However, the proposal makes the determination of the public interest an interpretation of one individual, the public director. More importantly, there is the problem of selecting and maintaining the independence and moral integrity of the director. Moreover, this approach would not enhance the self-respect of the workers to the same degree as worker participation.

Another approach that has been suggested is the formulation of code of ethics for each corporation. A code of ethics which is followed and implemented would surely help make firms more ethical.

A code of ethics would surely be part of making corporations more moral but it can hardly be the best solution. First, there is the problem of moral relativism; can there be one code of ethics for all firms in all societies? Even if this problem could be answered, there is the question of what is in the code of ethics, who writes the code and how it is promulgated? Most importantly, there is still the problem of motivating persons to conform to the code, discovering when it has been violated and enforcing it. Finally, a code does not enhance the self-respect of the employees as directly participating in the running of the firm.

Another objection to the model of corporate governance defended here is that government law and regulation is sufficient to control the actions of corporations. There are several theoretical and pragmatic problems with this approach. First, as the current financial crisis and other corporate scandals show, this is simply not the case.

---

407. Ackoff, Russell L., *Re-Creating the Corporation*, New York: Oxford University Press, 1999, pp. 25-43; Werhane, Patricia, & R. Edward Freeman, eds, *The Blackwell Encyclopedia of Business Ethics*, Malden; Blackwell Publishers, 1997, p. 622.
408. Stone, Christopher, *Where the Law Ends*, New York: Harper & Row, 1975, pp. 122-4.

In addition, as has been argued in previous chapters, the current political system is still under the dominant influence of the entrenched economic elite and more and radical campaign reform and the right to political leave is necessary before legislative enactments would perform the necessary social functions of controlling corporate actions.[409] Moreover with the growing global economy and the multinationals, legal control of corporate entities which can flee to any part of the world to find cheap labor and corrupt governments is becoming increasingly difficult.

These problems are exacerbated by the theoretical limitations of positive law. Legislative enactments are limited in that law as a system of general rules cannot deal perfectly with all specific circumstances. Further, law is by nature a reaction to a problem that has already occurred, and thus will always allow certain immoral actions to occur until the legislature acts. Thirdly, law is usually negative in formulation, telling what not to do, but moral behavior does not just involve the avoidance of evil, but the promotion of good to some degree. Moreover, the law can never completely express the full content of morality, but only that enforceable component; being moral means more than just being law-binding.

In addition, even when there is legislation which is passed, its implementation is thwarted by what has come to be called "regulatory capture."[410] Once congress enacts laws, regulatory agencies are engaged to implement the legislation by making various decision and rules. The regulatory agencies often have substantial discretion and often function as legislative and judicial agencies. Regulatory capture exists when government agencies which exist to regulate corporations for the public interest are often improperly influenced by the very industry it needs to control which then shapes regulation to promote the individual interest of the firm even when in opposition to the common good. This influence can be exercised indirectly by campaign contributions to the political elite which then selects regulators sympathetic to various industries and/or by promise of lucrative employment to underpaid government regulators or, of course,

---

409. Greider, William, *Come Home America*, New York: Rodale, 2009, p.225.
410. Talbott, John, R., *The 86 Biggest Lies on Wall Street*, New York: Seven Stories Press, 2009, pp. 29-31.

by outright bribery of the regulators.

Finally, there are the questions of sufficient motivation and the secrecy of illegal activities. Corporate leaders are often not sufficiently motivated to act legally or morally because the legal system does not provide sufficient penalties to act as a deterrent. In addition, the bureaucracy can act as a shield of anonymity protecting malefactors. Moreover, the anonymity problem is exacerbated by the problem of secrecy which illegal actions require. Participation of employees and the community in the very heart of corporate decision-making will greatly reduce the opportunity for anonymity and secrecy and thus reduce illegality.

Milton Friedman has objected to theories of the corporation similar to the one presented here.[411] Defending what he calls the "stockholder theory" against the stakeholder theory or the "socially responsible corporation" Friedman argues that the corporation has no moral or social responsibility because the corporation is not a real person and only real persons have moral responsibility.[412]

Friedman further argues that in a free market capitalist system, the executives and managers of a firm are the employees of the stockholders and their only responsibility is to increase profits, within the parameters of the law, the reason stockholders invested in the company to begin with. To take into account social responsibility, such as reducing pollution beyond what the law requires, or hiring the poor and not the most qualified, would be inefficient, reduce the profits of the company and thus harm the shareholders. For Friedman, it is the job of the government not corporations to make socially responsible laws to protect society.

For Friedman, to talk of the stakeholder model or the socially responsible corporation is to move from capitalism to socialism. To talk of the social responsibility of the corporation beyond obeying the law is to politicize the firm and reduce the power of the free market and this, Friedman fears, will lead to socialism. Friedman believes that the only correct way to require change in the behavior of firms is to pass new laws, which is the function of government, not

---

411. Friedman, Milton, "The Social Responsibility of Business is to Increase Its Profits," *New York Times Magazine*, Sept., 13, 1970, pp. 17-21.

412. Cf., Freeman, R.E., *Strategic Management*, Boston: Pitman, 1984.

the managers.

Furthermore, Friedman adds, that corporate executives simply do not have the knowledge to deal with the ethical and social problems. Again, for Friedman, this is the function of government and other social institutions. Friedman's arguments defending the traditional view of the corporation are significant and demand a reply.

First, Friedman's charge of socialism raises several points. To argue that departures from the traditional stockholder model to the stakeholder model will lead to socialism is arbitrary and an example of black and white thinking. It also begs the question that all forms of socialism (which he does not examine) are inferior to the current corporate paradigms. Socialism is usually defined as a social arrangement where that there is no private ownership of the means of production but rather government or social ownership of all (major) economic establishments and resources. The stakeholder model is far from such a social order and moreover and Friedman ignores that there are many different social and economic arrangements possible, within the large middle ground between the extremes of traditional capitalism and full socialism.

Friedman's charge of socialism also brings up the issue of the status of property rights, the corporation and the US Constitution. The Constitution does not say anything specifically about employee rights nor are business corporations explicitly mentioned. Chief Justice John Marshall of the Supreme Court in the landmark decision of *Dartmouth v. Woodward* (1819) interpreted the contract clause of the Constitution (Article I, section 10, clause 1) to mean that the corporation is "an artificial being, invisible, intangible, and existing only in contemplation of law." Later in 1886 (Santa Clara County v. Southern Pacific Railroad, 118 U.S. 394), the Supreme Court declared the corporation a "person" with the rights of the Fourteenth Amendment including the right to property and due process.

One central period of the Supreme Court known as the Lochner era had a dramatic impact on workers. In *Lochner v. New York* (1905), the court ruled that New York state law limiting working hours in bakeries was unconstitutional, claiming, among other reasons, that it was a violation of the freedom of contract. This questionable interpretation was abandoned during the Depression when the court allowed unprecedented federal regulation of the economy.

More recently, the Supreme Court has interpreted the idea of the right of eminent domain in a manner which can be used to justify the restructuring of the corporation. The Fifth Amendment of the US Constitution reads "...nor shall private property be taken for public use without just compensation." Eminent domain is the right for the government to take private property for public use if proper compensation is made. The right of eminent domain places an important limit on private property but what this limit is has varied in constitutional interpretations.

The original interpretation of the Fifth Amendment was narrowly construed to mean that the land and property taken must be used for a public purpose such as a road, military installation and the like. In rulings such as *Berman v. Parker* (1954), the Supreme Court interpreted the eminent domain clause more expansively allowing the taking of property to enable private developers to remove blighted areas and allow economic development. The court held that "public use" can be interpreted to be any action which promotes the "health, welfare, safety, moral, social, economic, political or aesthetic ends."[413] In *Strickley v. Highland Boy Gold Mining Co.* (1906), the court ruled that "public use" does not necessarily imply actual public use such as a highway, but some action that is of use or promotes the good of the general public. In a case more relevant here, *Hawaii Housing Authority v. Midkiff* (1984) concerned the Hawaiian government actions on the Island of Oahu. The government deemed the land ownership on this island to be so concentrated in only a few owners that it constituted and oligopoly. To rectify this problem, the Hawaiian government increased the number of owners by granting land to previous tenants on the land. The Supreme Court saw this as constitutional. The promotion of economic development was interpreted even more widely in the *Kelo v. City of New London* (2005) where public use was interpreted more expansively to include any legitimate public purpose.[414]

The proposal for employee and community participation in the running of the corporation does not imply the taking of property. However, it does place a limit on property but this limit is consistent with the right of eminent domain as interpreted by the court

413. www.law.cornell.edu/supct-
414. Ibid., p.2.

rulings explained above. These court rulings clearly expanded the idea of public use to encompass a public good and the preservation of the common good including health, safety and moral concerns. As argued above, the democratic corporation seeks the empowerment of workers, among other ends, to make the corporation more moral and law abiding, two essential components of the common good. To follow the logic of eminent domain, the "compensation" to the corporation would be the improved legal and moral stating of the firm, greater legitimacy and, if the empirical findings are correct, improved productivity and profits as well.

Part of the empirical support for the democratic corporation as efficient and as not necessarily a form of socialism is the experiment in Germany. Germany is by all accounts a vigorous capitalist state even though the German law (mitbestimmung) passed in 1974 requires worker representatives on all firms with over 500 employees.[415]

Secondly, to argue as Friedman does that only real persons can act in a socially responsible manner seems simply false. Corporations are considered legal persons and are led by real persons who certainly can act morally. Friedman seems to see the corporation as an amoral machine but that he has not proved. For even if it is viewed as a machine, it is a machine which can be controlled by persons and if something can be controlled by persons it is subject to moral norms.

Thirdly, Friedman believes it is the function of government and the law to make laws dealing with issues of social responsibility. However, as argued above, the law is not alone adequate to ensure the moral behavior of the firm.

Fourth, to argue that managers are employees of the stockholders is simply to restate the current model, not to argue against the reform. In fact, in cases such as *A. P. Smith v. Barlow*, the courts have upheld the right of managers to contribute to charitable causes without the expressed approval of the stockholders.

To argue that executives lack knowledge to act morally is arbitrary and, if so, is really a reason for the model of the corporation defended here. Although theoretical ethics is a field which requires some special philosophical training, acting morally usually does not. Managers can ask for the input of various experts and with the input

---

415. Kuhne, Robert J., *Co-Determination in Business*, New York: Praeger, 1980, pp.28-39; Cf. Pope Benedict XVI, "Caritas in Veritate" encyclical.

of the community and the employees can generate corporate actions that are consistent with these findings. Friedman simply assumes that the stockholders are concerned about one thing-profit, but this is often not true. Stockholders are often interested in questions of pollution, the rights of workers, etc., even if these concerns go beyond the requirements of law.[416]

Friedman' traditional model of the firm cannot adequately deal with the problem discussed in the current crisis that some corporations are "too big to fail." To say that some firm or institution is too big to fail means it would have vast negative consequences on stakeholders and society in general if it did fail. But if a firm is too big to fail than it has moved from the domain of private property into the realm of the social property. As such it has acquired a quasi-political status and as such it must share the governance of the political institutions. Friedman's model would presumably let these firms fail but that option has problems as well. If failure is allowed in institutions such as major banks and insurance firms, it could cause major social disruptions which could have severe political consequences. Secondly, if firms are not allowed to grow, given the reality of global competition of multinationals, domestic corporations would be at a clear competitive disadvantage.

Corporations are not eternal Platonic structures but human constructs created to achieve some goals. For the corporation to survive and thrive it must adapt to its changing social and moral environment and to this it must change and evolve to better fit into the new cultural context which places increasing value on the dignity and self-respect of workers and all persons. The democratic model of the corporation does not treat people as merely a means or tools of the firm but as ends in themselves with rights and dignity as human beings. A corporation which embodies these values will have greater legitimacy which will enhance its long term survivability and flourishing.

---

416. Cf. Pfeffer, Jeffrey, "Shareholders First? Not So Fast" *Harvard Business Review*, July-August, 2009, pp. 90-91; Michael Kinsley, ed., *Creative Capitalism*, New York: Simon & Schuster, 2008, pp. 7-16, et al.

# Chapter 14. The Contradictions of Libertarianism

"Freedom is not enough."
— President Lyndon B. Johnson

Many political philosophers of the left, right and center have built their theories on arbitrary assumptions, intuitions or prejudices. Some, such as the Tea Party and the Republican Party, start from their understanding of liberty, others, such as the Democratic Party, start from some conception of equality, still others start with some theory of virtue and so on. Not surprisingly, they all develop inconsistent theories which seem to cancel each other out. What these philosophers are seemingly oblivious to is the fact that all governments and societies must meet empirical challenges to survive and flourish. Proponents of these theories indulge in abstract conceptual argument and tend to ignore empirical and social science data which is vitally relevant in the field of political philosophy. Since political philosophy is developed to be implemented, facts, social conditions and tendencies must be considered.

Political theorists seem to have forgotten the generally agreed principle that "ought implies can": if some act or theory of government is presented as morally correct then it must be possible to do the act or implement the theory in a sustainable manner. That is, a political theory, by its very nature if it is plausible must be capable of being implemented and, if it is a stable and coherent theory, continue in its basic structure indefinitely. If, for various reasons, a theory cannot be implemented or when implemented is unsustainable and tends to corrupt and evolve into something inconsistent with the initial formulation of the theory, then there is a serious flaw in the theory. This, as will be shown below, is the case with libertarianism.

Libertarianism is a political theory which is fundamentally flawed in that it makes claims which are, when implemented, shown to be, in time, contradictory. The claims are not necessarily logically contradictory but pragmatically contradictory. Pragmatic contradiction is here understood as occurring when a theory is put into practice it has the opposite or inconsistent results of what is intended or desired by the adherents of the theory. In other words, the goals of the theory cannot be reached as the theory assumes but rather contradictory goals are reached when the theory is institutionalized.

There are of course different versions of libertarianism but in essence this view holds that persons have certain inalienable rights and that these rights and only these rights must be protected by the government.[417] This basic idea is complex and its full meaning is debated but for present purposes this idea is spelled out in the following doctrines: the right to freedom, the right to self-ownership, the right to property, the right to a free market, and the right to a minimal state to protect these rights. The right to freedom is usually defined as the negative right to non-interference by others in the exercise of one's autonomy; one has a right to action to the degree one does not harm others or restrict their rights. The right to self-ownership means one owns one's body and one's labor and has the right to control it as one sees fit including all forms of sexual relations between consenting adults in private and economic relations in the free market.

Libertarianism stands for not only the separation of church and state, but for greater separation of ethics and politics. They claim that many laws are a reflection of legal moralism, the theory that laws should enforce religious morality to defend many laws such as the condemnation of gay marriage, prostitution, etc., which violates, according to the libertarians, basic human rights. (This aspect of libertarianism is not critiqued here.) The right to property means

---

417. Machan, Tibor, ed., *The Libertarian Reader*, Totowa, NJ: Rowman and Littlefield, 1982.

people have the right to own, transfer, buy and sell property as they see fit. This right is not limited by the poverty or needs of others. The right to a free market means the government cannot restrict the free flow of goods and services, production or prices except to prevent fraud and coercion.

The right to a minimal state means the state cannot be anything like the modern welfare state. The welfare state through various forms of taxation provides social services such as education, health, social security, unemployment insurance, and other services which, according to libertarians, violate property and other rights. The only legitimate state, as the libertarians see it, is the night watchman state which protects the right to life, freedom and property and does not take wealth from the haves and give to the have-nots. Libertarians see the welfare state as government essentially stealing money from the wealthy through taxes and giving it to others who do not deserve it. They believe government should simply protect human rights and liberties against criminals and foreign attack, leaving everything else to the personal free decisions of individuals in a free market. Government would be a democratic system which consists of the minimum number of individuals and institutions consisting of the military, police and the courts to protect the minimal rights of the people.

These ideas seem attractive to many but the libertarian theory of government is simplistic, abstract and oblivious of crucial social and human realities. The problems of libertarianism are legion and many have outlined these flaws but what has not been examined are the flaws which emerge when the theory is implemented for it is in the implementation stage that certain realities impinge on the theory and radically reveal its internal contradictions. There are implications of libertarianism in the realm of politics, economy, the military and society which make manifest its weaknesses.

A libertarian society would certainly not be a meritocracy. A meritocracy is a social system which assigns individuals to positions in a society based solely on criteria which enables them to perform their function in the most efficient manner. These criteria usually are intelligence, education, skill, experience, industriousness, motivation and a moral character. These traits have been found to provide for high level of performance in meeting the needs of individuals and society with the least depletion of societal and individual resources.

Meritocracy is crucial because a modern society must maximize the acquisition of knowledge due to its highly scientific and technological nature. A high tech society requires high educational levels and training from most employees, but access to education in a libertarian society would depend on one's social class and economic means. The affluent and middle class could likely afford private education but many of the poor and those from the lower middle class could not and the quality of the education of the affluent would outstrip that of the middle class. This would transform a class society into a virtual caste society, a society with almost no class mobility for many.

Meritocracy requires class mobility for it requires that individuals most qualified fill any relevant position in society.[418] A fully actualized meritocratic society would entail what Rawls calls the "fair equality of opportunity" to education but libertarianism supports only a formal equality of opportunity.[419] Formal equality of opportunity is the legalistic equality of rights on paper where no one is legally denied employment or access to education on the basis of properties not relevant to job performance, such as race, gender, religion, ethnicity, class origins, and sexual orientation. That is, if society is, as Rawls believes, analogous to a race, a fair race is one where all start at the same starting line, but because of different social classes, family circumstances and natural talents, people do not in fact start at the same point. Fair or substantive equal opportunity includes the formal sense of opportunity but adds the equalization of the social starting conditions of all regardless of the class of origin.

To deny high level of education to some social classes would deny the full development of the potential of individuals in these classes. Of course, there are other reasons why this would be immoral as Rawls argues, it would deny these persons rights they have as free and equal individuals, it would also be irrational because these individuals could not contribute their maximal level of skill and talent

---

418. A meritocratic society does not necessarily exclude various welfare programs such as those which would be justified by Rawls' theory but these would be in addition to a predominantly merit based society.

419. Rawls, John, *A Theory of Justice*, rev. ed., Cambridge: Harvard University Press, 1999, pp. 62-3.

to society and as such these talents would be at least in part wasted. These segments of society could contain potential that would greatly enhance the economic, technological and other aspects of society but lack of educational opportunity leaves potential as mere potential.

Without meritocracy many persons would not be in the pool of applicants for important social positions. Such a society would not be able choose the most qualified to fill significant political, professional and other positions. A society would not be as efficient as it could be in the functioning of its economy, military and governmental operations (including the rights which the libertarians cherish, see below).

The libertarian dogmatic belief in the absence of regulation of the economy is a major facet of libertarian philosophy. They claim that the free market and the invisible hand of Adam Smith are sufficient to run an efficient economy. However, among other problems, without regulation, there would be nothing to stop the formation of monopolies and massive conglomerates. Monopolies, in addition to controlling the market and the process, would reduce technological innovation since innovation is primarily caused by competition between firms to maximize profits and market share. Once again, this would place the country in a negative relation in global competition with other societies.

The lack of education for many would also exacerbate the asymmetries which exist in the so-called free market. Exchanges in the market would place in even weaker position the uneducated or poorly educated and the poor for they would not have the information equal to the sellers or employers. Moreover, since the poor have less savings they have fewer options and often must take jobs due to lack of means to wait for a better offer. This would further impoverish the lower classes and create social inefficiencies for talents would not be maximally utilized.

Contrary to their claim, libertarian theory, if implemented, would lead to the creation of a government unable to perform its functions in a fully rational and efficient manner or even protect the rights libertarians value. A political system must perform certain necessary functions to be considered a government. First, it must be able to control a certain geographic area where the population lives. In order to control an area the society must be able to adapt to its external physical and social environment of other social groups.[420] All enduring social systems provide for group survival by successfully competing with hostile social groups and by allocating resources, extracting the necessities of life from the environment and producing the goods and services required or creating the framework for their efficient production.

Successful adaptation requires sufficient knowledge and resources to help provide for the needs and survival of the members of society. The ability of a community to adapt is enhanced by the expansion of the knowledge base and the resulting development of new technology can play a pivotal role in controlling the physical environment and extracting new resources to provide for social needs. But a libertarian society, being at least in part non-meritocratic, would have negative impact on the economy and not be maximally able to provide for these conditions of social survival and progress since the lack of high quality universal education would not maximize knowledge or problem solving skills. Further, since a libertarian society would not be efficient in providing the goods and services in general or maximally use the talents of individuals, there would be an increase in poverty among certain sectors of society. With poverty comes crime and an increase in an inefficient prison population as well as a loss of legitimacy (see below).

Another consequence of a non-meritocratic society is that it would not be able to compete successfully with other societies economically, militarily or culturally. Other societies which had a meritocracy would maximize human potential in knowledge, technology and efficient economic production and thus would be more successful in global competition for resources and technology development. Given these inefficiencies and the freedom of movement, a libertarian society would lose the elite educated population (and other classes) to more affluent countries.

The libertarian society would also be a society that was at a disadvantage in military conflicts with other societies. Failure to develop human intelligence maximally across society would mean possibly inferior personnel in the military as well as inferior technology. An

---

420. Parsons, Talcott, *The Social System*, New York: The Free Press, 1951, pp.191-203.

elite would likely prefer its own members in the leadership to p. tect its position and thus would choose loyal members rather tha. the most qualified. Even if it did chose the most qualified, given the pool chosen from who had an education would be smaller than the pool if there were universal education access to equally effective education.

Culturally, in the arts a libertarian society would also be in a disadvantaged. Diminished educational opportunities and lack of social connections to the elite would reduce the cultural opportunities for funding and institutions which would nurture the arts from the lower classes.

To implement this theory in the real world means to implement it in the existing world of class divided society of individuals with widely divergent education, wealth and power. Since even libertarians grant that people are self-interested these individuals would seek to protect their interests by themselves running for public office or selecting their own to do so. Further since private limits on campaign financing would be abolished and given that individuals are not perfectly moral, this means that in short order the political system would be captured by the economic elite who would draft laws and structure the political system to correspond to their interests.

This capture of the institutions of government would threaten the freedoms libertarians cherish. A government run by an elite which, as libertarians themselves often emphasize, all persons, is self-interested and morally limited, would rule in its own favor and gradually reduce the freedoms of the middle and lower classes, especially as the lower classes become increasingly a threat to their hegemony. Libertarians would agree that the basic self-interest of persons would trump any interest they may have initially in any ideology.

This domination of government by one class and its consequences is explored by the theory of the "iron law of oligarchy."[421] The iron law of oligarchy states in essence that all political systems tend to develop into oligarchies. An oligarchy is a type of government where a small wealthy elite has most of the power. Although the larger thesis that all governments develop into oligarchies is more controversial and not defended here, the aspect of the law of oligarchy relevant

---

421. Michels, Robert, *Political Parties*, New York: The Free Press, 1968.

.e is the more modest claim that in every large-scale bureaucratic government, an educated elite is necessary since a bureaucracy is necessary to run such a government and society. Given the need for an educated elite and the general ignorance (given the absence of universal high quality education under libertarianism) and apathy of the alienated masses, power will tend to concentrate in an elite which will seek to keep and expand its power. When one combines the self-interest of humans, the need for bureaucracy with an uneducated and uninformed and impoverished general populace, the government has a tendency to become ruled by a small group which will rule not in the general good but in their own self-interest.

Although the law of oligarchy has been criticized, it plausibility in this context of libertarianism is more apparent.[422] Given the absence of a meritocracy and the consequent absence of equal access to equal education for all classes, there would inevitably be a tendency to concentration of power in an educated elite. Moreover, the law of oligarchy is supported by another tendency that libertarianism will expand the concentration of the media. The deregulation of the economy, a central element of libertarianism, would lead to greater media concentration. The free press, the fourth estate, is essential for the communication of ideas and of critiquing the government. As the economy increases into conglomeration and monopoly formation the media would likely become dominated by the elite and offer little criticism of the government. This would inevitably lead to lack of diversity of opinions but no lack of opinions supportive of the status quo. The government would have no fear from the media in expanding the power of the elite and undermining the freedoms of the other classes. Control the flow of information is a presupposition and enhances oligarchy and so increases the likelihood of the law of oligarchy.

The elimination of all limits on election campaign contributions, already started in *Citizens United v FEC*, which libertarians demand, would further enhance the domination of a relatively closed elite and enable oligarchy. The economic elite would support those candidates sympathetic to its needs and interests that others would

---

422. Leach, Darcy, "The Iron Law of What Again? Conceptualizing Oligarchy Across Organizational Forms", Sociological Theory, Sep. 2005; 23,3, pp. 312-37.

not have a fair chance at being elected into government. Evidence is overwhelming that those candidates who spend the most amount of money usually win elections and given the concentration and control of the media makes the election of the elite a virtual certainty.[423] The massive concentration of wealth and resulting political power to protect this wealth and power especially against the growing masses of impoverished workers who are preoccupied with simply trying to survive and increasingly leave the political elite to perpetuate their power in a virtually absolute form.

The law of oligarchy is also enabled and exacerbated by the problem of "concentrated benefits and diffused costs."[424] Libertarians use this to critique the welfare state but it would be an even greater problem in the minimal state. The government is capable of giving special interests (political supporters, constituents, etc.) tax breaks and other enormous financial benefits, and, because the cost is spread over the large population, the voter hardly feels the impact of the cost of these special favors which comes in the form of a slight increase in taxation.

This fact adds to the corruptibility of government, which would increase under libertarian government. Due to the fact that large segments of the population would lack the education and the leisure time to keep informed of government activities, they would offer little or no resistance to these policies. Since the government would be staffed by an inbreed cast system, the tendency to give favors to its own class would be even a greater reality. Again violating the rule of law and reducing the freedoms of the non-elite masses.

Another problem with modern bureaucratic governments which tend to oligarchy is that of the "iron triangle."[425] The iron triangle is the relationship that allegedly often exists between Congress, the regulatory bureaucracy and the interest group or industry the bureaucracy is, in theory, regulating. This relationship is also known as "regulatory capture" when the control of the regulatory agency is taken over by the industry it is supposed to regulate. This means, in

---

423. Goidel, Robert K., et al., *Money Matters*, Totowa, NJ: Rowman & Littlefield, 1999, p.12.
424. Boaz, David, *Libertarianism*, New York: The Free Press, 1997, p. 194.
425. Ibid. pp.197-8; John R. Talbott, *The 89 Biggest Lies on Wall Street*, New York: Seven Stories Press, 2009, pp. 28-9.

short, that the regulators will tend to regulate in the interest of the industry not the consumer and the common good as the law specifies. This is what President Eisenhower referred to as the influence of the "military industrial complex" except that the influence goes beyond those areas.[426]

One way this triangular relationship is established is through campaign contributions. Corporations contribute funds for election of politicians who after they are elected influence regulators to rule in favor of the industry. Another way this relationship manifests itself is known as "the revolving door." In this situation congressmen, senators and their staffers who write the regulations go to work as a lobbyist for the special interest in the private sector for much larger salaries for the inside information and contacts he or she can provide the industry. Once again, the problem of concentrated benefits to the former staffer or senator or representative and the special interest, and diffused costs to the general public, plays a role here as well. These problems would be maximized due to the absence of a meritocracy and the control the government elite would have over the media.

Although the "iron" part of the "iron triangle" is not proven in all cases, there is evidence of such relationships existing to various degrees. The thesis here does not require that the strong version of the claim be established but only to indicate that such a relationship is more likely to develop under a libertarian system. To be sure, the libertarian ideology is against regulation except in some specific cases however, even these cases would be subject to the influence of the oligarchical elite since the government elite would be increasingly drawn from the same social class. Moreover, as suggested below, the concentration of and corporate control of the media and the absence of anti-trust legislation and total freedom in campaign contributions would empower smaller number of corporations whose influence would increase on all aspects of society.

Another concern with government bureaucracy is what Milton Friedman called the "tyranny of the status quo" the tendency for programs and bureaucracies, once created, to continue in existence

---

426. Eisenhower, Dwight, President, "Farewell Address to the Nation," 1/17/61.

even when their need is nonexistent.[427] Sunset laws, laws passed with the intent to eliminate these bureaucracies, tend not to be effective and so bureaucracy increases. Friedman used this to critique the government under the welfare state but this tendency would be even greater in a libertarian system. Although the libertarian system would have a different bureaucracy, it could have an even larger one due to the dominance of an elite who would pursue their interests without limits since the lower classes lack would lack education and the time to pursue public matters.

A libertarian government that is dominated by an elite would weaken its own legitimacy. Legitimacy is the idea that the power wielded by the government is perceived by the majority of the populace as morally and legally justified and generally as working for the common good. In other words, legitimacy is based on the perception that the government has the right to rule because it serves the common good, not exclusively the good of the governing class.

The lack of legitimacy would first be caused by the lack of universal education. Universal education, besides developing human intelligence and potential, also performs the functions of socialization. Human beings, because of their rationality and ability to organize and learn, are remarkably plastic and capable of adapting to a diverse range of environments and conditions by, in effect, creating their own environment, a cultural system. What adaptations and changes are made and how they are implemented is in part determined by the nature and effectiveness of socialization, the complex psychological and social processes which transmit the cultural system from one generation to the next.

A central function of socialization is the creation of sufficient motivation of the members to support and maintain the beliefs and values of the social system. Some of these beliefs will be moral beliefs which deal with the proper relationship between members and the regulation of means to achieve goals. The internalization of ethical norms and customs are central for legitimacy and social control where the majority of individuals accept the basic structure of the community, and work to support it against enemies internal and external to it. The socialization or internalization and institutionaliza-

---

427. Boaz, op. cit., pp. 196-7.

~ion of these basic values and beliefs are the necessary conditions for social functioning at any level. Successful socialization would limit potentially disruptive antisocial behavior. Human drives need to be shaped to conform to social system and not destabilize it through antisocial behavior.

For socialization to be successful, a society must produce, nurture and educate new members of that society. Without socialization into the cultural system society would cease to function efficiently, be maladaptive and incapable of confronting hostile groups.

Another cause of loss of legitimacy and social solidarity is due to the fact that libertarianism also ignores past injustices. The socioeconomic starting points of persons in society may be the result of past injustices, some of a systemic form such as genocide, slavery, racism, sexism, prejudice, ignorance, violence and ordinary criminality. To ignore these pervasive and profound injustices and structure a political system oblivious to these realities is to base a system on an unstable foundation which will contaminate the system with the illegitimacy of the status quo it was based on. Equal opportunity and welfare programs are seen by non-libertarians as, in part, a response to these injustices of the past but not open to the libertarian ideology.

Political systems in addition to controlling a geographic area, must also formulate, promulgate, interpret and enforce legal norms. In order to regulate human interaction, a stable society must promulgate norms viewed as legitimate by the society. The implementation and enforcement of these norms require an adjudication process provided by a court system to resolve conflicts between members. Within a cast society as libertarianism would produce, the legislative, executive and judicial systems would be dominated by the economic elite.

The rule of law ideal is part of the libertarian ideal. A society of ordered freedom and economic stability and efficiency cannot exist without all members of a society obeying the law where no one is above or below the law but all are subject to various forms of punishment for violating the law. A legal system as seen by the rule of law ideal must be a complete and consistent interrelated network of norms specifying how members of the community should behave

and how the legal system and governmental institutions themselv
should function. The rule of law stabilizes social interaction and pro
vides norms for social order. The idea of an institution itself would
be impossible without the rule of law for institutions are defined by
rules. The importance of the rule of law as setting limits on governmental power and promoting a stable social context within which
persons can pursue their goals with some security and predictability.

Inevitably, given human nature, self-interest, the incompleteness
and vagueness of the law, the subjectivity of interpretation, and one
class domination of government, the political system would drift toward favoring its own class and undermine the rule of law. The libertarian government would draw members of the judiciary from the
same class and would tend to formulate and implement laws which
directly or indirectly favor the ruling elite which would increasingly
alienate vast segments of society and further delegitimize the political structure. This would further destabilize society and greatly increase the likelihood of crime and revolt.

Another concern is whether a minimal government required by
libertarianism would be able to deal adequately with emergencies
that may arise. Natural disasters such as hurricanes and earthquakes
and social and economic crises require governmental planning, coordination and resources that libertarian government would likely
not have. The lack of full maximization of knowledge and technology
would also contribute to problems dealing with emergencies. Weak
legitimacy would also contribute to the problem for it would make
marshaling resources difficult the populace lacking sufficient socialization to establish a sense of community.

The libertarian society with weakened legitimacy would also
be at a disadvantage in another emergency, war. A society that was
dominated by a self-interested elite would increasingly lose legitimacy and be further destabilized by lacking the motivation for citizens to enlist and fight the enemy. As in the case of other emergencies, the libertarian night watchman government focused on keeping
government spending at the minimum would be handicapped by the
lack of a standing military of sufficient size, information of various
kinds, contingency planning, coordination protocols and other resources modern non-libertarian governments have. Again, the lack of

universal quality education with its socialization function would place such a society in jeopardy in time of war for a large segment of the society would feel little or no allegiance to the status quo and consequently not oppose the enemy with much enthusiasm, if at all.

A stable and viable form of government must be based on an accurate understanding of human nature. Libertarianism has a pre-scientific view of human nature and human development which undermines its entire paradigm. Their ideal of freedom fails to realize that freedom needs certain social, political, cultural and psychological conditions to be actualized. Libertarians seem to hold the view that no matter what familial, social, economic and political conditions one is born into, one can rise up and achieve almost anything if he or she sets their minds to it in the right libertarian political context. This 'pulling oneself up by one's bootstraps' philosophy seems to be contradicted by overwhelming scientific, sociological and psychological evidence that familial and social circumstances (e.g., access to education being an absolute essential) shape human personality, motivation, self-concept, self-esteem, criminal activity, mental health and life prospects. Rawls is clear that family background and other social and economic factors, which chance events he calls "the lottery of life" have an immense impact on human achievement.[428] Ignoring these factors would exacerbate social inequality to the point of destabilizing society for reasons discussed below. The fact is some people don't even have boots to pull on.

A fundamental problem is the libertarian understanding of liberty which, when implemented, would reduce freedom of the lower social classes. Let us define freedom as the scope and number of options, possibilities and actions open to persons. The libertarian understanding of liberty is that of negative liberty, the right to be free from interference from others and the government. But libertarians seem to be blind to the danger to liberty from poverty, disease, ignorance, social prejudice and customs of tribalism, racism and sexism and dysfunctional family backgrounds. Obviously these factors reduce the number of possible course of actions open to many persons.

Libertarians also do not seem to realize how Rawls' fair equal opportunity would maximize liberty generally. Rawls believes that lib-

---

428. Rawls, op. cit., pp.64, 265.

erty needs certain social conditions such as good family backgrour.
education, health, income security, etc., to be fully developed. If these
conditions do not create obstacles combined with a democratic system which protects the basic human rights, would create maximal
opportunities for free human actions.

Further, the values of liberty and rights would not have what
Rawls calls "equal worth" under a libertarian regime. Privileged individuals would have the resources such as education, health care and
a social network to enhance their political rights to run for public
office, while those less privileged would not.

Finally, libertarians also misread human nature in another basic
way, their emphasis on the importance of the single ideal of liberty.
Humans do tend to value liberty but they also value security, equality, survival, hope, friendship, community, stability, and in general,
happiness. The very starting point of libertarianism is arbitrary and
unfounded.

Decreased legitimacy and increased poverty would increase crime
resulting in a destabilized society. Increased crime would move the
ruling elite to more repressive measures to control the lower classes.
This would be a vicious cycle for it would further weaken legitimacy
which would further increase anti-social activity which would further evoke repressive measures and so on. The libertarian ideal could
easily evolve into a fascist state, the exact opposite of the libertarian
hope.

Libertarians claim that private charity can perform many of the
functions of the welfare state. Although this is true in some cases, the
charity institutions cannot provide free universally high quality education, economy or military. These types of social services can only
be provided by a government which has the vast resources, information and coordination to implement the necessary laws, institutions
to provide the educational opportunities. In addition, the self-interest of people, which the libertarians assume, will keep charity at a
low level.

Finally, libertarianism is irrational in another way. It is irrational
since rational human beings would choose a political system which
is not inconsistent with their survival and welfare. It is irrational to
ignore possible future circumstances which could negatively impact

one's welfare and survivability. Since life is uncertain no one is exempt from financial and other types of problems, it is rational to buy into an insurance policy to protect one against worst case scenarios. This is one of the functions of the welfare state which provides minimum income for unemployment, retirement, etc. Private insurance would not be feasible to provide this security for all since the lower classes could not afford it and, moreover, no matter which class one currently occupies, one could always find oneself in the underclass at some point in the future. Without a safety net poverty would increase, and with poverty comes crime, instability and social unrest.

A libertarian society would also become what Popper called a "closed society."[429] According to Popper, all societies confront problems or obstacles in meeting their needs, whether at a societal or institutional level, hence problem solving must be a key dimension of successful societies. Popper added to this claim his uncontroversial contention that human knowledge is incomplete in all areas, including politics. He reasons from these two facts that a rational society, i.e., a society which acts on the basis of knowledge or warranted beliefs and takes the most efficient means to achieve ends, is one which seeks to maximize problem solving capacities and therefore one which must also maximize knowledge acquisition. Such a society Popper called an "open society" a society which values education and knowledge and is receptive to new ideas, all necessary elements of problem solving and knowledge expansion.

An open society, unlike a closed society, is designed on the model of modern science which, for Popper, is the most successful human enterprise that has ever been developed for solving problems. Science, according to Popper, is an open and rational discipline where all ideas can be entertained and evaluated by rational standards. An open society must be, therefore, Popper argues, a free and democratic society with a free press and a great deal of personal freedom where the power of government is clearly limited and the rule of law is present. It would be a society where the development of knowledge and critical reasoning are valued as key virtues as central to problem solving.

---

429. Popper, Karl, *The Open Society and It's Enemies*, New York: Routledge, 7e, 2002, pp. 12-9.

It has already been established that a libertarian society wou not be able to maximize knowledge. Moreover, a libertarian societ would be a closed society for, as suggested above, the ruling elite would also control the media and the dominant private educational institutions, the economy and, of course, the government. To maintain its control it would need to control the ideas disseminated in the society and so would evolve into a closed society to protect its power. Hence, libertarianism would evolve into a fascistic state of limited freedoms if any, the exact opposite it intends.

These criticisms of libertarianism must not be interpreted as a carte blanche approval of the welfare state status quo. The current welfare system has many deficiencies which the implementation of many of Rawls' ideas, especially of fair equality of opportunity, would go a long way in correcting.

There are, of course, other criticisms of libertarianism others have articulated and need not be repeated here.[430] But given its theory of human nature and freedom and the likely devastating consequences to democracy if it were to be implemented, most of the ideas associated with libertarianism seem destined for the trash bin of history.

---

430. See *Reading Nozick*, Jeffrey Paul, ed.,Totowa, NJ.: Rowman & Littlefield, 1981; Amartya Sen, *The Idea of Justice*, Cambridge: Harvard University Press, 2009.

# BIBLIOGRAPHY

Ackoff, Russell, L., *Re-Creating the Corporation*, New York: Oxford Univ. Press, 1999.

Adler, Stephen J., *The Jury*, New York: Random House, 1994.

Alexander, Herbert, *Financing Politics*, Washington, DC: Congressional Quarterly, 1976.

Alperovitz, Gar, *America Beyond Capitalism*, New York: Wiley, 2006.

Amar, Akhil Reed, *America's Constitution*, New York: Random House, 2005.

Aristotle, *Nicomachean Ethics*.

Auerbach, Jerold S., *Unequal Justice*, New York: Oxford Univ. Press, 1976.

Bartels, Larry, *Unequal Democracy*, Princeton: Princeton Univ. Press, 2008.

Basler, Roy, ed., *The Collected Works of Abraham Lincoln*, New Brunswick: Rutgers Univ. Press, 1953-5.

Bauerlein, Mark, *The Dumbest Generation*, New York: Tarcher/Penguin, 2008.

Bayles, Michael, *Professional Ethics*, Belmont: Wadsworth, 1981.

Bedau, Adam, *The Death Penalty in America*, Boston: Northeastern Univ. Press, 1997.

Bell, Daniel, *The Coming of the Post-Industrial Society*, New York: Basic Books, 1973.

Boaz, David, *Libertarianism*, New York: The Free Press, 1997.

Bodenheimer, Edgar, *Jurisprudence*, Cambridge: Harvard Univ. Press, 1974.

Bork, Robert, *The Tempting of America*, New York: The Free Press, 1990.

Bowie, Norman, E., ed., *Business Ethics*, Englewood Cliffs: Prentice Hall, 2002.

Bradley, Bill, *The New American Story*, New York: Random House, 2008.

Caro, Robert A., *Master of the Senate*, New York: Vintage, 2003.

Currinder, Marian, *Money in the House*, Boulder: Westview Press, 2009.

Dahl, Robert, *How Democratic Is the American Constitution?*, New Haven: Yale Univ. Press, 2003.

Amico, Robert, *Contemporary European Philosophy*, Boulder: Westview Press, 1999.

Davis, Richard, *Electing Justice*, Oxford: Oxford Univ. Press, 2005.

Dean, John W., *Broken Government*, New York: Viking Press, 2007.

Devlin, Patrick, *Trial by Jury*, London: University Paperback, 1966.

Diamond, Larry, *The Spirit of Democracy*, New York: Times Books, 2008.

Dobbs, Lou, *War on the Middle Class*, New York: Penguin Books, 2006.

Domhoff, William, *Who Rules America?*, 6e, New York: McGraw-Hill, 2009.

Douthat, Ross, & Reiham Salam, *Grand New Party*, New York: Doubleday, 2008.

Drehle, David von, *Triangle*, New York: Atlantic Monthly Press, 2003.

Drew, Elizabeth, *The Corruption of American Politics*, New York: Overlook Press, 2000.

Dworkin, Ronald, *Is Democracy Possible Here?*, Princeton: Princeton Univ. Press, 2006; *A Matter of Principle*, Cambridge: Cambridge Univ. Press, 1985; *Law's Empire*, Cambridge: Harvard Univ. Press, 1986.

Eitzen, Stanley, & Janis E. Johnston, *Inequality*, Boulder: Paradigm, 2007.

Emmanuel, Rahm, *The Plan*, New York: Public Affairs, 2006.

Epstein, Lee, & Jeffrey Segal, *Advice and Consent*, Oxford: Oxford Univ. Press, 2005.

Farrand, Max, *The Framing of the Constitution of the United States*, New Haven: Yale Univ. Press, 1913; *The Records of the Federal Convention of 1787*, New Haven: Yale Univ. Press, 1966.

Freeman, R. Edward, *Strategic Management*, Boston: Pitman, 1984.

Freeman, Samuel, *Rawls*, New York: Routledge, 2007; *John Rawls: Collected Papers*, Cambridge: Harvard Univ. Press, 1999.

Friedman, Milton, "The Social Responsibility of Business is to Increase Its Profits," *New York Times Magazine*, Sept., 13, 1970, pp. 17-21.

Goidel, Robert K., & Donald A. Gross, & Todd G. Shields, *Money Matters*, New York: Rowman & Littlefield, 1999.

Golden, Daniel, *The Price of Admission*, New York: Crown, 2006.

Golding, Martin, *Philosophy of Law*, Englewood Cliffs: Prentice Hall, 1975.

Gore, Al, *The Assault on Reason*, New York: Penguin Press, 2007.

Green, Mark, *Selling Out*, New York: Regan Books, 2002; *Losing Our Democracy*, Naperville: Sourcebooks, 2006.

Greider, William, *Come Home, America*, New York: Rodale, 2009.

Gross, Donald, & Robert Goidel, *The States of Campaign Finance Reform*, Columbus: Ohio State Univ. Press, 2003.

Gumble, Andrew, *Steal This Vote*, New York: Nation Books, 2005.

Hall, Kermit, ed., *The Supreme Court of the United States*, New York: Oxford Univ. Press, 1992.

Hare, R.M., *Moral Thinking*, Oxford: Clarendon Press, 1981.

Hartmann, Thom, *Unequal Protection*, New York: Rodale Press, 2004.

Haskins, George Lee, *Foundations of Power*, New York: Macmillan, 1981.

Hill, Bob, *Double Jeopardy*, New York: Avon Books, 1995.

Hill, Steven, *10 Steps to Repair American Democracy*, Sausilito, CA: Polipoint Press, 200€

Hollings, Ernest F., *Making Government Work*, Columbia: Univ. of South Carolina Press, 2008.

Huff, C. Roland, Arye Rattner, Edward Sagarin, *Convicted but Innocent*, London: Sage, 1996.

Jacoby, Susan, *The Age of American Unreason*, New York: Pantheon Books, 2008.

James, William, *Will to Believe*, New York: Dover, 1956.

Jencks, Christopher, & David Riesman, *The Academic Revolution*, New York: Doubleday, 1968.

Johnston, David, Cay, *Free Lunch*, New York: Portfolio/Penguin, 2007.

Kaiser, Robert G., *So Damn Much Money*, New York: Knopf, 2009.

Kalven, Harry, & Hans Zeisel, *The American Jury*, Boston: Little, Brown, 1966.

Kant, Immanuel, *Foundations of the Metaphysics of Morals*, L.W. Beck, trans., New York: Prentice Hall, 1989.

Kronman, Anthony, *Education's End*, New Haven: Yale Univ. Press, 2007.

Krugman, Paul, *Conscience of a Liberal*, New York: Norton, 2009.

Kuttner, Robert, *The Squandering of America*, New York: Vintage Books, 2008; *Obama's Challenge*, White River Junction: Chelsea Green Publishing, 2008.

Kuhne, Robert J., *Co-Determination in Business*, New York: Praeger, 1980.

Lapierre, Dominique, & Javier Moro, *Five Past Midnight in Bhopal*, New York: Warner Books, 2002.

Larson, Magali S., *The Rise of Professionalism*, Berkeley: Univ. of California Press, 1977.

Laski, Harold, *A Grammar of Politics*, New Haven: Yale Univ. Press, 1931.

Lee, Frances, E., & Bruce Oppenheimer, *Sizing Up The Senate*, Chicago: University of Chicago Press, 1999.

Lijphart, Arend, *Democracies*, New Haven: Yale Univ. Press, 1984; *Patterns of Democracy*, New Haven: Yale Univ. Press, 1999.

Litan, Robert, E., ed., *Verdict*, Washington, DC: Brookings Institution, 1993.

Lodge, H.C., ed., *The Federalist Papers*, New York: Putnam & Sons, 1888.

Loevinger, Jane, *Ego Development*, London: Jossey-Bass, 1976.

Loewen, James, *Lies My Teacher Told Me*, New York: New Press, 1995.

Loury, Glenn C., *Race, Incarceration and American Values*, Cambridge: MIT Press, 2008.

Lowery, David, & Holly Brasher, *Organized Interests and American Government*, New York: McGraw Hill, 2004.

Machan, Tibor, ed., *The Libertarian Reader*, Totowa: Rowman & Littlefield, 1982.

Madison, James, *Notes of the Debates in the Federal Convention of 1787*, New York: Norton, 1987.

Main, Jackson Turner, *The Upper House in Revolutionary America*, Madison: Univ. of Wisconsin Press, 1982.

\nn, Thomas E., & Norman J. Ornstein, *The Broken Branch*, Oxford: Oxford Univ. Press, 2006.

Marx, Karl, *Economic and Philosophical Manuscripts of 1844*, Martin Milligan, trans., Amherst: Prometheus Books, 1988.

Michels, Robert, *Political Parties*, New York: The Free Press, 1968.

Middlekauff, Robert, *The Glorious Cause*, New York; Oxford Univ. Press, 1982.

McDonald, Forrest. *Novus Ordo Seclorum*, Lawrence, KS: University Press of Kansas, 1986.

Morehouse, Ward, & M. Arun Subramanian, *The Bhopal Tragedy*, New York: The Council on International and Public Affairs, 1986.

Moyers, Bill, *Moyers on Democracy*, New York: Doubleday, 2008.

Myers, David G., *Exploring Psychology*, New York: Worth Publishers, 1990.

Nozick, Robert, *Anarchy, State and Utopia*, New York: Basic Books, 1977.

Obama, Barack, *The Audacity of Hope*, New York: Three Rivers Press, 2006.

O'Brien, David, *Storm Center*, 4e, New York: Norton, 1996; *Constitutional Law and Politics*, 4e, New York: Norton, 2000.

Paine, Thomas, *Common Sense*, Ontario, Canada: Broadview Press, 2004.

Paul, Jeffrey, *Reading Nozick*, Totowa: Rowman & Littlefield, 1981.

Parsons, Talcott, *The Social System*, New York: The Free Press, 1951.

Pennock, J.R., & J. W. Chapman, *Due Process*, New York: NYU Press, 1977.

Plato, *Laws*.

Polsby, Nelson, & Aaron Wildavsky, *Presidential Elections*, New York: Free Press, 1991.

Popper, Karl, *The Open Society and Its Enemies*, New York: Routledge, 2002.

Posner, Richard, *How Judges Think*, Cambridge: Harvard Univ. Press, 2008.

Rawls, John, *A Theory of Justice*, Cambridge: Harvard Univ. Press, 1971; *Justice as Fairness*, Cambridge: Harvard Univ. Press, 2001; *Political Liberalism*, New York: Columbia Univ. Press, 1993.

Reich, Robert, *Supercapitalism*, New York: Knopf, 2007.

Rothkopf, David, *Superclass*, New York: Farrar, Straus, Giroux, 2008.

Rothman, Robert, A., *Inequality and Stratification*, 4e, Upper Saddle River: Prentice Hall, 2002.

Sabato, Larry, *A More Perfect Constitution*, New York: Walker & Co., 2007.

Sachs, Jeffrey D., *The End of Poverty*, New York: Penguin Press, 2005.

Sandel, Michael L., *Justice: What's the Right Thing to Do?*, New York: Farrar, Straus, Giroux, 2009.

Scalia, Antonin, *A Matter of Principle*, Princeton: Princeton Univ. Press, 1997; *A Matter of Interpretation*, Princeton: Princeton Univ. Press, 1997.

Schumpeter, Joseph, *Capitalism, Socialism, Democracy*, 3e, New York: Harper, 2008.

Sen, Amartya, *The Idea of Justice*, Cambridge: Harvard Univ. Press, 2009.

Shields, Todd G., *Money Matters*, Lanham, MD: Rowman & Littlefield, 1999.

Sirota, David, *The Uprising*, New York: Three Rivers Press, 2009.

Smith, Bradley A., *Unfree Speech*, Princeton: Princeton Univ. Press, 2001.

Spence, Jerry, *With Justice for None*, New York: Times Books, 1989.

Sterba, James, *How to Make People Just*, Totowa, NJ: Rowman & Littlefield, 1988.

Stone, Christopher, *Where the Law Ends*, New York: Harper & Row, 1975.

Sunstein, Cass, et al., *Are Judges Political?*, Washington, DC: Brookings Institution Press, 2008.

Talbott, John, R., *The 86 Biggest Lies on Wall Street*, New York: Seven Stories Press, 2009.

Tamanaha, Brian, *On the Rule of Law*, Cambridge: Cambridge Univ. Press, 2004.

Todd, Chuck, & Sheldon Gawiser, *How Burack Obama Won*, New York: Vintage Books, 2009.

Toobin, Jeffrey, *The Nine*, New York: Doubleday, 2007.

Vago, Steven, *Law und Society*, Upper Saddle River: Prentice Hall, 2003.

Tribe, Laurence, & Michael Dorf, *On Reading the Constitution*, Cambridge: Harvard Univ. Press, 1991.

White, G. Edward, *The Marshall Court and Cultural Change*, vol. 3-4, New York: Macmillan, 1988.

Whittington, Keith, *Constitutional Interpretation*, Lawrence: University Press of Kansas, 1999.

Wilkinson, Richard, & Kate Pickett, *The Spirit Level*, New York: Bloomsbury Press, 2009.

Zakaria, Fareed, *The Post American World*, New York: Norton, 2009.

Zinn, Howard, *A People's History of the United States*, New York: Harper, 1995.

# INDEX